CLASS,
POWER
AND
PROPERTY

CLASS, POWER
AND
PROPERTY

ESSAYS ON CANADIAN SOCIETY

Wallace Clement

Ⓜ METHUEN

Toronto   New York   London   Sydney   Auckland

Canadian Cataloguing in Publication Data
Clement, Wallace.
   Class, power and property

Bibliography: p.
ISBN 0-458-96880-3

1. Social classes — Canada.   2. Power (Social sciences).
3. Canada — Economic conditions.   I. Title.

HN110.Z9S622   305.50971   C83-098366-X

Printed and bound in Canada

1 2 3 4 5   83 88 87 86 85 84

Contents

Preface

Understanding Canadian society has only become a widespread academic preoccupation in the past fifteen years. The publication of John Porter's *The Vertical Mosaic* in 1965 sparked tremendous interest, while a growth in postsecondary education and the number of Canadian scholars allowed these interests to develop (at least until the late 1970s when cutbacks to education began to dampen the fires). During this time many young Canadian academics have taken an active interest in their own society. They have surmounted restrictive disciplinary bounds, particularly with the re-emergence of an active Canadian political economy tradition, and have set as their tasks the understanding and interpreting of the society in which they live.

My own inquiries about Canadian society have been punctuated by three studies, which have appeared as *The Canadian Corporate Elite, Continental Corporate Power* and *Hardrock Mining*. In addition, I have written a number of papers for journals, collections or conferences. These papers have often filled gaps between the larger studies, developing their implications in specific directions and indicating other issues to investigate. This collection draws together some of these papers, published and unpublished, and provides an overview of my understanding of Canadian society.

As the reader will discover, there is a relationship between the papers and an evolution from a focus on power to one on class. It is my contention that there is an important complementary relationship between power and class frameworks. These papers also indicate a concern for understanding the state, not fully evident in the three books. Several of these papers address the nature of the state and state policies in Canada. The entire undertaking remains a 'work in progress' as the final two papers indicate; it is less a conclusion to the previous work than a blueprint for future research.

There is continuity within the collection of papers in that all are directed at understanding inequalities in Canadian society. It is the way these in-equalities have been conceptualized that has evolved. I do not mean to suggest that now it is somehow incorrect to view inequalities in terms of power (the earlier focus), only that such a view is inadequate when not located in a broader context. Power analysis tends to view the powerful as all-powerful rather than as people engaged in a dynamic relationship with those whom their decisions affect. Whether it is economic or state power that is examined, there is a temptation to abstract power from both the conditions that make it possible and those it affects. The powerful do not operate in a vacuum. They are powerful in relation to others, and those 'others' are not simply passive.

Class analysis, unlike studies of power, compels the investigator to locate the inherently social relations of a society. Studies using this approach to Canadian society have had an uneven but blossoming career, as I seek to demonstrate in the paper "Canadian Class Cleavages." There has been a tendency to examine the capitalist class, the working class and the petite bourgeoisie as distinct phenomena rather than, as class analysis should de-mand, in relationship to one another. The final four papers contribute to this more dynamic class approach. "Transformations in Mining: A Critique of H.A. Innis" attempts to demonstrate the explanatory capacity of class analy-sis in contrast to the staples approach. It also incorporates within a class analysis the valuable insights contained within the staples tradition. "Subordination of Labour in Canadian Mining" is a concrete study of Cana-dian mining, building on the class transformations identified in the earlier paper but following them through the contemporary struggles between man-agement and labour. While the focus is on mining, the paper's purpose is to illustrate broader changes occurring primarily within advanced capitalist societies with the real subordination of labour through the intensification of production by mechanization and automation. "Class and Property Rela-tions" is a more abstract discussion of class structure through an exploration of various property forms of class and their implications for class analysis. "Property and Proletarianization" applies some of the theoretical insights from the previous paper to farming and fishing as case studies of transforma-tions occurring within simple commodity production. These final two papers represent the current direction of my thinking on Canadian society, while the earlier papers trace the path I used to get there.

Quite obviously, "The Changing Structure of the Canadian Economy," which is a historical review of economic power in Canada, and "Inequality of Access," which is a comparison of the economic elites of 1951 and 1972, were written within the power perspective. There is a tendency in both papers to overstate the degree to which changes in the elite reflect changes in the rest of society. These papers also tend to ignore the workings of classes besides the capitalist class that demonstrate how classes have implica-tions for the development of one another.

The next paper locates contemporary Canada within international economic forces. "Uneven Development: A Mature Branch-Plant Society" examines Canada's relations abroad, particularly with the United States but also in the form of Canadian investment in the Third World. In addition, it examines some implications of Canada's pattern of development regarding regions, the state, and class formation. This paper is an extension of themes touched upon but not developed in *Continental Corporate Power*. It draws together concerns emerging from my earlier work and acts as a bridge from a power to class analysis.

While continuing to some extent to examine the characteristics of the powerful, the paper on "The Corporate Elite, the Capitalist Class and the Canadian State" marks the beginning of a broader focus on class and, as with the paper following, of an analysis of the state. It introduces the concept of property relations, a theme which is explored in more detail in the final two papers. "An Exercise in Legitimation: The Bryce Commission's Justification of Corporate Concentration" examines specific state policies and the assumptions underlying the operation of the Canadian state. It is argued that Canadians were not well served by this royal commission. Its research was for the most part shallow and uncritical; the commissioners from the outset were committed to justifying the present high levels of corporate concentration and laying the groundwork for even higher ones. An examination of the commission's arguments does, however, provide the opportunity for a broader questioning of state policies regarding foreign ownership, corporate concentration, financial control, regulation and the mass media.

Woven throughout this collection of essays on Canadian society are the themes of class, power and property. These themes are used to examine contemporary patterns in the Canadian economy and state but emphasize the way Canada arrived at its current situation. A historical dimension is central to Canadian political economy, since it is basic to understanding social change and the dynamics underlying our present circumstances. Each essay is grounded in an attempt to explain and understand concrete features. Canadian political economy is still at a fairly primitive stage of theorizing about society. A good deal of empirical work has been completed, although much remains to be done. We are at a period of consolidation, where it is necessary to draw together this empirical work and begin to fashion a more comprehensive understanding. Some of the papers in this collection are attempts in this direction, but they far from satisfy the challenge. Canada is a particularly interesting nation. It occupies an unusual place within the world system and contains within it much diversity. It also contains much conflict and struggle. Its potential is enormous and possibilities many. To realize its promise, Canadians must become more aware of who they are and where they stand, both in a class and national sense. They must learn to assess their positions as members of society and act in their collective best interest. The point of these

papers is to help Canadians in understanding their best interest and, hope-
fully, to stimulate them to act accordingly.

Wallace Clement
January 1982
Ottawa

Acknowledgements

"The Changing Structure of the Canadian Economy" originally appeared in the *Canadian Review of Sociology and Anthropology — Aspects of Canadian Society* (a special publication on the occasion of the VIII World Congress of Sociology, 1974), pp. 2-27.

"Inequality of Access: Characteristics of the Canadian Corporate Elite" originally appeared in the *Canadian Review of Sociology and Anthropology* 12:1 (1975), pp. 33-52.

"The Corporate Elite, the Capitalist Class, and the Canadian State" originally appeared in *The Canadian State: Political Economy and Political Power*, edited by Leo Panitch (Toronto: University of Toronto Press, 1977), pp. 225-48.

"An Exercise in Legitimation: The Bryce Commission's Justification of Corporate Concentration" combines two previously published papers: "An Exercise in Legitimation: Ownership and Control in the Report of the Royal Commission on Corporate Concentration," in *Perspectives on the Royal Commission on Corporate Concentration*, edited by Paul K. Gorecki and W.T. Stanbury (Toronto: Butterworths and Company for the Institute for Research on Public Policy, 1979), pp. 215-36; and "Justifying Corporate Concentration: Canada and International Capitalism," in *Canadian Public Policy* 5:1 (1979), pp. 120-26.

"Subordination of Labour in Canadian Mining" originally appeared in *Labour/Le Travailleur* 5 (1980), pp. 133-48.

Chapter 1
The Changing Structure of the Canadian Economy

Originally published in 1974, this paper represents the historical and corporate background later developed in The Canadian Corporate Elite. *Subsequent studies, particularly Tom Naylor's two-volume* The History of Canadian Business, *developed the themes outlined here. Some of the underlying assumptions of this type of analysis have been challenged in recent writings, particularly the articles by Leo Panitch, David McNally and Ray Schmidt in* Studies in Political Economy, *number 6 (Autumn 1981). The major weakness of this paper is its exclusive concentration on the capitalist class and the failure to clearly document the alliances and struggles between commercial and industrial capital on the one hand and Canadian and foreign capital on the other. These weaknesses are addressed in the paper "Canadian Class Cleavages: An Assessment and Contribution," included as chapter 6 of the present volume. The purpose of the following paper was to establish the historically specific structural conditions under which mobility into the economic elite occurred. As such, the focus on condition as well as opportunity represented some advance over John Porter's approach but was still constrained by the limitations of an elite analysis.*

Canada's economic development has involved a series of changes in its organization and control; these structural transformations have recast opportunities available to Canadians for upward mobility and access to power. This paper presents an analysis of how two distinct yet intersecting processes central to stratification theory developed in Canadian economic history.[1]

---

[1] A series of studies are now completed that update parts of John Porter's *The Vertical Mosaic*. Dennis Olsen of Carleton University has finished a study of the bureaucratic, political and judicial elite called *The State Elite*. I have updated the media elite from 1961 to 1972, and along with a detailed analysis of the corporate elite, this appears in *The Canadian Corporate Elite*.

The dual processes of condition and opportunity will be examined to understand how they 'fit' with one another historically. It will be argued they are ordered in such a way that condition places limits on opportunity.

Frank Parkin argues in *Class Inequality and Political Order* that "inequalities associated with the class system are founded upon two interlocking but conceptually distinct, social processes. One is the allocation of rewards attaching to different *positions* in the social system; the other is the process or *recruitment* to these positions" (1972:13). Although paralleling Parkin's concepts of "position" and "recruitment," the notions of condition and opportunity are broader. Condition refers to the framework within which a society is organized, and focuses on the structural level of stable sets of social relations. Since this analysis is primarily concerned with economic structures, condition refers to structured inequalities within corporations and power differentials between them. The entire social structure, of course, includes a wider system of institutions. Opportunity focuses on the individual level, but on the individual as representative of particular social types, whether these are distinguished by class origin, ethnicity, sex, region of birth, or so forth. Concern here involves the freedom persons with these ascribed characteristics have to move within settings created by the social structure. In liberal democracies, where the economic system is predominantly capitalist, condition parallels the class structure, and opportunity the ability of persons with different class origins to move within the class structure. The way society is organized provides some people with the ability to accumulate power and privilege and to transfer these to their children through wealth, stockholdings, social 'position,' access to education and occupational contacts. The prerogatives of power within capitalism provide that private property, and the advantages associated with it, is a key nexus between condition and opportunity. Private property is at the basis of the economic system in capitalist society, and the advantages it affords some are the limits it imposes on others.

Social Forces and Social Change
The argument here is that new social forces produce changes in condition and open the social structure, thus providing the opportunity for social mobility. This includes downward and upward mobility, each of which occurs if old power holders are displaced by new ones. New social forces may also create parallel structures alongside old ones, thus expanding the types of structures present at any time. Conversely, dominance by traditional, established social forces consolidates the structure and places restrictions on mobility. Consolidation of power can occur in one of two ways. Old social forces can dominate and contain new forces, or social forces can crystallize, whereby new forces of one era become established forces of the next. This serves to restrict avenues of mobility for new entrants and is analogous to the absence of downward mobility in a stable system.

By a social force, it is meant a source of power; for example, the forces of production. Power is the capacity to mobilize resources such as capital, wealth, personnel, knowledge, technology, ideology or military forces in the favour and to the advantage of those making allocative decisions. As a social structure stabilizes, the points of access become established, institutionalized avenues become set, and those with power are able to dictate the qualities required for entrance. Quite understandably these qualities tend to resemble the characteristics of those already in power, with the limiting case in this respect being common kinship.

Access to economic power by particular social types can be complemented by other social institutions, such as education. If education becomes defined as a prerequisite for mobility and if access to education is restricted to certain social types, then this will further restrict mobility. Since the powerful are better equipped to have their children go to particular schools (private and university), this further reinforces the probability that subsequent generations of the advantaged will take the 'reins of power.' New social forces represent the emergence of new sources of power. If these new sources of power emerge and remain autonomous from existing powers, new social types will develop in power positions; but if new forces are 'captured' or absorbed by traditional power holders, this will strengthen the powerful's position and further stifle mobility for outsiders.

Within this framework the changing structure of the Canadian economy will be analysed with reference to concentration of power within the economic system, the transformation from entrepreneurial to corporate capitalism, and restrictions placed on the development of an industrial system within Canada by indigenous financial and foreign industrial capitalists. Distinctions will be drawn between portfolio and direct investment that correspond closely to differences between financial and industrial capitalists. Within Canada these types of investment and capitalists have created an almost unique combination of indigenous financial institutions, branch-plant manufacturing and resource industries. Branch plants create a combination of comprador elites in manufacturing and resource sectors and independent indigenous elites in finance, transportation and utilities. This paper elaborates and traces the development of these processes to provide an analysis of the current structure of corporate elites.

Importing Colonial Structures

Following initial trading ventures, the European mercantile thrust of the fifteenth century soon evolved into colonial rule. Based on state power, mercantilism equated economic power with national power and encouraged development of strong commercial classes that gathered surplus by providing intermediary services between world resources and the home country. In Canada the St. Lawrence was established as a fur-trading route organized by

Montreal merchant capitalists. Rigid French mercantilism prevented diversified economic development and created a distorted social structure in which the colonial elite was part of the colonizing elite, with the colonial elite dominant in economic, political and military affairs. The colonial ruling class was related through marriage and commerce to the French merchants and aristocracy (Pritchard, 1972:37).

With the Conquest of 1760, North America became a British possession, and this change brought a new social structure, which became superimposed on the remnant French colony. Conquest, Hubert Guindon says, "involved the takeover by the British of the political and economic institutions of New France. This was greatly facilitated by the massive exodus of the middle-class entrepreneurs and political administrators of New France" (1968:52). One colonial rule had given way to another. The new and old forces were both external to Canada, and indigenous mobility was not facilitated by replacing one set of outside rulers by another.

Transformations were occurring, however, that provide interesting parallels with later developments. This can be best illustrated by contrasting the structures of two great fur-trading companies, the Hudson's Bay Company (HBC) and the North West Company (NWC). The NWC was a syndicate formed in Montreal in response to increasing capital requirements of extended continental trade and, as a joint enterprise, resembled earlier fishing expeditions that had gathered capital to finance expeditions and split profits at the end of a period. Its organization required constant refurbishing by expanding trade and, unlike the HBC, did not form a rigid bureaucratic framework extending back to the United Kingdom. The HBC was syndicated at the ownership level by thirteen men who had obtained a royal charter in 1670. It is important to contrast the effects of capital accumulation by these two types of structures and the effects they had on capital formations and elite configurations. For the HBC, "profits on the original subscribed capital stock, actually paid, of between 60 and 70 percent per annum from the years 1690 to 1800" were returned to the United Kingdom, and much of this surplus became the capital for reinvestment within the United Kingdom and abroad. On the other hand, "profits of the North West Company were derived from great fortunes which later were conspicuous in banks, steamboats, railways, and other capitalist channels" within Canada (Myers, 1972:61-63).

Differences between these two organizations represent the difference between the future development of an indigenous economic elite in Canada and an external elite in the United Kingdom, both based, to a large extent, on capital appropriated in Canada. Although each relied on foreign capital, operations of the HBC were directed from the United Kingdom, with capital flowing back along the same path; the NWC borrowed its capital, thus retaining capital accumulation and control within Canada, forming the basis for an indigenous capitalist class. This provides the pattern for the development of elite stratification in Canada and illustrates the importance of relating stratification to the means of capital accumulation. The NWC can be regarded as a new indigenous social force that emerged parallel to the external colonial powers represented by the HBC. The NWC provided an avenue to power for indigenous Canadians distinct from the colonial power of the HBC. The effects can still be seen today, with capital accumulated through the NWC providing an initial basis for developing an autonomous financial and transportation structure, while the HBC, still owned primarily in the United Kingdom,[2] is now engaged in retail and wholesale trade.

The formation of an economic system in this earlier period had other effects still evident today. As a colony, Canada had to fit the dominant mode of production prevalent in the United Kingdom. Mercantilism provided English fur-trading interests in Canada with capital, securing advantages and market outlets the post-Conquest French merchants lacked. The alliance between English-speaking Montreal merchants and British commercial interests provided a strong and complementary power base on each side of the Atlantic; export of staples proved beneficial to both and reinforced colonial dependence. The mercantile empire, with its focus on circulation rather than production, stultified industrialization in the colonies through a policy that prohibited exporting "manufactured machines and the emigration of skilled artisans," thus maintaining the "dominance of merchant-capital at the expense of industrial capital, which would compete with Britain. The merchant class and rich Loyalists in Canada aligned themselves with the colonial ruling class, the church, and the landowning elites" (Naylor, 1972:6). Indigenous economic interests were committed to existing British rule and advantages they received from mercantilism by acting as mediators between Canadian staples and U.K. commercial houses. None had a vision of developing a strong indigenous industrial system, since, under the protection of British mercantilism, their needs were met by the colonizers' industrial structures. Their interest was in developing a strong transportation system focused on the St. Lawrence and, later, a transcontinental railway as their contribution to the overall mercantile scheme.

Canada's Ruling Class and Nascent Industrialists: From Entrepreneurial to Corporate Capitalism

External pressures from westward expansion by the industrial nation to the south created within Canada a series of what Hugh Aitken described as "forced moves" of "defensive expansionism" to prevent U.S. encroachment on western territories. These events, Aitken argued, stimulated the rapid extension of transportation systems within Canada and strengthened political union to provide the basis for "very large public investment and has

---

[2]The Hudson's Bay Company was taken over in 1979 by Kenneth Thomson, heir to the Thomson newspaper empire, jointly headquartered in Canada and the United Kingdom.

brought the political leadership into intimate alliance with influential business groups" (1965:496-97). To combat pressures from the south, the ruling class required guaranteed capital for canal and railway construction. This brought state and economic interests in Canada together to petition Britain's commercial houses.

Several well-documented accounts of Canada's social structure exist for this period, particularly for relations between political and economic elites, who clearly formed a ruling class. Evidence of a ruling class is provided, for example, by the host of railway charters issued by the state to sitting legislators for the period 1845-58. A ruling class based in commerce and politics can be contrasted with nascent industrialists. It was within an economy dominated by imperial-oriented merchants that emerging industrialists had to struggle. The ruling class was the old, established social force based in commerce and the state, while the nascent industrialists were an emerging social force.

Stanley Ryerson's analysis of the "embryonic industrial bourgeoisie" in Upper and Lower Canada and the Maritimes stresses that development of "incipient industrialism" was greatly retarded by the existence of a Canadian ruling class based in mercantile capital (1968). Gary Teeple maintains that the ruling class "preferred to trade their articles rather than produce them" (1972:61). Manufacturing developed at a pace and direction imposed by the mercantile oligarchy, which extracted its surplus through trade and commerce rather than production.

G. Tulchinsky's study of the Montreal-based merchant class between 1837 and 1853 finds this a period "with significant growth of new insurance, banking and telegraph companies, as well as capital expansion amongst the older banks"; in addition to extending the St. Lawrence by means of a canal system, steamer service was introduced to the United Kingdom, and there was the beginning of railways to service the "Montreal argonauts'" quest for "commercial ties with her restless hinterland" (1972:125). Although personal investment in commercial activities of the city was a prerequisite for membership in the ruling class, "prominence, reputed wealth, service in organizations like the Board of Trade or in provincial or municipal politics seem to have been other important criteria for directorships in the companies" (129-30). The "cadre of leaders" was headed by three families, the McGills, Molsons and Torrances.

> Most prominent members of the Montreal commercial fraternity were favoured with considerable advantages. Family business connections in Montreal combined with some experience and often backed by grammar school (or college classique) education, paved the way for their easy entry and accelerated advancement to positions of leadership in the city's commercial affairs. In most cases it seems that they were in command of or had access to substantial capital. [130]

Tulchinsky emphasizes relations between particular types of commercial activities, such as those of merchants, shipbuilders, import-export dealers and railway promoters, arguing that the same people were interlocked within these and none expressed interest in industrial activities. Most prominent businessmen were Scottish in origin, with Americans representing the second largest group, followed by English, Irish, and English-speaking Canadians. French Canadians were not significant in commerce, although they were important in the business community through their activities in the medical and legal professions (132-33).

Further evidence of the 'tightness' of the ruling commercial and political circles is also available. Aitken notes the state was not equally accessible to all business interests at this time, but only to mercantilists at the exclusion of industrial entrepreneurs (1965:495), and Tom Naylor argues that "the list of eminent financiers and railwaymen of the period is a veritable 'who's who' of Canadian politics for two generations. And, without exception, the linkage runs from merchant capitalism to finance, transportation and land speculation" (1972:17). It was within an economic system dominated by these powerful interests that the emerging industrial entrepreneurs had to develop. The promise of the National Policy was that relief would be provided by its tariffs, railways, and immigration policies.

Torn between British capital and American markets, the Canadian ruling class generated the National Policy of 1879, a policy that asserted the independence of Canada from the encroachment of U.S. westward expansion and declared that central Canada was to rule the western hinterland. Mercantilists, with state support, proceeded to assert a vision of Canada, placing the St. Lawrence at the centre of an east-west nexus of trade.

The tariff policy associated with the National Policy was not intended to prevent foreign capital from entering the country. It was designed to promote a Canadian market and industrialization within Canada. With implementation of the tariff, branch plants from the United States were actively encouraged to enter Canada, meeting with some success and producing what Naylor calls "industry in Canada but no Canadian industry" (1972:25). Naylor is overstating his point; of course there was some Canadian industry prior to and catalysed by the policy, but industrial pursuits were not led by the ruling class. Powerful Canadian interests were instead engaged in pursuit of finance and transportation. Manufacturing was mainly undertaken by smaller Canadian entrepreneurs and already-developed firms from the United States.

Stephen Scheinberg notes that the National Policy was intended to develop foreign investment but "foreign economic domination was never perceived as a real threat during that period. American investment was stimulated, but not in amounts that would raise fears. Macdonald, of course, does not bear the responsibility for the failures of twentieth-century Canadian leaders to readjust to changed economic circumstances" (1973:221-22). Scheinberg may be overly generous to Macdonald and his associates, but he is correct in regard to the failure of later elites to adjust. Macdonald and his associates failed to adjust their assumptions to an industrial age. They preferred to import 'wholesale' an already-developed industrial system from the United States rather than support their own nascent entrepreneurs. In other words, traditional dominant interests in Canada failed to encourage and sustain new indigenous social forces in manufacturing. Rather, they chose to dominate and contain them by taking advantage of their weak capital and market position, consolidating industrially based entrepreneurial firms into joint-stock complexes suited to the pursuit of finance capital.

T.W. Acheson demonstrates how the National Policy, in the short term, generated within the Maritimes a developing industrial structure emerging from the limited capital of second-generation Maritime merchant families. The Maritime ambition was to generate a powerful industrial system led by the East, as in the U.S. model. The power of the Montreal ruling class proved too great an obstacle to such high aspirations. Maritime entrepreneurs were too limited in their capital reserves, according to Acheson, to survive the recession of 1885 and "acquiesced in the 1890's to the industrial leadership of the Montreal business community" (1972b:4). Their success to that point under the National Policy was substantial; by 1885 they were strong in cotton mills, sugar refineries, rope refineries, rope factories, glass works, and steel and rolling mills (14). Montreal interests, however, entered the region, taking control of coalfields and railways; as Acheson says, "The community manufactory which had dominated the industrial growth of the 1880's ceased to exist in the 1890's" (19). There was in its place a "growing shift from industrial to financial cap'*alism. Centred on the Montreal stock market, the new movement brought to the control of industrial corporations, men who had neither a communal nor a vocational interest in the concern" (23-24). As intended, the National Policy did produce industry within Canada, but the ruling financial elite failed to allow its development. It stifled emerging entrepreneurial talent by maintaining tight control of capital sources and taking control of firms after they developed. With the shift in manufacturing from entrepreneur-controlled firms engaged in production to financier-controlled conglomerates, companies themselves became commodities to be bought and sold.[3] This further limited the entrepreneurial talents of Canadian industrialists. The emerging social force was literally absorbed by the traditional power holders.

Just as small firms in the Maritimes were bought out and consolidated, the same process was also occurring in central Canada under the guidance of finance capitalists. The Steel Company of Canada, for example,

---

[3]Acheson provides numerous examples of this consolidation process in the Maritimes between 1880 and 1920, whereby external financiers bought and sold firms, using the bond and stock markets of Montreal (1972b:15-27). Consolidating firms and turning them into joint-stock companies served as the modus operandi of the financiers, who extracted their profits on transactions of capital and stocks.

was pieced together by members of the ruling class in response to the demand for rail lines and rolling stock for westward expansion. Financiers such as Max Aitken amalgamated several developing manufactories into a steel empire; nascent industrialists were not able to resist the thrust toward corporate capitalism (see Kilbourn, 1960:18, 48ff).

Acheson's excellent study of the industrial elite[4] of 1885 and 1910 captures the shift from entrepreneurial to corporate capitalism.[5] He documents the squeeze this places on nascent industrialists and tests its impact on social mobility. Occupational inheritance for the 1885 industrial elite was prevalent; "most Canadian industrialists inherited rather than acquired their status in society; nearly one-third were sons of manufacturers, more than a fifth were raised as children of men engaged in a variety of other business occupations" (1972a:150). This group tended to import skills and capital to Canada to take advantage of industrial opportunities. Rather than representing mobility for indigenous Canadians, the members of the industrial elite experienced 'horizontal mobility' from similar positions in their place of origin. Social mobility was intimately linked to immigration, with immigrants composing over half the elite, while four-fifths had foreign-born fathers. Acheson found only limited mobility within the indigenous population. Overall, he identifies three groups: "The smallest consisted of a group of old Canadian industrial and commercial families in their native lands who succeeded in transforming their status to the new society through a form of horizontal mobility. Finally, a third group, largely of Scottish or native Canadian farm or minor industrial origins, succeeded over a lifetime in achieving a significant degree of vertical mobility" (171).

Aside from its influence on the National Policy, this group was not politically effective; in fact, its members considered themselves the "working class" of businessmen (151): Acheson reports: "In a survey of Canadian wealth conducted in 1892, the *Canadian Journal of Commerce* gave pride of

---

[4] Acheson's studies are of the industrial elite. He says, "Industrialist is used in this study to refer only to those figures who played leading roles within the manufacturing sector" (1973:190). There is contained within his studies a direct analysis of industrialization in early Canada and not directly an attempt to study finance and transportation elites.

[5] Entrepreneurial capitalism is characterized by innovative individuals who organize, own and manage relatively small businesses engaged in competition on the marketplace with numerous other enterprises in a high-risk situation. Corporate capitalism, the production of the centripetal movement of centralized capital, is characterized by legal entities known as joint-stock companies, which are largely and highly concentrated. They are controlled by ownership of shares, and management is hired by controlling ownership. A few large corporations have the majority of the market, thus reducing both risk and competition. As the process of accumulation of capital occurs either in financial institutions or through the competitive victory of some entrepreneurs over others, acquisitions, mergers and takeovers occur, thus concentrating capital into fewer and larger units. This results in the movement from entrepreneurial to corporate capitalism. Entrepreneurial activity continues in the era of corporate capitalism, but the tendency is for this to be absorbed in the continual process of concentration.

place to the transportation entrepreneurs whose personal resources frequently exceeded several millions of dollars. The remaining Canadian millionaires are all 'merchant princes'—wholesalers and shippers" (164). In contrast, the industrialists had fortunes between one and four thousand dollars; it is evident the industrial elite at this time was not only separate from the ruling class but did not contend meaningfully with it for power.

Between 1879 and the First World War, Canada's industrial structure underwent great transformations, the earlier period being characterized by small establishments and the later by joint-stock companies and the rise of corporate capitalism. Following his 1885 study, Acheson repeats his procedures for 1910 to capture the effect of transformations in the economic structure on the industrial elite.

Only 51 per cent of the industrial elite in 1885 were native-born, but by 1910 this increased to 74 per cent; the proportion of native-born fathers increased only slightly from 22 to 27 per cent (1973:193, 195). Many of the 1910 elite were sons of the immigrants so prevalent in 1885.

> About half of all the industrialists of 1910 entered businesses—manufacturing, mercantile, financial, transportation, or construction firms—which were owned by their fathers or uncles. Some of these concerns were already large joint stock corporations; most were relatively small family firms which were used as a base from which the entrepreneur later expanded his activities. Most of the remaining industrialists, and particularly those of more limited means, began their careers in the service of one of the joint stock companies. [202-3]

The transformation from entrepreneurial to corporate capitalism consolidated the economic structure, and this had its effect on mobility into the elite. Simultaneous with the concentration of corporate structures was a closure in access to decision-making positions. While in 1885, 68 per cent of the fathers of those in the industrial elite were professionals, businessmen, manufacturers or managers, by 1910 this climbed to 84 per cent. Correspondingly, the 32 per cent whose fathers were farmers or craftsmen had been cut by half to 16 per cent, thus representing a decline in the ability of those from petty bourgeois origins to move into the bourgeoisie. At neither point did any of the elite members have fathers who were labourers (206). Of the 129 members of the industrial elite,

> at least fifty-three members of the elite of 1910 were clearly identifiable as sons of leading Canadian industrialists or merchants. In addition to these, some twenty-one members of the 1885 elite remained among the 1910 industrialists. Still another indication of the hardening social fabric was the growing incidence of intermarriage among the offspring of leading entrepreneurs. In all, at least fifteen marriages, each involving two leading industrial families, occurred among the members of the elites of 1885 and 1910. [206-7]

Acheson's study verifies the increasingly important component of financiers among the industrial elite. This indicates the ruling class of financiers, railway magnates and state elites were moving into manufacturing concerns, but only after these concerns had been established by entrepreneurs. The effect was to close off opportunities for those without upper-class backgrounds. During a brief period the industrial field was open, and immigrants with skills and some capital were able to establish themselves as a new social force; but as the ruling class moved in and consolidated these emerging firms, avenues began to close, manufacturing became concentrated, and opportunities were limited. Even the short period when the structure was open did not provide mobility for many indigenous Canadians, particularly French Canadians. The industrial elite, like the ruling class, was overwhelmingly Anglo. With only 7 per cent French in 1885, this dropped to 6 per cent by 1910, although the French represented 29 per cent of the population (197).

Foreign Portfolio and Direct Investment
Differences in the effect of portfolio and direct investment parallel those outlined earlier between the two great fur-trading companies. The implications of these types of investment are most apparent in the types of institutional structures they develop and the nature of the elites who control them. Portfolio investment, although tied to a veto power of lending financiers, produces more freedom than does direct investment. Portfolio investment, typically bonds, is 'self-liquidating' in the sense that earnings from investments are used to pay off debts. This creates institutions in the economy controlled by indigenous businessmen able to form an indigenous capitalist class. Direct investment brings with it a 'package' of direct control and foreign capitalists. Rather than self-liquidating, it tends to accumulate and expand on the original investment; while creating economic activity, it does not necessarily create an indigenous capitalist class.

Two important trends in foreign investment in Canada are the increasing orientation to direct investment and, simultaneously, the increasing proportion of investment from the United States. For example, between 1913 and 1926, U.S. investment as a percentage of all foreign investment increased from 22 per cent to 53 per cent. There is a strong tendency for U.S. investment to be direct and U.K. investment to be portfolio. It is at the level of capital formation that basic differences exist between Canada's relationships with the United Kingdom and with the United States. One relationship breeds increasing autonomy, the other dependency. The ruling finance, transportation and political elite was built and flourished on U.K. portfolio investment, while the U.S. direct investment represents the entrance of U.S. control in the industrial and resource sectors. Direct investment produces what has come to be known as a branch-plant economy.

While the Canadian financial ruling class was taking control and consolidating firms, powerful U.S. industrialists to the south were transferring their own concentrated industrial system into Canada as branch-plant operations and through buying out viable firms that were consolidated on a continental basis. A Canadian industrial capitalist class did exist at the turn of the century as an emerging social force, but between U.S. industrialists and Canadian financial capitalists their survival was limited. Only a few, who allied with the ruling class, were able to continue in manufacturing.

At the time of Confederation, only 7.5 per cent of the total foreign investment[6] was direct. This climbed steadily to 30 per cent by 1926, reaching 50 per cent by 1952 and nearly 60 per cent by 1965. Paralleling the shift from portfolio to direct investment was the shift from the United Kingdom to the United States as the source of investment. While the United States had controlled only 8 per cent of of all foreign investment in Canada in 1867, this jumped to 53 per cent by 1926, 77 per cent by 1952, and almost 80 per cent by 1965. U.S. direct investment has been a growing social force within Canada since the turn of the century and especially in the postwar era. Given the nature of control associated with direct investment and the types of structure it creates, it can be anticipated that important transformations have occurred in the structure of power for the Canadian economy. The important questions are whether this new social force has displaced traditional Canadian elites based in finance and transportation, has been absorbed by the old elite or has developed a parallel structure alongside the traditional elite. John Porter's 1952 study of the corporate elite provides some indication of what has occurred.

Canada's Corporate Elite in 1951
Porter drew his list of dominant corporations from the period 1948-50, just at the beginning of the fantastic onslaught of U.S. direct investment in the 1950s and at the peak of the postwar industrial boom. He argues that the corporate elite was based in 183 dominant corporations that controlled the majority of economic activity in Canada (1955: 508; 1956). Manufacturing corporations, Porter notes, were highly influenced by U.S. control, which accounted for 40 to 50 per cent of their gross value. Financial institutions, however, represented a different pattern with only five U.S. residents and one from the United Kingdom out of 203 bank directors. Bank directors held 23 per cent of all directorships in dominant industrial corporations, while dominant insurance directors held 14 per cent of the dominant industrial directorships. Insurance directors also held 27 per cent of the bank directorships, while bank directors held 41 per cent of the dominant insurance directorships (1965:211). Of the total elite, 23 per cent were U.S. dominated, that is, either

---

[6]For investment statistics, see Levitt, 1970, and Statistics Canada, 1971.

U.S. residents or Canadian residents in U.S. subsidiaries, while only 4 per cent were U.K. dominated. These findings suggest that U.S. capitalism made significant inroads into the Canadian corporate structure, but the Canadian component remained powerful in the financial sector, its traditional strength. Initially, it would seem that a parallel structure had been struck, with U.S. control in large parts of manufacturing and Canadian control of its traditional forte.

Porter's study provides an analysis of the Canadian resident members of the corporate elite for 1951. He finds that "the professional and financial groups make up almost 60 per cent of the economic elite. Another 14.8 per cent of the elite are individuals who were born in or close to it," thus indicating mobility was strongly biased towards those from finance backgrounds (1957:380-81). He also finds only 6.6 per cent of the elite to be French Canadian (one-third of the population). Other ethnic groups had insignificant numbers in the elite (one-fifth of the population), and the rest were Anglos. This illustrates that ethnic origin was as significant for access to the economic elite in 1951 as it had been in 1885 and 1910. Whatever the effect of U.S. investment, it did not change the ethnic balance in Canada at the upper levels of economic power; nor did it undermine the class base of the elite. The upper class, composed of the kin of earlier elites and big business-men, still held a predominant place in the power structure. Porter found that 38 per cent of the elite had upper-class family origins, and this increased to 50 per cent when those who attended private schools were included.[7] The middle class accounted for 32 per cent of the elite, and only 18 per cent were lower than middle class. Class of origin shifted significantly higher when only the most powerful members were included. For the top one hundred members of the elite, 67 per cent were upper class in origin, including those who attended private schools.

The high interlocking that Porter found within economic institutions is matched by elite cross-membership in terms of kinship ties, common educa-tional backgrounds in private schools, a few key universities and law schools, plus social groups such as private clubs (394). He also describes a number of relationships members of the economic elite had with one another and with members of other, particularly political, elites (1965:430-31, 526-29). Porter maintains, "Social goals are now established by a much smaller number than in the days of entrepreneurial capitalism. Because of the traditional rights of private property, enshrined in the myth that corporations are individuals, the corporate elite hold the creative privileges available" (1961:34). Porter's

---

[7]Fee-paying private schools of the Headmasters' Association in English Canada and classical colleges in Quebec were institutions where upper-class children received their education. The high cost of sending children to these privileged establishments restricted access to those whose parents were wealthy enough to pay high tuition and boarding costs. The class origins of the 1951 elite are compared with the 1972 corporate elite in the following paper, chapter 2.

findings indicate that by 1951 corporate capitalism had become well entrenched in Canada and that a financial elite still based in an upper class with strong political connections remained the keystone of the economic system. There are indications, however, that significant inroads had been made by U.S. industrialists into the manufacturing sector, traditionally the weakest sector as far as the Canadian economic structure was concerned. The period just following Porter's study confirms the trend to increasing U.S. control of industry and also indicates it has made intrusions into the resource sector as well. The implications of this will be analysed in the following section.

Parasites, Satellites and Stratification:
Current Trends in Canada's Economy

Following the historical development of a strong indigenous financial elite and a weak indigenous industrial elite, the 1950s witnessed the development of foreign control in manufacturing and resource sectors. As a strong social force in Canadian society, foreign-controlled multinational corporations[8] have a prominent place among Canada's dominant corporations. This serves to dislodge or prevent the emergence of a portion of the indigenous economic elite. Between 1952 and 1960 there was a dramatic inflow of U.S. capital into Canada, with U.S. direct investment rising by $6,017 million to $10,549 million compared to only $1,535 million U.K. direct investment by 1960. It is the almost doubling of U.S. direct investment, carried mainly through multinationals, in the span of only eight years that has had such a great impact on the Canadian economy and social structure. Foreign investment during the 1960s followed mainly the same pattern as the earlier decade. From 1960 to 1965, U.S. direct investment further increased by $3,196 million.

It is often argued that multinationals bring extensive capital into capital-poor areas, either geographically or developmentally defined, but the example of Canada suggests otherwise. Between 1960 and 1965 total new capital inflows from the United States amounted to $4.1 billion, but counter to this, outflow in the form of remittances to U.S. parent corporations amounted to $5.9 billion, a net outflow of capital from Canada to the United States of $1.8 billion (Levitt, 1970:94). In addition, most of the 'foreign' capital for expansion was obtained within Canada. Capital sources for expansion of foreign-controlled firms totalled $43.9 billion between 1946 and 1967, and only $9.7 billion or 22 per cent was from foreign sources. For the period 1960-67, this declined to only 19 per cent (Information Canada, 1972:25). Canadian

---

[8]"Neo-mercantilism" is a term sometimes used to describe the political economy of multinational corporations, but a distinction between the current stage and its namesake lies in the creation of an indigenous labour force, since the earlier form was primarily in the sphere of circulation, while the latter is in production. This has important implications for the structure of the labour force that develops. Leo Panitch has made this point privately.

capital and capital generated from retained earnings of foreign-controlled firms in Canada finances the majority of foreign-controlled investment and expansion.

Current Elite Structures

One point of analysis insisted on by elite theory is that it is not adequate to examine underlying economic processes and institutional structures alone, but that analysis must be taken to the level of relations between sets of people, particularly those holding the command posts of dominant institutions. Essential to elite analysis is the structure of decision making and the study of those holding key positions. It is only at this point that the structure of inequality can be analysed in terms of social stratification. For example, to argue that multinational corporations dominate part of Canada's economy would be incorrect. Elite theory insists it is those who head these corporations, the directors and senior management, who command the resources of these organizations. It is this essential de-reification of corporate structures that is integral to an analysis of social stratification.

As indicated, Canada in the 1960s witnessed a great transformation in its economic power structure. As a consequence of these developments, three major elites can be identified. First is the indigenous elite, closely associated with the dominant, Canadian-controlled financial, transportation and utilities corporations, with smaller representation in manufacturing and resource sectors. Second is a comprador elite, the senior management and directors of dominant foreign-controlled branch plants, mainly in the manufacturing and resource sectors. This group is subservient to a third group, the parasite elite,[9] which controls major multinationals that dominate important sectors of the Canadian economy through branch plants.

The difference between the use of portfolio and direct investment by the United Kingdom and the United States has already been emphasized. In terms of investment, it may be accurate to describe Canada's relationship with the United Kingdom as 'satellite,' since it was U.K. portfolio investment that developed an indigenous corporate elite. However, the notion of satellite does not capture the quality of Canada's relationship with the United States in the postwar period. The U.S. case involves direct control and development of a satellite elite within Canada, but this elite has only secondary power within the overall multinational framework. The powerful elite associated with U.S. direct investment is actually a foreign elite appropriately described

---

[9]A parasite, according to the dictionary, is something that receives advantage from its "host" "without giving any useful or proper return," thus reducing the host's potential for development. What is important is that this concept describes a particular relationship where actions of one party serve its own self-interest to the detriment of other parties. It is argued that this relationship most aptly describes how multinational corporations relate to structures of decision making and potential for development.

as a parasite. Comprador elites[10] are top managers and directors of branch plants who follow directives and policies from the multinational head-quarters. Their functions are mainly advisory and administrative, since they manage the affairs of subsidiaries; branch plants are simply subsidiaries of parent corporations that cross national boundaries and as such are subject to the same constraints as other subsidiaries.

Elite formations in a situation of high foreign control include parasite elites that control parent multinational corporations, comprador elites that manage branch plants, and an indigenous elite that controls national corpo-rations and may or may not be linked with foreign corporations in addition to its primary activities. Further elaboration of this structure would exist where the indigenous elite is itself multinational in character and acts as a parasite elite towards another nation. More complexity may also be intro-duced if the elite structure is international and members of an indigenous elite cross national boundaries and sit on boards of foreign-controlled parent companies.

With regard specifically to Canada, the traditional economic elite has never been seriously threatened in its stronghold by the burst of U.S. direct investment, and in fact it enjoyed a favourable position of servicing the industrial boom stimulated by U.S.-controlled investment.[11] Even in the few instances where their autonomy has been challenged, as in the Mercantile Bank affair and insurance company takeovers in the early 1960s, close alliances with political interests have allowed the members of this elite to capitalize on this privileged position and bring pressure to bear for legislation ensuring their protection. The fragmentation of the elite that has occurred does not necessarily, or often, breed conflict. On the contrary, the position of the indigenous elite, particularly the major section based in finance, transpor-tation and utilities, is reinforced by the industrial development occurring with U.S. direct investment. It is the smaller Canadian entrepreneurs based in industries that have not established themselves as dominant who feel the squeeze of U.S. penetration. Unable to maintain their autonomy, those in this group are frequently forced to sell their firms and join the ranks of the comprador elite or live off the proceeds from their sale.

In the meantime, other interests, not as well developed as the traditional

---

[10]The term 'comprador' has its origins in an analysis of China in about 1850 when there existed a 'hybrid society' of the Imperial system and foreign powers who used compradors as a way of mediating or as a 'wedge' for their interests in order to conduct business within that country (see Moore, 1966:176).

[11]In addition to providing capital backing to foreign firms, both parents and branch plants, the indigenous elite has been active in supplying utilities such as natural gas and hydroelectric power, and providing extensive transportation services such as ship lines and railways, and communication networks such as telephones and telecommunications, not to mention the services of trust and mortgage companies.

upper-class Anglo elite, are restrained from attaining economic power. These include, for example, French Canadians, members of 'third' ethnic groups, people from underdeveloped regions of Canada, such as the Maritimes and the West, and other members of regional and social hinterlands—not to mention the majority of the population not from the upper class.

Structured Inequality: Dominant Corporations and Their Interlocks
Control over major sources of capital, especially banks and insurance companies, as well as paramount positions within other key sectors of Canada's economy, serves as the power base of the corporate elite. With increasing economic concentration, the structure has become increasingly closed, thus making it more difficult for those outside the inner circles to break through. Tight controls prohibit other members of society from effective participation in economic decisions of consequence, decisions about the future, and the direction of the Canadian economy.

Presiding over the corporate world, members of the current corporate elite use as their means of power central institutions of the Canadian economy— 113 dominant corporations, their subsidiaries, affiliates, investments, and interlocking directorships with smaller corporations. Each of these 113 separate legal entities obscures the fact that at the top a small number of people with common social origins, common experiences and common interests oversee the direction of economic life. The 'corporate mirage' of competing, struggling corporations obscures the reality of elite power and masks overriding factors that bring those at the top together to govern these legal fictions.

Corporate Concentration
In the two decades since John Porter identified the central corporations in Canada, mergers and acquisitions have been prevalent among dominant corporations. For example, Domtar, itself an affiliate of Argus Corporation, has acquired three other dominant corporations as defined in 1948-50; John Labatt Limited has acquired three others, while Power Corporation has acquired four. Most prominent has been George Weston Limited, which includes no less than six earlier dominant corporations. Overall, of the 183 dominant corporations identified by Porter, 41 have been reduced to 17 companies through acquisitions and mergers. It should be remembered that this consolidation is only among the very largest companies that have also been absorbed. The centripetal movement represented by merger and acquisition centralizes the means of exercising power and further aggregates the scope of power held by the corporate elite. Over these twenty years there has been a consolidation of power by traditional elites; however, there has simultaneously been the increasing penetration of U.S. capital, representing a new social force within Canada. These two social forces, one new and the other traditional,

have developed side by side but have been located in relatively distinct sectors of the economy, as will presently be demonstrated.

Identifying Dominant Corporations

Dominant corporations are the largest companies within each corporate sector and the largest when compared across sectors. Corporations were divided into sectors by Standard Industrial Classification and compared to aggregate statistics for each sector. Classifications and aggregate data were provided by CALURA (Corporations and Labour Unions Returns Act Division of Statistics Canada). Using a 'composite index' of assets and revenue, 113 dominant corporations were selected as the largest within their sectors and within the economy as a whole. Assets and revenue controlled by the dominant corporations were then expressed as a percentage of all assets and revenue in their sector. The result of this procedure appears in Table 1.1 The high proportions in this wide range of economic activities illustrate the enormous power concentrated in only 113 dominant corporations. These proportions should be regarded as conservative for a variety of reasons:[12] sectors with the greatest concentration are also those with the greatest assets and revenue compared to all sectors. These 113 dominant corporations are the basis for the remaining analysis in this paper.

Directorship Positions

Directorship positions represent actual numbers of openings on the boards of corporations and are not equivalent to the number of persons, since one individual may, and often does, hold more than one position simultaneously. Examining directorships, including senior management, defined as dominant in 1951, Porter found that 170 corporations included 1,304 positions held by Canadian residents and an additional 309 held by persons resident outside Canada. In 1972, 113 dominant corporations include 1,454 positions held by residents of Canada, with an additional 301 held by outsiders. This represents an overall expansion in the number of elite positions since 1951 but a contraction in the number of dominant corporations. Two factors account for the larger number of positions. First, several new sectors in finance, including sales finance, mortgage and trust companies, have come into prominence during the period, and these tend to have larger boards than most companies. Another factor is that corporations defined as dominant in 1972 are relatively larger than those for 1951, and this typically means a

---

[12]These proportions are conservative because they do not take into account (1) the numerous interlocks members of the corporate elite have with middle-range companies, (2) the franchise, buyer and seller relations with smaller companies, (3) control dominant firms have by 'setting the pace' within particular corporate sectors, (4) control exercised by dominant corporations with less than 50 per cent holdings in smaller companies, and (5) influence on small companies by controlling access to the major sources of capital (see Clement, 1975:437-45, Appendix X).

Table 1.1
Assets and Revenue of 113 Dominant Corporations in Canada by Sector as Percentage of all Assets and Revenue, Year End 1971

Sector	Assets (percentage)	Revenue (percentage)
Finance		
Banks	90	91
Life insurance	86	81
Sales finance	90	—
Mortgage, trust companies	80	—
Trade		
Retail	39	45
Wholesale	15	11
Transportation and Utilities		
Utilities	66	81
Railways	89	87
Transportation (including pipelines)	90	31
Communications	97	93
Mining		
Metal mining	56	64
Mineral fuels	48	40
Manufacturing		
Paper products	52	57
Food and beverages	66	56
Petroleum	90	94
Non-metallic minerals	44	30
Primary metals	55	57
Transportation equipment	59	59
Machinery	66	58
Electrical products	35	31
Other manufacturing	29	43

Source: See Clement, 1975:396-433, Appendices V-IX, for sources of data, methodology, and classifications.

larger board is created. It is important to note that aside from minimal legal requirements, the size of the board and number of senior management positions are based on decisions by those in control and vary with the number of contacts they decide to establish.

The total number of foreign-resident directorships has remained stable over the period, shifting only slightly from 309 to 301 in spite of rapid increases in the amount of foreign control. This indicates that a simultaneous shift has occurred in the way foreign investment is now controlled. Rather than directors coming to Canada from foreign residences to board meetings, an increasing proportion of foreign subsidiaries are managed by inside directors, both Canadian- and foreign-born, resident in Canada. In other cases

Table 1.2

Residence and Control of Dominant Directorship Positions by Sector, 1972[a]

Residence and Control	Finance		Utilities		Trade		Manufacturing		Resources		All	
	N	%	N	%	N	%	N	%	N	%	N	%
Canada	655	76.9	128	75.3	90	51.7	101	44.7	80	24.0	1,054	60.0
U.S.	103	12.1	38	22.4	66	37.9	73	32.3	175	52.6	455	26.0
U.K.	60	7.0	2	1.2	18	10.4	27	12.0	28	8.4	135	7.7
Other	34	4.0	2	1.2	0	0.0	25	11.1	50	15.0	111	6.3
Total	852	100	170	100	174	100	226	100	333	100	1,755	100

[a]Joint ventures have been included by residence of director without control differentiation. "Residence and Control" includes the positions occupied by persons who are resident in the area indicated or are Canadian residents in foreign-controlled firms. For example, "Canada" includes persons resident in Canadian-controlled firms, while "U.S." includes those resident in the United States and comprador positions in Canada in U.S.-controlled firms.

Canadian participation is substantial in these subsidiaries, as will be evident when interlocks are examined.

Analysis of directorship positions by birth found 1,277 positions held by persons born in Canada, 301 held by those born in the United States, 113 in the United Kingdom and 64 born elsewhere. This leaves the impression that Canadian-born members dominate the boardrooms; however, when residence and birth are combined with control, a contrary situation is evident for some sectors. Porter found that in 1951, 27 per cent of the positions in dominant corporations were held by foreign residents or by Canadian residents in foreign-controlled corporations. In 1972 this *27 per cent had increased to 40 per cent.* When birth rather than residence is used, foreign control increases to 46 per cent of the positions. These figures represent the total of all sectors combined. When the analysis becomes sector specific, as Table 1.2 illustrates, important differences emerge that support the previous analysis concerning the particular concentration of traditional indigenous elites and the location of new social forces controlled outside Canada. For present purposes, only a table based on residence will be presented, although, as the above figures indicate, birthplace shifts the proportions toward greater foreign control, while the same pattern remains.

Wide variance between sectors and areas of control illustrates the validity of making such distinctions. Canadian residence and control account for about three-quarters of the positions in both finance and utilities (including transportation), while U.S. residence and control account for only about 12 per cent (the lowest U.S. participation) in finance and 22 per cent in utilities. It is evident that the core of indigenous Canadian capitalism is centred in its traditional forte of finance and utilities, accounting between them for three-quarters of all positions which are controlled in Canada by Canadian residents. Canadian control and residence account for about one-half the positions in trade, while U.S. participation increases to almost two-fifths and U.K. participation to about one-tenth. Canadian participation in manufacturing drops to 45 per cent, most of this accounted for by involvement in either pulp and paper or food and beverages; U.S. participation increases to about one-third, while "Other" area participation increases to about one-tenth, similar to that of the United Kingdom. The resource sector is important because over one-half the positions are controlled by U.S. residents or ownership, while Canadian participation falls below one-quarter; the United Kingdom remains at about one-tenth, while "Other" areas increase to 15 per cent.

The strongest overall indicator of the extent of compradorization remains the difference between the 27 per cent foreign-controlled positions based on residence in 1951 and the 40 per cent by residence and 46 per cent by birth in 1972. While this does indicate a significant increase in the amount of foreign, particularly U.S. control, a substantial segment remains Canadian in finance and utilities in spite of the erosion of power in manufacturing and resource sectors.

Corporate Interlocks[13]

(1) *Finance.* The nine chartered banks identified as dominant by Porter in 1951 had 203 directors, including five U.S. residents and one from the United Kingdom. In 1972 the five dominant banks total 231 directors, including seven U.S. residents, ten U.K. and one "Other." Although there are three times as many foreign residents now, they still account for only 9 per cent of all directorships in dominant banks. Porter found 197 Canadian residents with bank directorships held 297 directorships (22.7 per cent of all positions) in dominant corporations; in 1972 the 231 Canadian residents with bank directorships held 306 other dominant positions (25.1 per cent). In addition, over a quarter of the bank directorships are held simultaneously by a director of one of the eleven dominant insurance companies.

A strong explanation of why capital is difficult to secure for new ventures not undertaken by members of the elite is that banking circles are part of the established elite, making it almost impossible for outsiders to 'break in.' The elite members have both the contacts and legitimacy required for access to capital. Access to banks and insurance companies provides the advantage necessary to avail themselves of new investment opportunities. A tight financial system ensures bank investments will be stable and secure but also prohibits those outside the charmed circle from breaking into the elite. Banks and their extensive contacts with the elite provide a focal point for elite continuity and operate as major exclusion mechanisms.

Directors of the eleven dominant insurance companies had 27 per cent of the bank directorships in 1951 and 28 per cent in 1972; directors of banks, however, have had 41 per cent of dominant insurance directorships at both times. The greater proportion of bank directors holding key insurance directorships is due to the relatively small number of insurance (145) compared to bank (208) directorships. Because of the very close relation between banks and insurance companies, the tight circle around sources of capital becomes even tighter, encompassing the second major source of capital, the life insurance companies.

(2) *Dominant Corporate Interlocks.* There are a total of 1,848 interlocked directorship positions within the 113 dominant corporations in Canada. This enormous web of interconnections cuts across the formal structures of each dominant corporation; it is the existence of these multiple exchanges that permits the analysis to move from separate corporate entities to an interacting

---

[13]Corporate interlocks occur when one person holds two or more directorships simultaneously. In the following discussion only interlocking directorships are included, thus leaving aside the few cases where an executive of one dominant company does not sit on the company's own board but sits on the board of another dominant company. Typically, senior executives are simultaneously directors of their own companies. Interlocks discussed here are only among the 113 dominant corporations, but members of the elite also interlock extensively with smaller companies (see Clement, 1975:437-45, Appendix X).

Table 1.3
Corporate Interlocks between Dominant Corporations by Area of Control, 1972
(percentages)

Interlocks	Canada	U.S.	U.K.	Other
25 or over	41.4	5.8	10.0	14.3
10-24	29.3	22.8	40.0	57.1
Less than 10	29.3	71.4	50.0	28.6
Total	100	100	100	100
N[a]	(58)	(35)	(10)	(7)
Average	23.4	7.0	9.6	16.3

[a]Total of this table is 110 corporations, since three joint ventures are excluded.

set of powerful people, the corporate elite, who control and direct the Canadian economy.

Canadian-controlled companies are the greatest interlockers with other dominant companies. Core corporations with the highest interlocks are at the centre of the Canadian economy and provide institutional continuity for the entire elite. The five most interlocked companies among the 113 are the Canadian Imperial Bank of Commerce (ninety), the Bank of Montreal (seventy-three), the Royal Bank (sixty-three), the Canadian Pacific Railway (sixty-one), and Sun Life (sixty). Above all others, these stand as the core institutions of the economic elite. Not far behind are the Toronto-Dominion Bank, Bell Canada and Domtar with forty-six interlocks each. The foreign-controlled corporation with the highest number of interlocks is International Nickel (thirty-four), which is in the same category of over thirty interlocks as the Bank of Nova Scotia, Canada Life, Brascan, Argus, Huron and Erie, Dominion Stores, Trans-Canada Pipelines, Consolidated-Bathurst, John Labatt, Stelco and Massey-Ferguson. With twenty-five to twenty-nine are three foreign-controlled companies, Gulf Oil, Hudson's Bay and Canada Cement Lafarge, while Canadian-controlled Power Corporation, National Trust, Simpsons, Abitibi Paper and Molson are in the same range.

At the other end, there are seventeen Canadian firms with less than ten interlocks, and nine are family firms, including six of the eight with under five (13.8 per cent of the Canadian-controlled dominant companies). More than half the U.S.-controlled companies have less than five interlocks, while only 30 per cent of the U.K. companies and none of the "Others" have fewer than five. When the average number of interlocks by area of control is examined, companies controlled in the United Kingdom and "Others" are more integrated with the core of the Canadian elite than are those controlled in the United States. Canadian companies, as would be expected, have on the average the most extensive interlocking networks.

(3) *Multiple-Directorship Holders.* In 1951 Porter found that 203 members

of the corporate elite, or 22 per cent of the total, held more than one dominant directorship; together they held 600, or 46 per cent, of all dominant directorships (1965:589). This pattern is still evident in 1972, only more so. The proportion of directorships accounted for by people holding multiple directorships has increased from 46 per cent in 1951 to 54 per cent in 1972, indicating an increase in interaction at the upper levels of power from 1951 to 1972. There is also an increased proportion of the elite engaged in dominant interlocks, with a change from 22 per cent to 29 per cent. In other words, 274 members of the elite of 1972, representing 29 per cent of the total, hold 782 or 54 per cent of all dominant directorships. In 1951 three or more dominant directorships were held by 91 members of the elite, accounting for 28.8 per cent of all elite positions; in 1972, members are in the same category and hold 32.4 per cent of all dominant directorships. The implications of this shift are for further concentration of power at the top over the twenty-year period.

Conclusion

Two major processes have been occurring throughout Canada's economic history and particularly between 1951 and 1972. During these years, there has been a marked tendency for an increasing centralization and concentration of capital into fewer and larger firms, and secondly, there has been an increasing penetration of the economy by foreign, especially U.S., direct investment. These processes are associated with two social forces, one traditional and the other new. Traditional social forces are represented by the indigenous elite and are concentrated in finance, utilities and, to a lesser extent, in specific parts of the manufacturing and resource sectors. The new social force is represented by a comprador elite, the Canadian counterpart of a foreign-based parasite elite, concentrated in manufacturing and resource sectors.

Analysis has shown that during earlier periods, particularly in the 1880s, the social structure was relatively open and recent immigrants could enter manufacturing. However, as accumulation and concentration took effect, financiers consolidated smaller firms, thus closing avenues and limiting access. Since then, it has become increasingly difficult for other than the dominant Anglo upper class to enter the elite. The transformation of the economic structure, particularly since the growth of branch plants in the 1950s, has had an effect on the elite structure. This new elite has concentrated in sectors traditionally neglected by the indigenous elite. The comprador elite parallels rather than displaces the traditional elite, since it remains sector specific.[14] Since the traditional Canadian elite chose to gather its surplus in

---

[14]However, as was argued earlier, the parasite elite and its Canadian extension, the comprador elite, does inhibit the emergence of an indigenous elite in manufacturing and resources. It does displace a portion of the indigenous elite by buying out established dominant corporations, but this has largely occurred outside traditional areas of Canadian control.

the role of mediator rather than producer, it has committed itself, and Canada with it, to an economy wherein U.S. industrial capitalists represent a leading industrial force. The power of the indigenous elite has not been eroded in the process; quite to the contrary, it has further consolidated its position in traditional activities. The extremely high number of interlocks between the two major sources of capital, banks and insurance companies, as well as the extensive web between Canadian-controlled companies, illustrates that as corporations themselves become more concentrated so does the interaction between elites. Indeed, the fact that 29 per cent of the elite hold 54 per cent of the positions indicates that extensive elite interaction has been taking place among indigenous corporations in spite of the new social force represented by U.S. direct investment and the comprador elite. It should not be surprising in the following paper to find that avenues to the traditional elite have become more closed in the process; it will be interesting to note whether new social forces do bring new social types.

Chapter 2
Inequality of Access: Characteristics of the Canadian Corporate Elite

Continuing with the analysis begun in the previous paper, this one reports on the findings about economic elite characteristics. The results are the same as those reported in The Canadian Corporate Elite *(1975), although several footnotes have been added that reflect greater data coverage obtained when the study was later used for comparison in* Continental Corporate Power *(1977). In an unabashed way, this paper represents a classic elite analysis, concentrating on mobility into the elite without reflection on the consequences of power or the possibility of resistance by the non-elite, who, by implication, are powerless. It is very much modelled after John Porter's 1951 study, replicating as closely as possible his methodology. One significant difference, however, is the analysis of indigenous and comprador fractions of the elite, which is the most significant innovation of this study, aside from the obvious merits of being able to examine social change by having elite characteristics at two points in time. An important fact not sufficiently stressed in the paper is that the study is of the economic elite, not the capitalist class. The capitalist class is much larger and more diffuse than the economic elite, which is its most powerful edge. Of equal value to the understanding of corporate power, however, would be a study that examined fractions of the capitalist class based on size (not only the dominant fraction but medium and small capital as well). Even more important would be a study of the behaviour and actions of capital, not simply the characteristics of capitalists.*

Embedded in the capitalist economic order of Canada and perpetuated through the sanctity of private property, the corporate elite during the post-Second World War period has concentrated its base of power and consolidated avenues of access into its inner circles. Important transformations have occurred in the economic structure, and rapid industrialization has been evident; but the corporate elite remains as closed as it was in 1951, even tighter in some key respects. Contrary to liberal ideology, which holds that greater mobility will characterize 'post-industrialism,' Canada remains capitalist, industrial, and closed at the upper levels of corporate power. Many sociologists who celebrate existing structures assert that corporate capitalism, with time and industrialization, will reduce inequalities based on ascription. Talcott Parsons, for example,[1] argues that religion, ethnicity, regionalism, and social class based on ascriptive characteristics "have lost much of their force" (1970:14-15). Evidence now exists that shows this has not been the case for Canada between 1951 and 1972. Although only the upper levels of corporate power are examined in this study, other recent studies find that increasing inequality is a general phenomenon penetrating the entire social structure.

Leo Johnson (1973) has shown that income inequality between 1948 and 1968, and especially for the last ten years of the period, has involved a proportional shift in income distribution from the bottom income-earners to the top. Over the twenty-year period, "the only people who have received a disproportionately increased percentage of national income have been the richest one-third of Canadian income earners. The lower income workers have been the sufferers" (5). Recognizing that an overall shift has occurred in the amount of income received, Johnson focuses on the way this income is distributed and finds, for example,

in the 1958-1968 period, the bottom ten per cent of income earners suffered a loss in purchasing power of 35.6 per cent, while the second decile lost 6.6 per cent. On the other hand, the top deciles of income earners greatly increased their purchasing power . . . the top decile received, in addition to a 51.4 per cent increase in purchasing power, 72 per cent of all capital gains from the appreciation of share capital. [3-4]

Although members of the corporate elite are defined in terms of power and not by wealth, there exists a high correlation between the two in Canada. For example, a recent study of the presidents of Canadian corporations by Heidrick and Struggles Incorporated found that three-quarters of the presidents in corporations with sales of over $100 million had annual salaries over $100,000 (1973:6).

Enormous inequality in the distribution of income is not alleviated by the existing regressive tax structure, as a study by Allan Maslove (1972) for the Economic Council of Canada showed. His examination of taxation found that "the overall effective tax pattern is highly regressive to a Broad Income level of $5,000-$6,000. Taking Full Income as the base, regressiveness is evident up to an income level of $3,000-$4,000" (64). Given that 46 per cent

---

[1]For an excellent summary and discussion of similar positions taken by a variety of sociologists, see Goldthorpe, 1966.

of all family incomes in Canada are included in the under-$6,000 income class for 1969, the regressive tax structure affects a very large proportion of the population. Contrary to the ideology of progressive taxation, the 8.3 per cent of family units that received over $15,000 income in 1969 paid only 1.4 per cent higher than the average based on Full Income, and 8.4 per cent *less* than those earning under $2,000. Based on Broad Income, this highest group actually paid a lower proportion of taxes than did the average group (108-9, 128-29). In other words, the tax structure is hardly even proportional at the upper levels, and not progressive. Maslove summarizes his findings, saying that "the extremely regressive nature of the tax system at the low end of the income scale and the lack of progressivity over the remainder is the predominant conclusion to emerge from this study" (77).

It would not be correct to argue that the wealthy are paying higher taxes through the corporate structure. In fact, the corporate contribution to the total tax revenue has been rapidly declining in recent years. Rick Deaton (1972) has shown that "between 1962 and 1970, the corporate share of all Federal income revenue *fell* by roughly 38% while the individual share of Federal income tax revenue *increased* by over 23%." With respect to all provincial income tax revenue "between 1962 and 1970 the corporate share *fell* by over 60% while the individual share *increased* by roughly 83%" (32). The burden of taxation has been shifted from the corporate world to the individual. Given that individual taxation in Canada is regressive, this shift represents a further step in the direction of increasing inequality in favour of the rich and powerful.

The four trends outlined here — an increasing concentration of economic power, an increasing disparity in income distribution, a regressive tax system, and an increasing shift in taxation towards individuals as opposed to corporations — combine to provide a sense of uneasiness, not only about sociological theory, but also about the direction of Canadian society. These developments, and those to be outlined in this paper, should lead to a questioning of the future in store for Canadians if substantial social change does not occur.

Elites and Social Class

Corporate elite positions reflect Marx's analysis of the accumulation and concentration of capital into fewer and larger units and the 'Pareto principle' of 'separating the trivial many from the vital few.' The corporate elite are synonymous in many respects with the 'big bourgeoisie.' Within the 113 dominant corporations in Canada in 1972,[2] two dimensions of inequality are important. One involves positions within corporations, their stratification

---

[2] For a definition of dominant corporations, see the previous paper, chapter 1.

and power differentials, and the other, recruitment to these positions. The first is concerned with condition and the second with opportunity. In other words, the first is concerned about the structure of inequality, the second about the processes of maintaining inequality.[3] To show that a corporate elite exists demonstrates the existence of inequality of condition; to show that there is differential access to elite positions demonstrates that there is an unequal opportunity structure.

This dichotomy is similar to that outlined by Frank Parkin (1972) when he distinguished between the 'egalitarian critique' and the 'meritocratic critique.' The first focuses on "objection to the wide disparities of reward accruing to different positions," while the second is concerned about "the process of recruitment to these positions. . . . Seen from this angle, social justice entails not so much the equalization of rewards as the equalization of opportunities to compete for the most privileged positions" (13). Parkin suggests the importance of synthesizing the two critiques, since they are analytically distinct aspects of inequality but actually closely related. One concept used to integrate the two is kinship, whereby families are able to pass on their accumulated advantages intergenerationally, thus perpetuating class continuity through the ascriptive institutions of kinship and inheritance.[4] Of course, it is not kinship per se that perpetuates existing class structures. This is accomplished by the persistence of an economic order organized on the basis of corporate capitalism, which determines which types of occupations will be created, how many there will be, how the economy will expand, its direction and scope, and the level of technology that will exist. Class structures, therefore, are a product of the way a society's economy is organized, and class continuity, a product of the way privilege is transferred. In Canada, as with all capitalist societies, there is a high correlation between class structures and class continuity. Those with advantages are able to pass them on, while those without are not able to provide their offspring with the same privileges.

---

[3]The relationship between opportunity and condition has been examined in the previous paper.

[4]In a recent paper, Parkin (1974) has examined two types of 'social closure as exclusion.' One he calls 'class nomination,' whereby "ruling groups claim the right to nominate their successors, but not to transmit their statuses to their own lineal descendants . . . class nomination depends upon the use of exclusion rules which single out specific attributes of individuals, rather than the attributes of a particular social group." On the other hand, 'classes of reproduction' are "those exclusion practices which *are* based upon purely group attributes — lineage, race, religion, or whatever." He goes on to say the distinction "is of course a purely notional one; in most modern societies both sets of exclusion practices seem to operate" (4). In the following analysis of inequality of access to the Canadian corporate elite, it is apparent that both means of exclusion operate. For example, 'classes of reproduction' are evident in terms of both class and ethnicity and explain a great deal of the means of access to these elite positions, while for some others university education and particular career patterns based on 'class nomination' offer an explanation.

Hierarchies within economic organizations and the existence of dominant corporations create positions of power to which social classes are differentially recruited, thus perpetuating dominant classes and reinforcing power disparities. An examination of the inequalities of power associated with key corporate positions and the perpetuation of class advantages will illustrate a corporate elite with roots firmly embedded in the upper class.

Owners, Directors and Managers

Ownership and control are not as widely separated as has sometimes been suggested (see Zeitlin, 1974). Family firms among the dominant corporations in Canada still have a very prominent place. However, within some corporations, ownership has become dispersed, primarily within the upper levels of income earners, but controlling ownership typically remains concentrated. Dispersal of ownership, which does occur in some cases, is not spread evenly throughout the population. Indeed, in 1968 only 10.3 per cent of income earners owned even one share, and the top 10 per cent of income earners owned about three-quarters of all shares (Statistics Canada, 1970: Tables 2, 5). This results in a community of interest among a select group of large shareholders who provide binding ties transcending individual corporate entities. The small stockholder remains a rentier whose capital is mobilized as an investment for dividend and capital appreciation but not for control. Controlling ownership is presented usually by a block of about 10 per cent or more of the voting shares, if the remainder of the stock is widely dispersed. In this situation, a block of shares is able to control corporations that exceed the value of investment many times over. This, combined with the fact that there are 1,848 interlocked positions among the boards of the 113 dominant corporations in Canada (previous paper), makes an image of competitive capitalism difficult to maintain. In fact, 60 per cent of the executives in dominant corporations hold an outside directorship in at least one of the other 113 dominant corporations; moreover, members of the corporate elite also hold an additional 41 per cent of the uppermost positions (senior management and directors) in the next 175 largest corporations, many of them executive posts. In other words, the outside directors of one dominant company tend to be the executives of others. It is one thing to say a person is an outside director of a particular corporation and quite another to place that corporation within the entire network of large corporations where such persons are typically members of the executive of one or more other companies. Members of the corporate elite tend to have several roles simultaneously; many are owners, managers and directors all at the same time. Consequently, by broadening the scope of the study, the distinction between these three categories tends to lose much of its meaning.

Decision making remains a collegial activity involving those within the arena of power. Although the corporate elite is being defined as senior executives and members of the boards of the 113 largest corporations in

Canada, all within this group are not equal in their power. If share ownership were determined, the number of corporate elites would probably be substantially reduced. Senior executives and the boards of directors are, however, a strong indicator of stock ownership, since those who hold controlling blocks of shares are able to select the boards of directors for the corporation and these in turn appoint senior management. Porter argues, "Directors control the resources of corporations through particular legal instruments which give them the right to do so" (1965:229). The board of directors represents the interests of dominant shareholders directly and makes decisions of importance about the policy and direction of the corporation. Managers deemed important by the controlling interests, outsiders of importance, and the controlling ownership itself all sit on these boards.[5] It is the people who occupy these powerful positions in the 113 dominant corporations in Canada who are called the corporate elite.

Social Characteristics of the Corporate Elite

The findings of the present study show that access into elite positions has become more difficult for persons outside the upper class. Since 1951, there has been a crystallization of the upper levels of power beyond the already rigid power structure identified by Porter in 1951. Directors and senior executives were identified from the 113 dominant corporations operating in Canada, and it was shown that a total of 946 individuals resident in Canada hold 1,456 of the corporate directorships. Adequate biographical data was found for 775 persons (82 per cent), who between them account for 1,276 positions (88 per cent).[6] This compared favourably with Porter's coverage of 78 per cent of the members and 82 per cent of the positions for 1951.

Career Avenues into the Elite

Several important changes have occurred in the career patterns for members of the corporate elite. The proportion of members of the elite technically trained in science and engineering has declined. It would be expected that greater proportions of technical men would have made their way into the elite if specialized technical skills were now more central to decision making, as the post-industrial thesis would suggest, but this has not been the case.

Financial executives have remained stable, with one significant change occurring in terms of educational background for this group. While in 1951 only 45 per cent had attended university, in the 1972 group 60 per cent of the financiers, 70 per cent of the insurance company executives, and 57 per cent of

---

[5]See Clement, 1975:1–43, for a detailed discussion of the issues summarized here.

[6]A later re-analysis of these data with expanded sources increased coverage to 84 per cent of persons and 90 per cent of positions, plus additional information for those already included. See Clement, 1977:339.

the other financial executives have done so. While only a quarter of the banking executives have attended university, these seven represent a substantial increase from the one in twenty-three who had in 1951. Porter indicates that in 1951, 39 per cent of the financiers had elite connections, with such connections being most prevalent among the youngest group. This is borne out in the 1972 set of financiers, 46 per cent of whom have family connections in the elite. Bankers also have a high percentage (35 per cent) of elite connections. A high proportion of individuals in this group attended private school. Enjoying this advantage were twenty-three (46 per cent) financiers, nine (31 per cent) bankers, seven (23 per cent) insurance executives and eleven (37 per cent) other financial executives. Private schools have provided large numbers of the individuals in this category with common experiences at an early age, as well as allowing extensive contacts to be developed with other upper-class peers. These initial contacts have been fostered in later life within the confines of one or more of the exclusive national men's clubs (Rideau, Mount Royal, St. James, York, Toronto and National). Sixty-six per cent of the financiers, 90 per cent of the bank executives, 47 per cent of the life insurance company executives, and 70 per cent of the other financial executives belong to one or more of these six clubs.

Lawyers tend to be of upper-class origin, and many have inherited law firms and directorships from their fathers. There has been a substantial increase in the proportion of lawyers entering the corporate elite. This change is due almost exclusively to those who have law degrees but choose to enter the elite via the corporation legal department rather than the law firm. While only 9 per cent of the lawyers came through the legal departments of corporations in 1951, 24 per cent were internal recruits in 1972. This suggests an increasing number who have chosen law as a general education suited to the corporate world and not primarily as a means of entering private practice. Law partnerships, however, remain an important linking institution. Porter reports for 1951 that thirteen sets of partners had more than one member in the elite. This number has increased to twenty-three in 1972. Together they include 60 partners and 106 dominant directorships. Many lawyers share a common social experience in their educational careers; for example, four went to the University of Toronto for their LL.B.'s and then on to Osgoode Hall 'finishing school.' This included one pair of twins, John A. and James M. Tory, who followed their lawyer father's footsteps, together taking over five of his dominant corporate directorships. All the lawyers are trained in Canada, with half attending Osgoode Hall. About one-fifth go to the University of Toronto and one-fifth to McGill University. Private school education is not uncommon for lawyers in the elite; 46 per cent of those in law practice and 29 per cent of the internal lawyers have this advantage.

Similar proportions in both periods made it into the elite through the finance departments. In 1972, of the forty-four Canadian-born, thirty-three are chartered accountants, nine have economics or administrative training, and two appear to be inside trained, both of whom entered the corporate world after attending private schools. Only four of the fifteen foreign-born are chartered accountants. The others worked their way up as treasurers or comptrollers. For the most part, those entering the elite through the finance departments have entered as inside directors and remained there; they also have fewer interlocks with other dominant companies than do those with other career patterns.

Porter did not include commerce as a career pattern in 1951, noting that "comparatively few persons in the elite have been trained in commerce or business administration" (1957:381). Commerce careers have become more prevalent. Persons in commerce hold 5.1 per cent of the directorships in dominant corporations, 5.5 per cent of bank directorships, and 5.7 per cent of those in insurance. An additional thirty members of the elite have also received commerce degrees, but their main careers have been classified elsewhere.

Table 2.1

Main Career Patterns of the Corporate Elite, 1951[a] and 1972
(percentages)

	Canadian-born		Canadian- and Foreign-born	
	1951	1972	1951	1972
Engineering and science	19.3	12.1	22.3	13.9
Financier and finance exec.	18.0	17.9	16.7	17.9
Law	17.7	21.7	14.2	19.0
Finance department	6.0	6.6	6.7	7.6
Main career in other elites	2.1	6.4	1.8	5.8
Career in family firms	16.8	18.8	14.9	17.2
Own account	7.5	2.1	7.6	2.2
Commerce	—	4.6	—	4.4
Unclassified	12.4	10.1	15.6	12.0
Total	100.0	100.0	100.0	100.0
N	(611)	(673)	(760)	(775)

[a]See Porter, 1965: 275, Table 27.

More people have been classified in this study as having their main careers in another elite than was the case in 1951, but part of the reason for this is a redefinition in this study of what constitutes inclusion. In 1951 only fourteen persons (1.8 per cent) transferred to the corporate elite after having their main careers in the political, bureaucratic or military elite. In 1972, 5.8 per cent of the corporate elite entered by way of another elite, including eighteen from the bureaucratic elite and seventeen from the political elite as defined by Porter (1965) and Olsen (1980). An additional ten are classified as coming from the academic elite, including university deans, presidents and prominent professors, particularly from business schools. There are no members having their main careers in the military. Even using only the political and bureaucratic elite, the numbers when compared to Porter's findings have more than doubled, representing a greater degree of interlock between the corporate and state elites than existed twenty years earlier. Among the members of the political elite are eight former Cabinet ministers, five former provincial premiers, one former prime minister and three provincial political elites. 'Career switchers' hold 6.2 per cent of all dominant directorships.

The 133 individuals who have been characterized as gaining access to the elite through family firms have spent the majority of their business careers in corporations where their fathers, or in five cases maternal grandfathers, held key corporate positions.[7] This does not include those who began at or near the top of the class structure, nor does it include those who gained their access through their father-in-law's firm. There are 133 individuals in this category in 1972, compared to the 113 in 1951. The 1972 figure includes 126 of the Canadian-born (18.8 per cent) and only 7 foreign-born (6.8 per cent). Within the 1972 elite who are Canadian-born with their main careers in family firms, there are twenty-four father/son combinations, and thirty-two are brothers. In examining the entire group of 133 individuals who inherited their positions, it becomes evident that private schools play a large part in their careers. Eighty-five attended private schools (64 per cent of the group), and 108 attended university (81 per cent). The power of this group extends further than does that of any other group in terms of interlocking director-ships; they account for 18.7 per cent of the directorships in all dominant companies, 23 per cent in banks, with 35 per cent of the group holding dominant bank directorships, and 21.4 per cent of the insurance directorships.

Class Origins

Class origins are important from a number of perspectives. They show the extent of mobility existing at any given time and (if more than one time-frame is available, as in the present case) relative changes in class access to elite positions. For those concerned with mobility, it is assumed that talent is distributed throughout all classes in society and if everyone had an equal chance at access to the elite the total society would be better served. From the perspective of liberal democratic theory, the concern is focused on the value that everyone should have equal opportunity to participate in the manage-ment and direction of a society's future. From the social structural perspec-tive, class access is an important indicator of the degree of openness present in the flow between different classes or, put differently, the extent of class crystallization in a society. The more difficult it is for people outside the upper class to enter the elite, the greater the exclusiveness of power in a

---

[7]Additional data increased to 26.8 per cent from 18.8 per cent the proportion with careers in family firms (Clement, 1977:196n).

particular society. With greater crystallization of power, there is less opportunity for those outside the inner circles of power to actualize their concerns and desires, thus stifling equality of opportunity, which forms the basis of liberal democratic ideology.

Table 2.2

Class Origins of the Canadian-Born Members of the Corporate Elite, 1951 and 1972
(percentages)

	Population[a] (approximate)	Corporate Elite 1951	Corporate Elite 1972[c]	Percentage-Point Change 1951 to 1972
Upper class[b]	1-2	50	59.4	+9.4
Middle class	15	32	34.8	+2.8
Working class	85	18	5.8	−12.2
Total		100	100	
N		(611)	(673)	

[a]The population 'at risk' breakdown is based on a calculation of occupations in 1941, the census year closest to when most members of the current elite entered the labour force. At that time, 12 per cent of the labour force was engaged in middle-class occupations, including professional, managerial and proprietary. Only 8 per cent of the male population of the age group of the current elite had even some university. Taking into account the known high overlap between sons of the middle class and those entering university, the proportion from middle-class origins is estimated at about 15 per cent of the population. Working-class origins are less than middle class, thus including manual, service and primary occupations. Upper class includes members of one of the corporate, political or bureaucratic elites, also fathers with large but not dominant corporations, and their families. See also private schools in note *b* below, and note *b* in Table 2.3.
[b]Includes attendance at one of the Headmasters' Association private schools or classical colleges. See Table 2.3 for detailed breakdowns of class indicators.
[c]Additional evidence changed upper class to 61 per cent, middle class to 33 per cent and working class to 6 per cent (Clement, 1977:274).

Table 2.2 presents a summary of class origins for the elite in 1951 and 1972. Several dimensions collapsed here are presented in detail in Table 2.3. These tables provide conclusive evidence that access to the corporate elite has become more exclusively the preserve of the upper class from 1951 to 1972. Using the same criteria and indicators as Porter, the present study replicates as closely as possible the methodology used earlier. Comparing overall changes between 1951 and 1972, it is found for the Canadian-born members of the 1972 elite that 28.5 per cent had fathers, or, in a few cases, uncles, in the corporate elite at some time. This represents an increase of 6.5 percentage points from 1951 of the proportion of the elite enjoying the advantage of coming from a family directly in the inner circles of the corporate world in a previous generation. There is obviously a high degree of continuity when 192 members replicate their fathers' positions. Adding 16 members who had fathers either in the political or bureaucratic elite increases the proportion

Table 2.3

Class Origins of the Canadian-Born Members of the Corporate Elite, 1951 and 1972

Class Indicators	All			Top 100			Multiple Directorship			1951[f]	
	N	(Cumulative) N	%	N	(Cumulative) N	%	N	(Cumulative) N	%	(Cumulative) Top 100	All
Upper[a]											
Father in corporate elite	192	(192)	28.5	26	(26)	32.5	86	(86)	37.4	30.3	22
Father in other elite	16	(208)	30.9	1	(27)	33.8	7	(93)	40.4	37	24
Wife from elite family	39	(247)	36.7	5	(32)	40	16	(109)	47.4	46	31
Father in substantial corporation	68	(315)	46.8	12	(44)	55	30	(139)	60.4	54.4	37.8
Upper/Middle[b]											
Attended private school	85	(400)	59.4	8	(52)	65	27	(166)	72.2	67	50
Middle											
Father in middle-class occupation[c]	57	(475)	67.9	7	(59)	73.8	15	(181)	78.7		
Attended university[d]	177	(634)	94.2	16	(75)	93.8	37	(218)	94.8	85.2	82
Working[e] (left)	39	(673)	(5.8)	5	(80)	(6.2)	12	(230)	(5.2)	(14.8)	(18)
N	(673)			(80)			(230)			(88)	(611)

[a]Since the categories are presented as mutually exhaustive from top to bottom, some in higher categories could also be placed in lower ones.

[b]"Upper/Middle" refers to the fact that although private schools are not exclusively the preserve of the upper class, they are primarily upper class. The values as well as lifestyles are those of the upper class. It should be remembered that most current members of the elite would have attended private schools during the thirties.

[c]"Middle-class occupations" refer to that section of the population with the advantages of high skills and income. This includes fathers who were doctors, lawyers, engineers or managers, and also ministers, who are special cases, since they have high status and advantages such as reduction in their sons' tuition fees at private schools.

[d]Since only about 8 per cent of the male population in the age group of the 1972 elite had even some university training, it is reasonable to assume that using this as an indicator of middle-class origin is still confining the class of origin to fairly near the top of the class structure.

[e]Elite members in this category have none of the above attributes and are considered to be of working-class origin.

[f]For a detailed breakdown of Porter's findings for 1951, see Porter, 1965:292, Table 28. Porter collapsed "father in middle-class occupation" and "attended university," while these have been reported separately here.

to 30.9 per cent compared to 24 per cent in 1951. A further 39 not already included married into elite families. This means that 247 members of the 1972 elite embarked on their careers with the initial advantage of having elite connections. This represents about a six-percentage-point increase since 1951. Another 68 members not thus far included had fathers who were in substantial businesses which, as far as could be determined, were not dominant but of sufficient size to provide an initial upper-class avenue into the elite. This means that 46.8 per cent of the elite in 1972 began at or near the top of the class structure.[8] The 1972 figure for those who started with this initial advantage shows a full nine percentage-point increase over the 1951 findings. Of the remainder, 85 had attended private schools. This brings to 400, or 59.4 per cent of the elite, the number who had upper-class origins, a significantly higher percentage than the 50 per cent with the same origins in 1951.

A further 57 members of the elite had fathers who were engaged in middle-class occupations, such as engineers, doctors, lawyers, ministers or managers. This brings the total to 457, accounting for almost 68 per cent of the elite. There are also 177 persons not included to this point who had attended university. The addition of this group brings the proportion accounted for to 94.2 per cent, while the same indicators accounted for only 82 per cent in 1951. The remaining percentage accounts for those who have made it into the elite from lower than middle-class origins. While, in 1951, 18 per cent of the elite were in this bottom classification, only 5.8 per cent of the 1972 elite are in the same position. The majority of the population, of course, have less than middle-class origins as defined here, with over 80 per cent of the male population engaged in other than managerial, technical or professional occupations (see Kalbach and McVey, 1971:257). Each indicator shows that the 1972 elite is of higher class origins than twenty years earlier. The class structure of Canadian society has tightened in terms of gaining access into the corporate elite.

Table 2.2 illustrates that particularly the upper class, but also the middle class, is overrepresented compared to the general population. Moreover, this general overrepresentation has increased from 1951 to 1972. While there is no reason to believe that there have been any significant changes in the size of the upper class, the proportion of those with upper-class origins in the elite has increased by 9.4 percentage points over the period. The number of persons in the elite in 1972 who are of middle-class origin has increased by 2.8 percentage points, a change that could correspond to a change in the class composition of the population. Those with working-class origins represent a significant decline of 12.2 percentage points. The major difference between

---

[8]"At or near the top" refers to those who began their careers having previous-generation kin in one of the three elites or having a substantial business with a substantial business possibly dominant in the past but minimally 'middle range.'

the two periods can be found in the 6.5-percentage-point increase in the proportion with fathers in the corporate elite, and particularly those whose careers are in family firms, as discussed earlier. It is recognized that there is differentiation within the elite based on length of time in the elite, corporate position, control exercised as in the case of comprador and indigenous elites, corporate activities or functions, and between single- and multiple-directorship holders. These will now be examined.

Elite Continuity

Within the elite in 1972 there is a set of seventy-six members who appeared as well in the 1951 elite; that is, they have survived over twenty years in the corporate elite. Analysis of this group showed a conservative bias in the method of data collection on social origins in favour of lower class origins. Based on this, it can be asserted that the method employed by Porter and replicated here understates the extent of elite reproduction. This analysis also found that there is a dramatic difference between the class origins of the group that had been in the elite for twenty years and all members of the elite for 1951 and 1972. Exactly one-half of the first group had fathers who were themselves in the economic elite in an earlier period. This involves thirty-eight individuals, of whom thirty-five directly inherited directorships from their fathers. Inheritance is substantially more prevalent for those who have lasted twenty years or more than for all members of either the 1951 or the 1972 elites. It is found that 68.5 per cent of the core group had upper-class origins compared to 50 per cent and 59.4 per cent of the 1951 and 1972 elites, respectively. This suggests not only that upper-class members move to the top at an earlier age but that they last longer, providing greater historical continuity than even their high numbers in the elite as a whole would imply. It also illustrates that private property in the form of inheritance is a major legal device members of the upper class have for staying in powerful positions, and they use this to pass privileges on to their offspring. It is also important to note that within this group there are only three French Canadians and one Jew (less than 4 per cent) and no one from other ethnic groups aside from Anglo-Saxons. This illustrates that only Anglo-Saxons have high continuity within the elite, most likely because they control capital in terms of ownership, which they are able to transfer intergenerationally.

Corporate Positions

Few members of the elite could be said to be selected *meritocratically* in the sense that they have worked their way up through the corporate bureaucracy without the advantages of middle- or upper-class origins. Even all inside directors are not meritocratic. Rather they are of two types: first, sons learning the business; and, second, those engaged in a long, or relatively long, crawl to the boardroom. Based on an analysis of the differences between the class origins of insiders and executives, it can be said that even at the upper levels of power those with class advantages are more likely to make the break from the insider to executive level: 63.5 per cent of the outside directors and 62 per cent of the excutives have upper-class origins, while only 46.7 per cent of the inside directors enjoyed this advantage. If the sons who have careers in family firms are excluded, only 31 per cent of the inside directors originated in the upper class. It is evident that it is primarily sons learning the business and those of upper-class origin who are able to make the shift into the executive ranks from within the bureaucracy and similarly into the circle of outside directors. Given this phenomenon, it is doubtful that many of the insider comprador elites will break into the executive ranks of the multi-national corporations they work for.

Comprador Elites and Mobility
The comprador elite[9] is made up of those members of the elite who identified their main corporate affiliation as a Canadian subsidiary of a foreign-controlled parent. In cases where the 'principle occupation' was other than corporate, as in the case of a law firm, the designation was based on the country of control of the corporations in which the individuals held the majority of their dominant directorships.

When the affiliations of all Canadian-born members are analysed, it is found that 76 per cent are members of the indigenous Canadian elite, 15.8 per cent are U.S.-controlled comprador elites, 5.6 per cent U.K. comprador elites, and 2.6 per cent 'other' comprador elites.[10] When the various elites are divided by age, an interesting pattern emerges. Of those born before 1905, 84.9 per cent are members of the indigenous elite, with only 12.6 per cent U.S. comprador, 1.7 per cent U.K. and 0.8 per cent 'other.' In contrast, of those born between 1905 and 1920, 73.2 per cent are indigenous, a drop of over 10 per cent from the older group, while 17 per cent are U.S. comprador, 5.6 per cent U.K. and 4.2 per cent 'other.' The youngest group, born after 1920, begins to reverse the age relationship, with 76 per cent indigenous, 15.8 per cent U.S., 5.6 per cent U.K. and 2.6 per cent 'other.' The increasing compradorization of the corporate elite represented by the shift from the

---

9The current elite structures have been discussed in detail elsewhere, including the definitions and relationships between comprador, parasite and indigenous elites (see previous paper). The reason for using the main corporate affiliation — which was self-identified — as the major criteria for determining indigenous or comprador elites is that this is the main base of power the person has for operating within the elite. For example, when the presidency of a foreign-controlled company (a comprador position) changes hands, the outgoing president typically drops his indigenous directorships when he returns home and these are often picked up by his successor. In other words, outside directorships are usually dependent upon one base of power, the main corporate affiliation, from which the elite member operates.

10It should be noted that these figures refer only to Canadian-born members of the elite and to persons, not positions. The degree of structural compradorization by corporate sector has been examined in the previous paper, chapter 1.

oldest to the middle group is counteracted by the youngest group, which has the highest degree of inheritance and is consequently indigenous.

In spite of the high degree of inheritance within the youngest age group, there are still 8.9 per cent more comprador elites in this group than in the oldest, while an 11.7-percentage-point difference between the middle and oldest group remains the greatest gap. Although the overall trend from 1951 to 1972 has been toward increased compradorization of the Canadian corporate elite, there still remains a strong and vigorous indigenous core, evident in the existence of the youngest group of indigenous capitalists.

A very interesting difference exists between comprador and indigenous elites with respect to class origins. While 'only' 45 per cent of the comprador elite started out with upper-class advantages, 64 per cent of the indigenous elite had this initial advantage. For the middle class, a reversal occurs, with the comprador elite having 50 per cent of its members within the middle class, while only 30 per cent of the indigenous elite are in this category. Comprador elites are more middle class than indigenous elites. For the working class, there is a greater proportion of members from the indigenous elite than comprador, accounted for predominantly by Canadian institutions such as banks that have tended in the past to have lower-class recruitment through their ranks. For this reason it can be stated that compradorization is predominantly a phenomenon of the middle class. (See Table 2.4.)

Compradorization has permitted some members of the middle class, but not the working class, to participate in arenas of power, unlike the indigenous elite, who have higher-cl? .: origins and tend to exclude even the middle class. The process of compradorization is primarily a phenomenon of the middle class and does not have the same impact on the upper class. The implications of this will be developed in the conclusion of this paper. Although the comprador elite has power within the Canadian context, or at least represents the power outsiders exercise in Canada, within the continental or North Atlantic triangle framework this so-called elite has only secondary power, since it is dependent upon the externally based parasite elite.

Elite Size and Concentration
Table 2.5 includes two further divisions, the "Top 100" and "Multiple Directorships." Porter introduced the division of the Top 100, which is replicated here,[11] but another basis of differentiation that distinguishes between single- and multiple-directorship holders within dominant corporations has also been introduced. Although including only about 10 per cent of the entire elite in 1972, as it did in 1951, the Top 100 have a scope well beyond their

---

[11]The "Top 100" were selected in this, and in Porter's study, on the basis of holding top executive positions, particularly presidencies and chairmanships, within the largest of the dominant corporations, multiple directorships which included more than one of the largest dominant corporations, or a combination of each of these.

Table 2.4

Class Origins of the Canadian-Born Members of the Comprador and Indigenous Elites, 1972

(percentages)

	Comprador	Indigenous	Percentage-Point Difference between Comprador and Indigenous Elites
Upper class[a]	45.3	63.9	+18.6
Middle class	50.4	29.9	−20.5
Working class	4.3	6.2	+1.9
Total	100	100	
N	(161)	(512)	

[a]See Table 2.2, note *b*.

Table 2.5

Class Origins of Canadian-Born Members of the Corporate Elite by Subgroups, 1972

(percentages)

	All	Top 100	Single Directorships	Multiple Directorships
Upper class[a]	59.4	65.0	52.8	72.8
Middle class	34.8	28.8	41.1	22.0
Working class	5.8	6.2	6.1	5.2
Total	100	100	100	100
N	(673)	(80)	(443)	(230)

[a]See Table 2.2, note *b*.

numbers. They hold 342 of the dominant directorships, that is, 24 per cent of those held by Canadian residents, 59 of the directorships in the five big banks (28 per cent of the positions), and 36 insurance directorships (25 per cent). These figures are almost identical to those of 1951, the corresponding figures being 25 per cent, 29 per cent and 23 per cent, respectively. One difference between the Top 100 identified in 1951 and those for 1972 is that there were eighty-eight Canadian-born in the group for the earlier period but only eighty in the later one.

Of the 274 multiple-directorship holders resident in Canada, adequate biographical data was available for 267, representing a coverage of 97.5 per cent. These 267 individuals constitute 28.9 per cent of the total number of elites resident in Canada. Although Porter did not use multiple-directorship holders as an analytical distinction, he did report that 22 per cent of the Canadian residents had a total of 46 per cent of the dominant directorships in

1951. Multiple-directorship holders in 1972, while representing only 28.9 per cent of the elite, account for 53.8 per cent of all dominant directorships, 58.6 per cent of all insurance directorships, and 68.3 per cent of the directorships in five key banks. Enormous power is concentrated in this group and represents an increased number of directorships and a greater scope over 1951. Over half the group holds a directorship in one of the key banks. Together they hold over two-thirds of these important posts.

The core of the corporate elite can be considered as members of the Top 100 and those who hold multiple directorships. Since only fifteen members of the Top 100 are not overlapped with multiple-directorship holders, there is a core of 282 persons who wield enormous economic power, even relative to other members of the corporate elite.

There is a great similarity between the class origins of the Canadian-born members of the Top 100 in 1951 and 1972 in that 65 per cent of each group had upper-class origins. The most important finding is that almost three-quarters of those who hold multiple directorships are from the upper class, 13.4 percentage points more than the elite as a whole. Even when compared to the Top 100, 8 percentage points more of the multiple directors started in the upper class. Once again, class barriers became important within the elite. Members with upper-class origins have a much stronger probability of becoming multiple directors than do those from lower classes. This confirms the value of upper-class connections and the social network operating at that level. Another fact which confirms the vitality and power of the core group of indigenous capitalists is the fact that 86 per cent of those with multiple directorships are Canadian-born.

Closing Avenues to the Elite

A good deal of evidence arises from this study to indicate that the elite is becoming an increasingly closed group. This will be summarized here for banks, new corporate sectors, and regionalism.

Banks

Traditionally, the long crawl through the banks was one institutional avenue leading to the elite for those starting near the bottom of the class structure. Many bank executives used to begin at a very young age as clerks in local branches and work their way up over an average of forty years into the executive ranks. To some extent this is still possible, but over the years from 1951 to 1972 this avenue of mobility has become restricted. More executives than previously come from upper-class families, go to private schools and university, and enter the executive ranks at a much earlier age. For example, nine of the twenty-nine bank executives (31 per cent) attended private schools, and ten (35 per cent) have family connections in the elite. Three of the executives have postgraduate training, two at Harvard and one at the London School of Economics. Seven have undergraduate degrees. The tightening of the upper levels in the banks is part of a general trend in this direction. With more of the upper class being recruited into the elite and with this one avenue being closed off to the lower classes, there are indications that the future will see even greater monopolization of positions of power by the upper class.

New Sectors

Of interest from the perspective of social change is the effect that expanding the scope of activities covered by dominant corporations has on the composition of the elite. Three new sectors have been introduced to the analysis since 1951, including trust companies, mortgage companies, and sales finance and consumer loan corporations. By examining class origins of elite members from these 'new' financial fields, it is possible to determine whether their presence has had an effect on class access to the elite. Those individuals with directorships in only *one* of these sectors and holding no other dominant directorships will be examined. It is expected that class origins would shift lower, since virtually all those with multiple directorships are excluded by definition. In spite of these qualifications, a similar class distribution remains. Examining those from the upper class, 60.2 per cent of the subset are included, with 59.4 per cent overall, compared to 50 per cent overall in 1951. The evidence shows that no inroads have been made into the elite because of the increased importance of these new sectors; quite the contrary, nearly one-quarter of these 'new' positions are filled by sons of previous corporate elite members. At the other end of the class structure, only 8 per cent of the new group started with working-class origins, while 5.8 per cent of the entire group were in the same situation compared to 18 per cent in 1951. This suggests that expanding the scope of the elite does not mean new social types are necessarily recruited. They can, as this data indicates, be 'captured' by the traditional power holders. In Canada this is facilitated by the fact that these new sectors are all in finance, the traditional preserve of the indigenous elite. Another potential source of lower-class mobility is cut off, and upper-class control becomes more pervasive.

Regionalism

Analysis of regionalism in Canada also indicates that avenues leading to the elite are closing. By examining the disparity between birthplace of elites and the distribution of population at the time of their birth, it is possible to establish that regional inequalities exist in terms of access possibilities into the elite. Of the Canadian-born members of the elite, 68 per cent were born in Ontario or Quebec, 23 per cent in the western provinces, and only 9 per cent in Atlantic Canada. When this is compared to the 1921 distribution of population, the census year closest to when most of the elite under study were born, it is found that the central provinces are overrepresented by about eight percentage points, while the West is underrepresented by five percentage points and the East by three percentage points. There is a thirteen-percentage-point difference between the Centre and the western periphery and eleven percentage points between the Centre and the East, with the Centre overrepresented in each case.

For present purposes, it is important to analyse differential class access by regions as distinct from disparities in numerical representation. Table 2.6 shows that, as would be expected, Ontario and Quebec, with their longer-established and more-crystallized class structures, have more elite members from the upper class with 62.7 per cent than Atlantic Canada, which is next with 59.3 per cent, and the West, which has the lowest number with only 50 per cent of the elite members born there having upper-class origins. There is a substantially greater difference between the West and the Centre (about 13 percentage points at the upper level) compared to the East and the Centre (a difference of only 3.4 percentage points). The findings suggest a high degree of similarity between the Centre and the East, based on the older established class structures in these regions. The West, on the other hand, as an immigrant society, did not have a rigid class structure relative to the other parts of Canada when the 1972 elites were growing up in the twenties and thirties, or even when they were embarking on their careers in the forties. An important conclusion that can be drawn is that as social structures mature and become more established, the chances decrease for those from the working and even middle class to enter elite positions. The small difference between the Centre and the East also indicates that it is not so much the level of development within the region that determines mobility as the maturity of the class structure. Measured in terms of economic development, the East would be more similar to the West than to Ontario and Quebec. The major determinant of mobility would then seem to be the length of time the class structure of a particular region is allowed to survive without encountering social upheavals rather than the level of economic development within the region. The more hierarchical the social structure, the less chance for mobility, regardless of the so-called opportunity structure, which is said to be correlated with the level of development in society. It can be argued that as the West begins to mature, another avenue of access to elite positions from lower class origins may also be cut off.

Career Avenues and Corporate Sectors
Of the 673 Canadian-born members of the corporate elite, 63 per cent, or 433, can be classified as having used one primary corporate sector as an avenue into the elite. This particular analysis is limited to those born in Canada because its purpose is to isolate indigenous avenues into the elite. Of the remaining 37 per cent Canadian-born not classified, 127 used law as the main avenue and 35 came from other elites. A further 78 could not be classified as having entered the elite through any one of the five sectors. These include some from construction, engineering firms, accounting firms, the

Table 2.6

Regionalism and Social Class of the Corporate Elite, 1972[a]

(percentages)

	Birthplace			
	West	Centre	East	All
Upper class	50.0	62.7	59.3	59.4
Middle class	44.3	31.8	32.2	34.8
Working class	5.7	5.5	8.5	5.8
Total	100	100	100	100
N	(158)	(456)	(59)	(673)

[a]For a discussion of more-detailed regional categories and residence as well as birthplace, see Clement, 1977:226-29.

media, architecture, real estate, advertising and other activities, including some who switched between sectors during their careers.

Sectors were divided in Table 2.7 into major divisions and separated by control in order to determine what main corporate avenues have been used by the Canadian-born elite to move into their present positions. Of those classified, 8.8 per cent came through utilities, 38.8 per cent through finance, 18.7 per cent through resources, 22.2 per cent through manufacturing, and 11.5 per cent through trade. When separated by control, this same group includes three-quarters who gained access to the elite through Canadian-controlled firms, about one-fifth through U.S.-controlled companies, and 3 per cent each through U.K.- and 'other'-controlled companies.

The findings indicate that by far the greatest corporate avenue is through Canadian-controlled finance corporations. Within the transportation and utilities sector, 92 per cent had their early careers in Canadian-controlled

Table 2.7

Career Avenues of Canadian-Born Members of the Elite by Corporate Sectors and Area of Control, 1972

(percentages)

	Sector					
Control	Finance	Utilities	Trade	Manufac-turing	Resource	All (%)
Canadian	94.6	92.1	88.0	58.3	38.3	75.1
U.S.	3.6	7.9	6.0	27.1	53.1	18.7
U.K.	1.2	—	6.0	6.3	3.7	3.2
Other	0.6	—	—	8.3	4.9	3.0
Total	100	100	100	100	100	100
Distribution	38.8	8.8	11.5	22.2	18.7	100
N	(168)	(38)	(50)	(96)	(81)	(433)

firms, while the remainder were in U.S.-controlled companies. This increases to 95 per cent through Canadian-controlled finance companies. Canadian-controlled companies in trade were also the main avenue for 88 per cent. In manufacturing the situation begins to change, with only 58 per cent using Canadian-controlled companies, and 57 per cent of these are in food, beverages and related products, while U.S.-controlled manufacturing accounts for 27 per cent. In the resource sectors, U.S. companies have the greatest career avenues, accounting for 53 per cent, over half of all those who have used U.S.-controlled companies. Canadian-controlled resource firms account for only 38 per cent of the avenues in this sector, with 68 per cent of these in pulp and paper.

Table 2.8

Ethnic Representation in the Corporate Elite

(percentages)

	Economic Elite		Canadian Population	
	1951	1972	1951	1972
Anglo-Saxon	92.3	86.2	47.9	44.7
French	6.7	8.4	30.8	28.6
Other	1.0[a]	5.4	21.3	26.7
Total	100	100	100	100
N	(760)	(775)		

[a]Porter says 0.78 per cent of his sample is Jewish; other 'third' ethnic groups "were hardly represented at all" (1965:286).

Aside from U.S. resource companies, which provide avenues for 10 per cent of the Canadian-born classified, and to a lesser extent U.S. manufacturing, which provides an avenue for about 5 per cent of the total, foreign firms have not been a major avenue to the elite for Canadians. Canadian-controlled companies, particularly in finance, utilities and trade, have been a more common avenue. The evidence would suggest that there remain independent Canadian-controlled avenues, open to at least upper-class Canadians born in Canada. There is still a core of Canadian elites who very much control the access into their select ranks.

Ethnicity and Inequality of Access[12]
In Canada, as in other societies built on conquest and immigration, ethnicity is interwoven into the class system, providing advantages for the conquerors while keeping the conquered and the newly arrived at the bottom of the so-called opportunity structure. Two elite systems based on the two charter

---

[12]A much more extensive analysis of ethnicity and the economic elite, as well as comparisons with the political and bureaucratic elites, is provided in Clement and Olsen, 1974.

groups provided their members with differential access to the corporate elite, while the 'third force' of other ethnic groups does not even have an elite of its own to operate in the national arenas of economic power.[13]

French Canadians
Although French Canadians constitute about one-third of Canada's population, only sixty-five members of the corporate elite could be classified as such, making the French component of the elite only 8.4 per cent. For 1951 Porter found there were fifty-one French Canadians representing only 6.7 per cent of the elite at that time. This represents a net increase of only fourteen persons, or 1.7 percentage points over the period 1951-72. The slight changes evident between the two periods have not decreased Anglo-Saxon dominance, since the slight decline in the total proportion of Anglo-Saxons in the corporate elite is completely offset by their decline in the total population over the same period. It has been shown elsewhere that the Anglo-Saxon 'index of representation' remains identical for each period; that is, they are just as overrepresented in 1972 as they were in 1951 when compared to their proportion in the population (see Clement and Olsen, 1974:25-26). Some may argue that while the French have not made it into the very top of the corporate world, they have made strong gains in the middle-range and smaller corporations. Once again the evidence is to the contrary. A study based on 12,741 names that appeared in the 1971 *Directory of Directors* (a much larger group than the 775 members of the corporate elite) found that only 9.48 per cent of these directors were French Canadians (Presthus, 1973:56).

Other Ethnic Groups
Although over one-fifth of Canada's population is made up of ethnic groups other than the two charter groups, they have almost no representation in the corporate elite, Jews being a notable exception. From the non-charter groups there are only thirty-two Jewish Canadians (4.1 per cent) and ten individuals from other third ethnic groups (1.3 per cent). In 1951 there were only six Jews (0.78 per cent) in the elite, an indication that they have made significant inroads into the elite from 1951 to 1972. There are, however, several factors associated with their mobility worth noting. Most of their inroads have been on their 'own account'; that is, mobility into the elite has not been through established corporations but through firms that have been established and have grown to national scope within one generation. A closer examination of these firms explains why Jewish Canadians account for 4.1 per cent of the elite

---

[13]Additional evidence indicates even greater inequality with 'Anglo' rising to 86.6 per cent, French falling to 7.9 per cent, Jewish rising to 4.3 per cent, and 'other' remaining the same at 1.3 per cent (Clement, 1977:232n).

and only 1.3 per cent of the population. Of the thirty-two Jews, twenty-eight are associated with five corporations: one is a long-established firm in the beverage industry, three others are in trade, and a final one deals primarily in real estate. These are all tightly held family firms, with only six families accounting for twenty-five of the thirty-two Jewish members of the elite. Outside these family firms, Jews have very little power in the corporate elite, holding only five bank directorships (2.4 per cent) and two insurance direc-torships (1.2 per cent). They have gained access by creating a parallel structure alongside, and for the most part separate from, the indigenous Anglo-Saxon elite.

Education as Training and Social Networks

Less than 10 per cent of the male population in the same age group as the corporate elite have any education past secondary school, and about 5 per cent have university degrees; the few who did have the advantage of higher education were indeed privileged. Of course, if females of the corresponding age were included, the proportions who attended university would drop even lower, since only about 2 per cent of the women had the same advantage. The corporate elite has had two distinct characteristics in sharp contrast to the general population: it is almost exclusively male (only six women), and most of its members have graduated from university.

In 1951, 58.3 per cent of the corporate elite were university educated, with an additional 5.4 per cent having some other higher education past the secondary level, such as chartered accountancy degrees or technical training. By 1972, 80.5 per cent of the elite had university training and an additional 4 per cent had other postsecondary education. In other words, only 104 (15.5 per cent) of the Canadian-born members of the elite do not have more than secondary education; in 1951, 36.3 per cent of the elite were in this position.

The interesting question becomes, not how many were educated at university, but how those who were not managed to get into the elite. Of the 104 who did not have postsecondary education, one-quarter (26) attended private schools and a further one-fifth (21) inherited their positions. In other words, almost half had upper-class advantages and did not require university training as an avenue to the elite. Of those remaining, 14 spent an average of forty years in the banks before attaining an executive post, 2 entered the elite through insurance and other finance companies, 8 by becoming financiers, 6 on their own account, 2 from the political elite, and 18 through a variety of other routes.

Not only is university education important, but it appears that post-graduate training and professional degrees are also rapidly becoming pre-requisites of elite membership. Of the Canadian-born, 280 have additional training beyond their undergraduate degrees. This number accounts for 41.6 per cent of the entire Canadian-born elite. Of these, 183 have law degrees, including 15 who have postgraduate degrees beyond law, with 10 of them attending Harvard for M.B.A.'s. Altogether, 53 of those with postgraduate degrees went to the United States for their education and 34 of these to Harvard for M.B.A.'s. An additional 14 went to the United Kingdom and 2 to France for their postgraduate training, with the rest obtaining their degrees in Canada.

Age has an effect on whether or not members of the elite attended university, with 73.1 per cent of those born before 1905, 79.3 per cent of those born between 1905 and 1920, and 87.3 per cent of those born after 1920 attending. Together with the difference for the entire elite between 1951 and 1972, this provides conclusive evidence of the increasing importance of university education for elite membership.

Not all universities in Canada are equally endowed with the ability to pass on elite membership. Actually, only four universities passed on three-fifths of the elite attending university. Of those attending university, 27.1 per cent had their undergraduate education at the University of Toronto, while another 15.7 per cent went to McGill. While almost half obtained their degrees in one of these two places, there are eight other universities that had between 3 per cent and 5.4 per cent of the elite passing through their gates at the undergraduate level, together accounting for 34.7 per cent of those attending. Not only university attendance itself, but which university is attended makes a considerable difference for movement into the elite.

The Private World of Powerful People
The upper levels of power in Canada are surrounded by a society very different from that experienced by most Canadians; the elite are people who become involved at the executive level in a range of philanthropic and cultural activities. From private schools to private clubs, they lead a life quite apart from, although very much affecting, the existence of the vast majority of Canadians. Through a series of elite forums and political connections, they make decisions with implications well beyond the dominant corporations where they base their power.

Private Schools
Although they may be examined as educational institutions, private schools can also be seen as class institutions designed to create elite associations and maintain class values both by exclusion and socialization of the potential elite. Private school education is a lifelong asset for the select few who experience it. The thousands of dollars it costs parents to send their children pays off many times over in the 'social capital' accumulated during these formative years. What Porter refers to as "simply an item within the common experience of class" (1965:528) is the total package of upper-class training that occurs not only in the private schools but through experiences gained by living in exclusive residential areas of Canada's metropolitan centres (areas

such as Forest Hill, Westmount or Rockcliffe Park), by vacationing at exclusive resorts in Canada and abroad, and by being privy to a host of other experiences known only to the upper levels of the class structure.

Attending 'Dad's' old school is another form of inheritance that preserves elite continuity. The fee-paying private schools of eastern Canada are institutions that stem well back into Canada's history, with some, like Upper Canada College (UCC), founded in 1829, and Trinity College School, founded in 1865, providing the common class experiences for many generations of Canada's upper class.

The pervasiveness of private school attendance is on the increase within the elite. While 34.2 per cent of the Canadian-born elite attended in 1951, this figure has increased to 39.8 per cent, or 267, of the elite in 1972.[14] Included are forty-nine of the sixty-five French Canadians, who attended classical colleges,[15] about the same proportion as the forty-two who had in 1951. Of those attending English-speaking private schools, elite members went almost exclusively to one of the members of the Headmasters' Association and, within this group, primarily to the older schools of eastern Canada.

It is evident why 64 per cent of the elite members who had careers in family firms attended private schools. Providing the aspiring elite with a total environment for usually eight of the most formative years, private schools teach the sons of the upper class values appropriate to their position; they have 'strong characters built' and the opportunity to build lasting friendships with other upper-class boys they later meet in the boardrooms of Canada's largest corporations. As was already illustrated, the pervasiveness of private school attendance within the elite has increased since 1951, but at the same time concentration in fewer of the finer schools has also been occurring. While twenty-nine members of the elite had attended Upper Canada College in 1951, by 1972 this number had increased to thirty-eight. Other elite schools include the University of Toronto Schools, which can account for the private school education of twenty-eight members of the present elite, Trinity College School, accounting for twenty-one members, and ten others accounting for between seven and thirteen members each. Since many of these schools were founded as extensions of the Anglican church, it is understandable that 38 per cent of the Canadian-born members of the elite attending private schools would be Anglican, 47 per cent if French Canadians are excluded.

Common private school attendance is only the beginning for many careers that follow very similar career paths. For example, of five elite members who attended Appleby College at the same time, four went on to the University of Toronto, including two by way of Royal Military College. Five

---

[14]Expanded coverage increased these figures to 284 members and 41 per cent (Clement, 1977:240).
[15]The traditional classical college system was removed in the early seventies in Quebec. The effect of this and whether or not alternative upper-class institutions will develop are not known. Of course, this does not affect the current elite, most of whom were educated in the thirties.

members of the elite followed a path that leads directly from UCC to the University of Toronto to Osgoode Hall, while another twelve stopped short of Osgoode and went directly into the corporate world. Three UCC alumni are on the board of Crown Life together, and two of these are also on the board of the Bank of Montreal, where they meet a third former UCC graduate. There are also five UCC graduates on the board of National Trust, four of whom appear to have attended their alma mater at the same time. These are not uncommon occurrences within the boardrooms of dominant corporations; there are at least two former UCC students on no fewer than eighteen dominant corporations. This is not unique to UCC by any means; for example, seven present members of the elite were at Ridley College at the same time and between them hold twenty-five dominant directorships.

After private school and, typically, the University of Toronto or McGill, sons of the upper class are ready for the corporate boardrooms. Like their fathers, they then enter another private world — that of the exclusive men's clubs.

Private Clubs, Bastions of the Elite
Providing more than simply status to the upper-class male, the exclusive gentlemen's club is a meeting place, a social circle, where businessmen can entertain and make deals. It serves as more than a badge of 'social certification' in that the club is a place where friendships are established and old relationships nourished. Especially in the six national exclusive men's clubs, there is an opportunity for the corporate elite to come together socially at the national level, thus transcending the metropolitan or regional class systems. These six Canadian clubs are one of the key institutions that form an interacting, active, national upper class.

The high cost of club membership is typically borne by the corporation. Among a number of other benefits, a recent survey of company presidents in Canada found that "more than nine out of ten presidents hold a town club membership at company expense" (Heidrick and Struggles Inc., 1973:6).

Three of Canada's national clubs are located in Toronto, including, appropriately enough, the National, founded in 1874, the York, established in 1909, and the Toronto, whose origins are the oldest of all the national clubs, dating back to 1835. In Montreal are the Mount Royal (1899) and the St. James (1857). The sixth is the Rideau of Ottawa, dating back to two years prior to Confederation, and although not central to the corporate elite, it is national because of its location and heritage. Over half the corporate elite (51.1 per cent) belong to one or more of these six clubs,[16] with members from all across Canada belonging to each of them. Between them, the 396 members of the corporate elite who belong to one or more of these six clubs hold 689

---

[16]Expanded coverage, and adding the Vancouver Club, increased this to 60 per cent (Clement, 1977:242)

memberships, an average of almost two each. The total memberships of these clubs are not large, averaging 578 in 1947 and 644 in 1957, that being the last year for which complete records are available. Based on a projected growth, it is estimated that they average just over 700 members in 1972. In 1957 they ranged in size from 300 in the York Club to a high of 1,127 in the National Club.

As an indicator of the relative importance of each club, the elite membership in 1972 can be compared with that found by Porter in 1951. This is then suggestive of the relative importance these centres have as social circles for the corporate elite in 1972. The St. James Club has had a stable number of elite members over the 1951-72 period, 146 in 1951 and 133 in 1972, and the total membership has remained unchanged, with members of the corporate elite accounting for about 18 per cent of the total. The Mount Royal has also been consistent in the number of corporate elite, 150 in 1951 and 148 in 1972, but its total membership has increased over the same period, bringing the elite proportion from 34.5 per cent in the earlier period to about 27 per cent in 1972. In Toronto the situation is somewhat different. The Toronto has had an increase from 105 to 152 elite members over these twenty years; while its membership has remained stable, the elite proportion has increased from about 30 per cent to 35 per cent. A similar increase has occurred at the York, with an increase from 92 to 101 elite members. It maintains a steady membership, the corporate elite accounting for 31 per cent in 1951 and 34 per cent in 1972. Elite membership at the National, with the largest total membership of all, has fallen off somewhat, from 115 to 105, while the overall membership has increased substantially, thus reducing the proportion of corporate elites from 13 per cent to about 8 per cent. This movement away from the general trend of more elite participation in the Toronto-based clubs may be due to a 'dilution' factor of too many outsiders at the National. The most significant change occurs in the Rideau. Porter mentioned that the Rideau, with 81 members of the corporate elite, was located in Ottawa, "off the path of industry and commerce" (1965:305). While the total membership in the Rideau has been growing substantially over the years, it has only 50 members from the economic elite in 1972, less than half that of the other national clubs and 31 less than it had in 1951. This may suggest that the Rideau, or more importantly the federal government, has declined as a key social domain for the corporate elite.

There are other clubs with substantial numbers of elite members, but they are not as important to the national upper class. For example, the Granite Club of Toronto has 82 elite members but over 6,000 total membership. Several other clubs are more regional in scope, each having between 20 and 50 elite members. These clubs number twenty-one, with some, like the St. Denis Club of Montreal, which has 27 members who are from the French Canadian corporate elite (41 per cent of all French Canadians in the elite), being quite specialized. The Halifax Club or the Vancouver Club are more closely meshed with the local rather than the national upper class, although leading members of the local upper class also tend to participate at the national level as well.

Conclusion

In the previous paper, it was shown historically that as the economic structure becomes more concentrated, mobility declines, while new economic forces tend to bring new social types into positions of power. This paper has shown that this relationship also holds true for changes in the economy between 1951 and 1972. The traditional, established, indigenous Canadian elite based in finance, transportation and utilities has concentrated and consolidated its power in these sectors, and as a result, mobility has declined, as evidenced in the overall shift from 50 per cent of the elite having upper-class origins at the time of Porter's study to 60 per cent with the same origins at the time of the 1972 study. On the other hand, new social forces have emerged as a result of expanded foreign investment in manufacturing and resource sectors, which accounts for greater openness in the comprador elite. It was shown that 45 per cent of the comprador elite have upper-class origins, compared to 64 per cent of the indigenous elite, while 50 per cent of the compradors originate in the middle class, compared to only 30 per cent of the indigenous elite. In other words, the overall access to positions of economic power has become increasingly upper class in spite of the tendency for compradorization to be more middle class. Other structural transformations, such as the parallel structure created by a few Jewish Canadians and the effect of long-established social structures on limiting mobility (as was illustrated in the analysis of regionalism), have also been suggested.

It has become increasingly evident that the men who fill corporate elite positions are predominantly of upper-class extraction or have become accepted into the upper class in terms of lifestyle and social circles. The process by which the upper class is able to maintain itself may be understood as one of co-optation and inherited advantage. Porter has argued, "Class continuity does not mean that there is no mobility. Rather it means that there is sufficient continuity to maintain class institutions" (1965:285n). As long as the upper class remains in control of dominant corporations and is able to keep its social class institutions such as private schools and clubs intact, it will be able to maintain itself, in Parkin's terms, as a 'class of reproduction' and ensure conformity through 'class nomination' of those members of the middle class, and occasionally lower class, deemed acceptable and, conversely, excluding those who are not. This means accepting the lifestyle, attitudes and values of those of the upper class. As guardians of institutions of power and avenues of success, they are able to dictate that the system should operate as they see fit, that is, as a system of exclusion and monopoly for their own privileges and prerogatives of power. The economic elite in Canada is that section of the upper class which operates the major economic institutions of Canadian society on behalf of, and in the interests of, the upper class. As long as economic power is allowed to remain in its present concentrated state, there appears to be no hope for equality of opportunity or equality of condition in Canada.

Chapter 3

Uneven Development: A Mature Branch-Plant Society

Taking a broad sweep of Canadian society, the following paper examines various implications of Canada's uneven development. After first setting Canada within the historical world system, the paper turns internally to regionalism as an expression of uneven development, then briefly returns to the contemporary international level by situating Canada once again within its world context. Two other spheres of social life that have also been influenced by uneven development are then examined — the state and class formation. This paper is a compilation of several themes I explored in various papers after publishing Continental Corporate Power. *While class, the state and regionalism were evident in the earlier works, they are examined here directly. Regionalism is not analysed in any detail in the latter papers in this volume; but the theme of the state is central to the following two papers, and class is the dominant concept in the final five papers. This paper's assumptions remain somewhat trapped within an elite perspective but are struggling to escape. The way the state is examined remains fairly simplistic, and the class analysis is confined by the limitations of occupational categories. There is, nevertheless, an attempt to translate the implications of uneven development into an understanding of Canadian society as a whole rather than confining the analysis to the most powerful.*

Uneven Development in the Historical World System
Foreign domination has distorted the Canadian economy and hence its class structure. This distortion did not begin with U.S. branch plants, although they are in part a reflection of the initial distortion resulting from dominance by the United Kingdom and a focus on resource extraction. To come to an understanding of Canada's current position, it is necessary to provide a brief historical sketch of Canada's uneven development. It will be seen that the sphere of circulation and service has been overdeveloped within Canada by

the indigenous capitalist class, while there has been an indigenous under-development of the sphere of production and the vacuum has been filled by U.S. capitalists in the areas of manufacturing and resources. The manufacturing sector is truncated and the resource sector geared to external requirements; both are vulnerable to the whims of metropolitan capitalists. It will be argued that a fraction of the indigenous Canadian capitalist class has benefited by the penetration of foreign capital and has struck an *unequal* alliance with U.S. capital, while another fraction of Canadian capital has been 'squeezed out' by these two dominant fractions. It will further be argued that the distortions of the capitalist class are also reflected in regionalism and Canada's international investments. Finally, some tentative observations concerning the implications of uneven development for the Canadian state and class formation will be offered.

Until the First World War, British capitalists used Canada as an outlet for their surplus capital and manufactured products and as a source for important resources. These resources were commercial staples, such as fish, fur, timber and grain. In order to extract these resources it was necessary to create an infrastructure of roads, ports, shipping, railways, brokerage houses and financial institutions. The vehicle by which the capitalists of the United Kingdom created this infrastructure was portfolio or loan capital. This was interest-bearing capital that Canadian capitalists borrowed to invest, in turn, in the necessary infrastructure, typically under the guarantee of the Canadian state. Over time, this invested capital paid a return and the initial loans to British capital could be repaid, leaving Canadian capitalists in command of these institutions.

Thus, Canada developed as a trading nation dependent on resource extraction and the whims of the world market; in turn, it served as an outlet for the goods of Britain, retarding its own manufacturing capacity. Even when and where this capacity was developed locally, little was done to sustain it. Indeed, the dominant fraction of Canada's capitalist class bought out much of this early manufacturing capacity and extended its holdings because it controlled the critical transportation networks essential for access to the national market and the necessary capital for expansion. As will be expanded upon later, many areas of Canada, particularly the Atlantic provinces, experienced a de-industrialization around the turn of the century, while other areas experienced the imperialism of central Canada in the form of the railway and the development of a wheat economy with the products destined for Europe.

Within Britain important changes were taking place. The first was the decline of mercantile capitalists, the counterpart of the indigenous Canadian capitalist class in the sphere of circulation, and the rise of industrial capitalists. This was marked by a movement toward free trade, which undermined the protected position and secure markets Canadian capitalists had had within the British Empire. The second change was the decline of Britain as the imperial centre and the rapid rise of the United States to this central position.

Initially, Canada had simply been a dumping-ground for U.S. surplus production. Tariff walls were created in reaction and this stimulated the establishment of branch-plant operations within Canada to maintain these markets. After the First World War these branch plants became important outlets for Canadian capital, both as investments and as buyers of Canadian manufacturing plants. This was particularly the case in high-technology, secondary manufacturing. They were seen by dominant Canadian capitalists and the Canadian state as a surrogate for indigenous industrialization. They represented industrialization from without; local industrialists lacked the technology, financial resources and access to markets these branch plants could provide. Small-scale Canadian manufacturers continued to survive so long as there were local or regional markets they could serve. Once the economy became a national and then rapidly a continental one, they could no longer compete. Foreign-controlled branch plants soon came to dominate the sphere of production.

The shift in capital terms is illustrated with the following figures: in 1926, 66 per cent of the outside capital invested in Canada was in the form of portfolio investment, 30 per cent in direct investment and 6 per cent miscellaneous. By 1974 direct investment accounted for 60 per cent, portfolio for 34 per cent and miscellaneous for 6 per cent. Canada's external dependence had simultaneously shifted from Britain to the United States.

While the indigenous fraction of Canada's capitalist class was nurtured on British portfolio investment and found its niche in finance, transportation and utilities, U.S. investment had a very different impact. Direct investment, as expressed in the branch plants of multinational corporations, involves an entire 'package' consisting of technology, access to markets, access to capital, and management. Unlike portfolio investment, over time direct investment expands and widens the scope of control for its owners. In Canada 80 per cent of the foreign direct investment is owned in the United States. In time this investment eventually expands at a rate faster than new investment, using both internally generated capital and capital borrowed within the investing country, and actually drains off more capital than is invested from without. This position was reached in Canada during the early 1960s. Branch plants do not require the development of an indigenous capitalist class for their operation, since they remain externally controlled. They serve, rather, to displace existing capitalists in the activities they engage in or prevent them from emerging. In Canada these firms found a welcome ally in the dominant indigenous capitalist class, anxious to invest in their secure operations and to benefit from the activity they generated.

U.S. corporations began to penetrate the Canadian economy with great intensity after the Second World War. This penetration was motivated by two forces. The first was the push for an expanded market for their manufacturing capacity; the second, a search for resources to feed industrialization at home. Both were designed to expand U.S. hegemony and maintain profitability. The first was simply an expansion of tendencies that had existed since the turn of the century but on a grander scale. The second was a conscious reaction to the experience of the Second World War and the Korean War, after which the U.S. government began to assess its future resource requirements. The Paley Report (*Resources for Freedom*) identified twenty-two key resources, with Canada designated as a major source for twelve of these. Table 3.1 illustrates the central position Canada represents in U.S. mineral requirements.

In 1946, 35 per cent of Canada's manufacturing was foreign controlled, but this rose to 50 per cent by 1953, and 56 per cent by 1957; in mining and smelting, the increases during the same years rose from 38 per cent to 57 per cent to 70 per cent. Thus, in the course of a decade, the productive cornerstones of Canada's economy ceased to be Canadian and became foreign dominated.

This development was welcomed by many Canadian capitalists. They participated in foreign control in a variety of ways. For example, by 1970 Canadian capitalists had committed some $5.8 billion to U.S.-controlled companies in Canada, representing 21 per cent of the value of U.S. direct investment. They also benefited from the secure loans they made, guaranteed by the foreign parents, the transportation and utilities branch plants used, and the access to technology and foreign markets they produced.

Alone, national financial capital is inherently weak. It requires secure, long-term capital outlets. Rather than risk supporting indigenous Canadian industrialists who were less stable, and given the inviting option of U.S. companies, financial capitalists in Canada frequently exercised their option and supported the larger and more secure companies from the Unites States. By feeding some and starving others, Canadian financial capitalists played a large part in the formative stages of the current arrangements. Financial capital is typically found to be closely integrated with national industrial capital, particularly during the era of corporate capitalism. But this is not the only outlet — only to mention giant transportation and utilities projects or, in Canada's case, externally controlled industrial capital in manufacturing and resources, or even the state and its sponsored activities, illustrates the variety of alliances and outlets possible for financial capital.

While some Canadian capitalists benefited from U.S. penetration, the overall condition drew Canada into a dependent position within the world system. Table 3.2 illustrates the indebtedness of the Canadian economy. As is evident from this table, Canada's indebtedness to the United States often exceeds its total indebtedness, indicating that even when Canada is in a favourable position vis-à-vis the rest of the world, its relationship with the United States places it in a dependent position.

What implications for Canada's class formation stem from this pattern of uneven development? This is a question that has seldom been asked except

Table 3.1

Canadian Minerals and the United States

(1970-73 average)

Commodity	Canadian Exports to U.S. as % of Canadian Production	Imports from Canada as % of U.S. Imports	Imports from Canada as % of U.S. Consumption
Asbestos	41	97	87
Nickel	46	63	57
Potash	71	95	57
Gypsum	74	77	29
Zinc	34	55	24
Iron ore	46	51	16
Silver	71	52	52
Sulphur	23	72	9
Lead	24	31	16
Copper	21	37	7

Source: Canada, Department of Energy, Mines and Resources, *Mineral Industry Trends and Economic Opportunities* (Ottawa, 1976), p. 21.

Table 3.2

Canada's International Indebtedness, 1926-77

($ billions)

	Assets	Liabilities	Total Indebtedness	Indebtedness to the U.S.
1926	1.3	6.4	5.1	2.8
1930	1.5	8.0	6.5	4.0
1939	1.9	7.4	5.5	3.6
1945	4.0	8.2	4.2	4.4
1950	5.9	10.2	4.5	5.9
1955	7.1	15.2	8.0	8.7
1960	8.9	25.6	16.6	14.3
1965	12.9	35.6	22.4	20.2
1970	23.9	52.1	28.2	28.9
1976	47.5	96.0	48.5	41.5
1977	52.5	106.0	53.5	—

Sources: Statistics Canada, *Canada's International Investment Position*, various issues (Ottawa, 1926-67, 1968-70, 1971-73 and 1974); *Globe and Mail*, 7 April 1978:B1.

in regard to the capitalist class. It is evident that foreign ownership, because of its impact on capital formation and structure and on the uneven development of the Canadian economy, has a strong impact on class formation and class structure but has a much more indirect impact on class relations. Put differently, foreign ownership has had a strong impact on the instruments of production but relatively less on the relations of production.

Both foreign and private Canadian investment are predicated on capitalist ownership of the means of production, although the relative concentration and stage of development of each source of ownership tends to differ significantly. Foreign ownership dominates in most resource-based activities and in secondary manufacturing. Moreover, it is much more heavily concentrated in the largest firms within these industries. Since foreign ownership is most commonly in the form of a branch plant of a much larger multinational corporation, many of the functions and activities associated with the entire corporation, such as research and development or marketing, are often performed outside the country. An obvious consequence is the 'exporting' of a large number of highly skilled jobs in these areas. Canadian capitalists, on the other hand, tend to be overdeveloped in finance, transportation, utilities and general services.

Closely corresponding to patterns in the economy is control of the labour movement. International unions, an anachronism for U.S.-headquartered unions, are concentrated in the same industries that U.S. corporations dominate, while in the areas where Canadian capital or the state dominate, national unions or no unions at all tend to be predominant. The specific implications for Canada's class formation, aside from the implications for the capitalist class, which will now be discussed, will be analysed in a later section.

Canadian capitalists, particularly the powerful ones in the sphere of circulation, have aligned themselves with U.S. corporations and invested heavily in them. "Canadian investment in common shares of United States corporations comprised 85 per cent of Canadian portfolio investment in all foreign stocks. Investments by Canadians in United States stocks and bonds totalled $2,967 million at 1974 year end, or 76 per cent of total Canadian portfolio investment in foreign securities" (Statistics Canada, 1978b:26). Table 3.3 illustrates that most of this investment has gone into very large holdings, with over half in investments of over $5 million. Of the $5,367 million Canadian investors have in U.S. corporations, $2,988 million (56 per cent) is in manufacturing corporations and $847 million is in petroleum and natural gas (16 per cent). Since these same corporations are the ones that penetrate the Canadian economy and create branch plants, it is reasonable to assume that a good deal of the financing is coming indirectly from Canadian capitalists through their investments in the parent corporations in the United States.

It must be made clear, however, that the nature of this relationship is a most unequal one. Table 3.4 illustrates the extent of this inequality. While part of the Canadian capitalist class does participate directly in the expansion of U.S. corporations and benefits from this expansion, the overall effect is to drain capital from Canada to the United States. In 1974 the net drain of capital was $1,481 million. The effect is to make Canada capital poor and more reliant on external capitalization. The circle of direct investment is a

Table 3.3

Canadian Portfolio Holdings of United States Corporation Stocks, 1972

($ millions)

Size of Canadian Holding	Number of U.S. Corporations	Book Value $M	%	Market Value $M	%
Over $10m.	43	1,036	42	2,139	40
$5-$10m.	39	281	11	661	12
$1-$5m.	267	671	27	1,468	27
Below $1m.	1,123	339	13	860	16
Not classified		169	7	239	5
Total		2,487	100	5,367	100

Source: Calculated from Statistics Canada, *Canada's International Investment Position, 1974* (Ottawa, February 1978), p. 26.

Table 3.4

Continental Investment Patterns, 1969-74

($ millions)

	Canadian Receipts from United States			Canadian Payments to United States			Payments over Receipts
	Direct	Portfolio	Total	Direct	Portfolio	Total	
1969	62	198	260	514	629	1,143	883
1972	66	319	385	605	818	1,423	1,038
1974	116	417	533	1,058	956	2,014	1,481

Source: Calculated from Statistics Canada, *Canada's International Investment Position, 1974* (Ottawa, February 1978), p. 45.

vicious one, leading only to greater and greater dependence.

It is important to note, however, the mediating role some Canadian capitalists have had in this structure of dependence. Much of their capital is invested in U.S. corporations, and these Canadian capitalists are also given positions on the branch plants of these companies in Canada. In fact, of the indigenous fraction of the dominant capitalist class in Canada, 31 per cent sit on the boards of U.S. branch plants in Canada. In addition, 7 per cent of the members of the Canadian economic elite hold positions directly on the boards of companies in the United States. Of the 113 dominant Canadian companies, 63 (or 56 per cent) are interlocked with U.S. dominants; of the 194 dominant U.S. companies, 73 (or 38 per cent) have interlocks with dominant Canadian companies (Clement, 1977:172-80). The direction of these ties is mainly from U.S. manufacturing to Canadian finance and back again, suggesting that at least part of Canada's capitalist class is able to operate within the continental economy.

Uneven Development as Regionalism

Uneven development has two main manifestations in Canada. These are expressed in its regional inequalities and in the sector-specific activities of fractions of the capitalist class, as discussed above. Regional uneven development is marked by the fact that the centre of Canadian manufacturing and finance is located in the 'golden triangle' between Windsor, Toronto and Montreal. The rest of the country is heavily reliant upon key resources typically foreign-controlled and destined for external markets. For the North, it is mining and minerals, following traditional furs; in British Columbia, it is wood, pulp and paper, mining, fish, agriculture and some hydro; it is natural gas, petroleum and potash, along with grain, on the Prairies; it is mining and pulp and paper in the northern areas of Manitoba, Ontario and Quebec, along with hydro; in Atlantic Canada, it is pulp and paper, agriculture, fish, some coal, and hydro. These regions feed the golden triangle and U.S markets with their resources and, in turn, consume the manufactured products from these centres. The economies of these different parts of the country, in turn, produce different types of class structures in these regions (see Clement, 1978) and have consequences for the nature of the Canadian state.

Both forms of uneven development result in large measure from the effects of foreign pressures that have penetrated and shaped Canada. Initially, France and then the United Kingdom colonized what is now Canada in search of staple commodities, and used it as an outlet for their surplus capital, which was invested in building the nation's infrastructure — its roads, canals, ports, railways and financial institutions — essential to moving these staples abroad from Canada. These colonizers provided a ready outlet for Canada's commercial staples — fish, fur, timber and wheat — while the colonies were a ready market for their manufactured products.

William Lyon Mackenzie characterized the dependent condition of British North America well when he said in 1824:

> Our foreign commerce, confined and shackled as it is, and it has been, is entirely in the hands of the British manufacturers. . . . Our farmers are indebted to our country merchants, our country merchants are deeply bound down in the same manner, and by the same causes, to the Montreal wholesale dealers. Few of these Montreal commission merchants are men of capital; they are generally merely the factors or agents of British houses, and thus a chain of debt, dependence and degradation is begun and kept up.
> [Quoted in Ryerson, 1968:106-7]

Because the primary form of capital used by the United Kingdom in Canada was portfolio or loan capital, this necessitated the development within Canada of an indigenous capitalist class and a stable state structure that could guarantee these loans and oversee their investment. This arrangement continued until, in 1846, marked by the abolition of the Corn Laws in Britain, there was a movement toward free trade and an end to Canada's privileged position within the empire. Canadian capitalists then floundered in search of another imperial centre to which Canada could become attached. Many signed the Annexation Manifesto of 1849 calling for commercial union with the United States; they settled for the Reciprocity Treaty of 1854. Soon followed Confederation, whereby central Canadian capitalists would become their own colonizers, turning east and west. The foundation of their economy remained that of mediators between Canada's resources and foreign markets, but alongside this, there was beginning to be developed small-scale manufacturing interests that had grown to serve the Canadian market. These were basically local in nature and tied to the local populations in Ontario, Quebec and the Atlantic provinces.

The position of small-scale manufacturers was, however, a precarious one. Dominant central Canadian capitalists controlled the transportation networks essential for getting goods to market and the pools of capital necessary for expansion. In addition, the United States by this time had become an important industrial nation, itself searching for outlets for its products and sources for raw materials. These two factors combined to cause the demise of indigenous Canadian industrialization, particularly in Atlantic Canada.

T.W. Acheson has summarized the position of Atlantic Canada within Confederation:

> Crisis occurred in the depression of 1874-79, when the British and American markets for Canadian wood products and grains experienced a sharp downturn. To further aggravate the situation many American businessmen, faced with contracting domestic markets, began dumping large quantities of manufactured products on the Canadian market at substantially reduced prices. The combination of failing markets and foreign competition drove hundreds of manufacturers into bankruptcy and seemed to threaten the very survival of the small and comparatively inefficient Canadian manufacturing sector. [1977:91]

In light of the fluctuating demand for Canadian staples and the dumping of surplus production by U.S. capitalists on the Canadian market, Sir John A. Macdonald devised the now famous National Policy of 1879. This policy was based on a program of tariffs to bring industry into Canada, railways to produce a national economy, immigration to fill the West, and production of wheat destined for the world commodity markets. It served to stimulate manufacturing within Canada but, as will be seen, did little to sustain it. As Acheson has illustrated:

> The National Policy increasingly fulfilled its promise of making the entire domestic market available to Canadian producers. Thus, in reaction to the problems of an international economy which was unable to consume Canadian staples, and in response to the demands of a variety of concerned business interests, the Canadian government moved to restore the traditional metropolis-hinterland economic relationships. . . . The effect of the reorganization was to create a new economic metropolis, centred in Montreal, replacing the traditional British and American centres. [1977:93]

All did not fare equally well under this new structure: "The Canadian metropolis was unable to perform most of the functions usually associated with a dominant centre. . . . The most critical metropolitan failure was the inability of the Central Canadian market to consume the output of these new regional industries" (Acheson, 1977:95). The result was the destruction of Atlantic industry, its takeover by central Canadian capitalists by the time of the First World War, and its replacement by branch-plant industries and central Canadian banking consortia.

John Baker has shown the scale of this demise. In Atlantic Canada "there was a decline in the number of persons employed in manufacturing, from 69,529 in 1890, to 43,179 in 1920 (reaching a low of 24,538 in 1933)" (1977:201). The root of this was in the overproduction of manufacturing output in central Canada and in the control by the financial capitalists of central Canada. Following Confederation, the new federal state implemented policies resulting in "the effective prohibition of independent community banking [as had existed in Atlantic Canada] and the establishment of a branch banking system, controlled from Montreal and Toronto" (Baker, 1977:298). These centrally controlled banks caused a shortage of loan capital and higher interest rates, thus undercutting the ability of Atlantic manufacturers to compete.

Alongside the exodus of banks from Atlantic Canada to central Canada was the equally devastating impact of the railway. As Henry Veltmeyer has argued:

> Between 1917 and 1921 production and employment in Maritime manu-
> facturing industry fell by nearly 40%. As the consolidated corporations
> began to close their Maritime branches and to concentrate their production
> facilities in central Canada, numerous other Maritime plants were forced
> into bankruptcy by the ruinous freight rates applied by the Canadian
> National Railway. As a result, by 1926 eight of the leading industrial towns
> and cities along the International Railway provided 45% fewer jobs in
> manufacturing than they had at the beginning of the decade. [1979:21-22]

In Atlantic Canada, a once thriving manufacturing base reverted to staples production, and with that, dependency. Whereas staples had accounted for 32 per cent of the Atlantic output in 1911, this grew to 38 per cent by 1951 (see Acheson, 1977:98). Not only did the region return to staples production, it also turned to the U.S. market as its primary outlet. By 1966 two-thirds of Atlantic exports were sent to the United States, and forest, mining and fish products accounted for 85 per cent of its exports (see Acheson, 1977:113n). The decline in manufacturing coincided with the mass exodus of many workers to other parts of Canada and the growth of the state and service sectors. More than anywhere else in Canada, Maritime workers were employed in these sectors and experienced the highest rates of unemployment. The consequence of such a pattern of development, James Sacouman argues, has been that "capitalist underdevelopment in Atlantic Canada has for many years capitalised two exportable commodities: raw materials and human labour" (1979:110).

The weight of the National Policy shifted many benefits to central Canada. By the time its effects were fully felt, central Canada housed the major financial centre of the nation and established a monopoly over manufacturing, extending its power over the East through branch operations and exports. By 1910 four-fifths of Canada's manufacturing capacity was located in Ontario and Quebec. Increasingly, this capacity was no longer controlled by small-scale Canadian capitalists. Some had shifted into the hands of Canadian finance capitalists in the steel, pulp and paper, and food and beverage industries as they expanded into corporate ventures by buying out many small operators and creating monopolies. Outside these areas of industry, U.S. capitalists led the way, particularly in the technology-intensive secondary manufacturing and resource sectors. This served to reinforce and aggravate the problems of regionalism in Canada.

An explanation for the difference in the patterns of development within central Canada between Quebec and Ontario has been offered by John McCallum, who argues: "Ontario industry developed on classic lines as the agriculture-based economy grew. . . . Markets, capital materials and labour were overwhelmingly local. Meanwhile, industrial growth in Quebec was based mainly on elements external to the province" (1980:6).

He argues that superior wheat production provided the necessary market in pre-Confederation Ontario for the development of local capital and manufacturers to supply agriculture. Furthermore, "in Ontario the shift from wheat to other commodities was a case of successful diversification around the staple product, or avoidance of the 'staple trap' " (52). Ontario developed a local market for its industry; Quebec, however, lacked such "a back country" (99) essential to industrialization.

Sharply in contrast to Ontario was the experience of the West during its wheat boom; there the Canadian Pacific Railway (CPR) monopolized development and aggrandized central Canada. The initial health of Ontario's local manufacturing eventually gave way to the onslaught of U.S. direct investment as a process of consolidation took place, drawing industries out of many small towns in central Ontario into the major metropolitan centres of Toronto and Hamilton. These major centres then used the rest of Ontario, and indeed the rest of Canada, as their market, thus displacing local industries (as in Atlantic Canada) and preventing others from emerging (as in the West).

By 1931 two-thirds of U.S.-controlled manufacturing plants were located in Ontario, with Quebec accounting for another 16 per cent. Today Ontario receives 62 per cent of the taxable income from U.S.-controlled manufacturing companies even though it has only 36 per cent of the population (see Clement, 1978). All other regions are significantly underrepresented. Thus, the penetration of the Canadian market by U.S. branch plants in Ontario served to draw even more economic power into the centre, further distorting the economy and failing to build a truly national market, since Canada was immediately drawn into a continental market where the United States dominated.

Central Canadian capitalists, both indigenous and foreign controlled, extended their dominance to the West. Following a path blazed by the Hudson's Bay Company, the CPR was given control over most of the West's productive land. In the vision of central Canadian dominance, the West was turned into a resource hinterland so that central Canadian capitalists could continue their historic role as mediators of Canadian resources for the markets of the world and the West would be a market for central Canadian-produced goods. This left western farmers vulnerable. As Paul Phillips has shown:

> The farmer had to sell his output, mainly grain, on an unprotected (European) international market, but had to buy his finished goods on a highly protected domestic market increasingly dominated by American manufacturers. What is significant, of course, is that the western producer had no control over either his market or his supplier. . . . caught between the fluctuating world grain prices and more stable finished-goods prices, the western producer suffered wide variation in real income. [1977:21]

Added to their burden was the discriminatory freight rates imposed by the CPR whereby the wheat rate "was almost three times that for comparable distances in competitive eastern areas" and consuming "half of the farmer's gross income from his grain crop" (Regehr, 1977:118-19). At least until the Second World War, the agrarian petite bourgeoisie, as expressed in the Social Credit and Co-operative Commonwealth Federation parties, dominated the politics of the West in reaction to the domination of their markets, transportation systems, financial sources, and implement supplies by central Canadian capital. While unable to protect themselves totally against the exploitation of this system, they did manage to create important institutions to moderate its impact with, for example, the introduction of the Wheat Board and the cooperative movement.

Today freight rates continue as a major obstacle in industrial development in the West. As fewer and fewer farmers are needed to work the more-mechanized farms, people are forced off the land and into the urban areas but find little employment in manufacturing industries. It has been difficult to attract manufacturers to the region because the freight rates make it more profitable to remain in central Canada and ship to regional markets. For example, the rate per hundred weight to ship iron and steel products by rail from Toronto to Vancouver is 168¢ but from Toronto to Saskatoon the rate is 247¢. Ensuring that a minimum of processing will occur with the grains, it costs 92¢ per hundred weight to ship from Saskatoon to Moncton, while the rate for mill feed is 162¢ (see Regehr, 1977:132-33). Besides freight rates, however, the historical legacy of central Canadian manufacturing ensures that the entire country will be served from one location that monopolizes the markets, thus preventing the development of regional competitors.

Since 1947, however, the West has had petroleum as an important lever in its dealings with central Canada. This industry, as one of the key industrial staples, is dominated by foreign, largely U.S.-controlled oil companies. When western oil came on stream, a world oil monopoly had already been established. Western oil simply became another domain for the Seven Sisters already in command of the markets and technology necessary to develop these resources. While petroleum gave the West an important counterpoint against central Canada, it in fact drew the West into a greater structure of domination (albeit one that would produce tremendous wealth). As Larry Pratt has convincingly argued, "Canadians are not receiving fair value for the exploitation of their resources; that it is the handful of multinational companies holding almost exclusive leasing privileges in the tar sands, that are dictating the conditions for their development" (1976:17). The costs of dependence are important, as provincial governments remain dependent upon single resources for their survival. Multinational companies often shift the risk and costs to the state while at the same time ensuring their own profitability. "Thus government must shoulder the enormous financial burden of building the massive infrastructure required to service and supply these remote projects, providing equity and debt financing, royalty holidays, guaranteed returns and prices, ensure labour stability, train a work force, underwrite environmental studies and costs — all of which carried a price tag in the billions" (Pratt, 1977:95).

The fact that several important Alberta-based, resource-related firms have emerged during the past decade is certainly an important occurrence. It cannot be overlooked, however, that control over the vast majority of energy remains with a few large multinational energy companies. The provincial state clearly has expanded its revenues as a result of capturing more rent from its energy, but so have the international oil companies. The dividends from these corporations are the property of their foreign parents. Rents collected by the state may provide the potential for alternative strategies but, depending upon how these revenues are used, need not lead to greater control over the destiny of the province's economy. The minimum that such a strategy should achieve is the maximization of petroleum-related industries, such as equipment manufacture and an extensive petrochemical industry, using the petroleum to manufacture final products. The maximum could be investment of these rents in non-petroleum activities that would produce jobs, build a diversified industrial base and reduce external dependence. Neither strategy has been systematically implemented with these rents.

The main factor accounting for the prosperity of Alberta in the 1970s has been the effectiveness of the Organization of Petroleum Exporting Countries (OPEC) and thus the rapid rise in world oil prices. This, of course, is not the result of policies carried out by the Lougheed government, nor of the rise to power of a 'new middle class' in Alberta, nor even of the demise of the multinationals. Whether an apparently 'successful staple,' such as energy in Alberta appears to be, will lead to an equalization of power with central Canada remains to be seen. Much will depend on how successfully the West pursues the strategy of capturing the advantages of forward and backward linkages and whether or not the exceptionally high cost of energy will bottom out. In either case the balance of economic power rests with the international oil companies, not likely candidates to seek a balanced Canadian economy.

A repeat of Canada's history of uneven development is again taking place in the North. The Berger Report calls the North "an area of production remote from the main markets of Canada and from the homes of those who own and invest in its resources. . . . The first great staple industries in the North were the fur trade and whaling; then followed by mining; now there is gas and oil" (1977:117). Each of these staples has left its stamp on the North, but the most recent developments in mining and minerals have been the most disruptive, serving exclusively outside interests. As Mel Watkins has shown, the fur trade involved the native people as gatherers of fur. They acted as independent commodity producers, selling their products to the fur-trading companies, thus giving them a measure of autonomy and control over their homeland. With mineral production, however, capitalists demand "both rights to the use of land and people who will work for a wage" (1977: 88). The linkages generated by this search for industrial staples benefit industrialized parts of the country but have only disruptive effects on the traditional economy of the native people. Moreover, the benefits of this development accrue primarily to the United States, and not even to industrialized Canada. As Edgar Dosman has shown, "In most well-established countries, the development of a peripheral region would be a largely domestic issue. In Canada, however, the development of the North was inextricably linked to the issue of the Canadian relationship with a foreign power, the United States" (1975:xiv). This is because the United States is the major recipient of Canadian gas and oil exports and because the companies controlling these resources are U.S. controlled. As has been characteristic of the entire Canadian economy, the exploitation of natural resources for foreign markets has placed Canada in a vulnerable position in the world system. In the North this means the destruction of the native people's final homeland, their last refuge from a mode of production that destroys their traditional culture and livelihood.

Uneven development obviously has different consequences for the various regions of Canada. Southern Ontario's successful diversification from its initial reliance on wheat to a powerful industrial base has not been matched elsewhere. Indeed, the concentrated industrial power of this area, along with its far-reaching control over finance and transportation, has been a major reason why the rest of the country has become so reliant on resource extraction, has failed to develop a strong industrial base (as in the case of the West), and has had its industrial base destroyed (as in Atlantic Canada). The industrial capacity of southern Ontario has, however, been built upon the uncertain sands of foreign ownership. With the recession of the late 1970s, much of that industry has been shaken as foreign firms retrench, leaving behind shells of factories and laid-off industrial workers. The totally foreign-dominated automobile industry has been hardest hit. As of July 1980, 23,200 auto workers were on indefinite layoffs, and fifteen plants were closed in the previous half year alone.

While southern Ontario has — with justification — been the traditional locus of regional antagonism in Canada, in the post-OPEC period attention has shifted to oil-rich Alberta. Both areas, it needs to be stressed, have foreign-controlled corporations dominant in their major industrial and resource activities. While the fortunes of one currently appear to be on the rise and the other on the wane, neither is really a 'master-of-its-own-house.' Both are subordinate to the powers of the multinationals.

Uneven Development in the Contemporary World System

A further expression of Canada's uneven development is evident in its relationship with the rest of the world. Investment from Canada falls into two types, closely corresponding to the relative strengths of Canadian and foreign capitalists within the Canadian economy. The first is real Canadian investment abroad, located primarily in finance, transportation and utilities. At the pinnacle of this are the five dominant Canadian banks. As the people from the Development Education Centre have argued:

> The Canadian banking trusts chose very early an international strategy, rather than bearing the risks of boom and bust in the Canadian 'staples' economy or in underwriting a potential national manufacturing strategy. Profits were more stable and insured in cooperation with Wall Street or London, no matter whether the action was at home or abroad. [1977:50]

The fortunes of Canada's banks abroad followed those of first the British and then the U.S. empire. For example, "branches and sub-branches of Canadian banks in the Caribbean and Latin America peaked at 140 in 1926; that figure was not reached again until 1958" (Chodos, 1977:11). Today, riding on the crest of U.S. hegemony, Canadian banks have grown to be the third largest in international financial circles. The five dominant Canadian banks, which control over 90 per cent of Canada's banking, all earn a fifth or more of their total revenues from foreign operations, and this share has been increasing. The international operations expanded at a rate of 667 per cent between 1966 and 1976, considerably faster than the 394 per cent growth in their domestic operations for the same period.

Besides the indigenous Canadian investment abroad, there is a second rather unusual form of 'Canadian' investment abroad. This is 'go-between' investment whereby branches, typically of U.S. companies, are used to control other branches in the rest of the world. As early as 1929, companies like Union Carbide, Ford Motor Company, Standard Oil of New Jersey, and Aluminum Company of America used Canadian subsidiaries as a means to avoid U.S. laws and take advantage of preferential Canadian tariffs. Today this pattern remains and a good deal of Canadian foreign investment in the manufacturing and resource sectors is usually controlled outside of Canada, with the Canadian branch acting as a go-between (Clement, 1977:115-17). Thus, foreign investment distorts not only Canada's national economy but its international relations as well.

Of Canadian direct investment abroad in 1974, 36 per cent ($3,363 million) was in the form of go-between investment. Table 3.5 provides a breakdown of Canadian and go-between 'Canadian' direct investment abroad by the geographical area of investment.

In Africa and Australasia, go-between investment actually exceeds Canadian-controlled direct investment abroad. Looked at differently, of the go-between investment, $445 million is in Commonwealth countries other than the United Kingdom and is located mainly in the manufacturing sector. There is an additional $320 million go-between investment in countries outside the Commonwealth and the United States, and this is located primarily in mining and petroleum. Much of this go-between investment is direct investment flowing from U.S. branch plants in Canada to Commonwealth countries to avoid manufacturing tariffs, and another part is in the form of resource investment in Third World countries.

Canadian direct investment abroad is also highly concentrated in a few giant corporations. As few as sixteen companies with investments of over $100 million each account for 67 per cent of the total. Only seventeen Canadian-controlled companies with investments of over $50 million account for 81 per cent of all Canadian-controlled direct investment, while eight go-between corporations with over $50 million in investments account for 44 per cent of this type.

Unevenness is a quality that characterizes not only Canada's internal development but its location within the world system as well. Now to be located within this overall pattern are the Canadian state and class formation.

The Relative Dependence of the Canadian State

It has been argued to this point that Canada is characterized by uneven development both internally and internationally. Another important area where this unevenness expresses itself is in the Canadian state. The most obvious expression is in federal-provincial relations and in conflicts among the provinces themselves. Uneven development as regionalism, discussed earlier, means that conflicting economic interests which are translated into political struggles become dominant issues. This fragmentation becomes further complicated by the demands of various fractions of the capitalist class, outlined earlier as yet another expression of uneven development. The

Table 3.5

'Canadian' Direct Investment Abroad, 1974

($ millions)

Area of Investment	Canadian Controlled	Go-Between	Total
North America	4,593	1,205	5,798
South and Central America	1,061	14	1,075
Europe	1,409	210	1,619
Africa	43	98	141
Asia	195	44	239
Australasia	185	249	435
Total	7,487	1,820	9,307

Source: Statistics Canada, *Canada's International Investment Position, 1974* (Ottawa, February 1978), p. 54.

problem is thus not simply to provide an analysis of the state but to create an analysis of society. It is an illusion to think the state operates independent of society. It is both generated by society and influences that society; in other words, the state is wedded to the socio-economic make-up of society. In the case of Canada, unevenness is a dominant feature.

Questions concerning the relative autonomy of the state have become important points of debate with the resurgence of Marxist theories of the state. This position acknowledges that the state in a capitalist society is used to further the general interests of the most powerful sectors of a society and in order to do so 'stands back' from the particular interests of some dominant sectors or fractions. In Canada this autonomy has not been much in evidence. Instead, there has been contradiction, confusion and conflict *within* the state itself. The fundamental role of the state in any capitalist society is not only to regulate or mediate relations between classes; the state is also crucial for regulating intraclass relations. In Canada this task is pushed to the extreme, given the fractions of the capitalist class already outlined. It is also important to take note of fractions of the state itself, especially differences between federal and provincial levels and between government and other parts of the state apparatus, such as regulatory boards and agencies, the judiciary and the public bureaucracy.

The major division within Canadian capital is between big- and medium-sized capitalists rather than between Canadian and foreign capitalists, and the overall weight of the Canadian state is such that it reinforces these dominant capitalists. Canadian capitalists, especially those in the giant banks, life insurance, trust and holding companies, back winners, whatever their nationality; their interests are inextricably bound to the international system of capital.

Basic to the Canadian state and its various branches is the need to balance contradictory requirements on the part of U.S. and Canadian capital.

The outcome has been that some Canadian capitalists who 'fit' the demand of U.S. capitalists have benefited by Canada's distorted development and struck an unequal alliance, while others have been left by the wayside. While it is important for the state's legitimacy to project an appearance that this does not occur or that it is acting to prevent it, in the end state economic policies have followed the demands of the most powerful sectors of the society. This is not simply because the state is ideologically predisposed to do so but because the most powerful are those that can make things happen, get things done. They are the backbone of economic activity and thus crucial to the viability of any capitalist state.

One outcome of such practice is a highly concentrated economy, a fact which does not bother the state (except that it has to legitimate it — such as was done recently by the Royal Commission on Corporate Concentration, to be discussed in chapter 5). Part of the concentration in Canada is internally induced and some is imported, but as far as the state is concerned, it is in the concentrated areas that 'planning' can take place, both by articulating the demands of capital to the state and providing the state with an input into the economy, such as through the Bank of Canada. But in large part the autonomy of the state's input is an illusion. The state under these conditions has its input on terms dictated by private capital; that is, ventures it advocates must be made profitable. Consequently, capitalists must be induced or subsidized in their activities or have conditions provided that artificially make them competitive internationally, as in the case of the uranium cartel. Under conditions of highly concentrated corporations as prevail in the key sectors of the Canadian economy, state policy is not acting upon an amorphous 'market.' Instead, a few dominant corporations, fully aware of their relationship to other dominant corporations, are directly involved in the state's plans.

It is quite apparent why the uneven development discussed earlier would lead to confusion on the part of the Canadian state in its performance of its accumulation function. Canada is an advanced industrial society whose mainstay is resources rather than manufactured products and whose industrial capacity is mainly foreign owned; it is a trading nation that sends over two-thirds of its exports to one country (the United States) and receives over two-thirds of its imports from that same country.

Resources, unlike manufacturing and finance, lend themselves to greater direct manipulation by state policies, particularly when they are in scarce supply. This is primarily because most resources are legally owned by provincial governments, thus allowing greater influence over their exploitation. In large part, however, actual control over these resources has been given over to capitalist firms. Any government coming to power or making decisions does not begin with a carte blanche. It inherits earlier commitments and agreements, often ranging over very long time periods, and it inherits markets dominated by these same firms.

Corporations are not simply passive to government direction. Aside from attempts at political manipulation, they make investment and development decisions based on their assessed returns on investment and continued control over resources. If they perceive conditions as negative, they will invest their development funds elsewhere — whether in another province or even another country. Thus, unless a particular province possesses a near monopoly over a resource, even a fairly valuable one, corporate policies can inhibit, if not prevent, its development. This is particularly important when the industry is highly concentrated and controlled by multinational corporations, as in the petroleum industry.

With the state setting the price of oil and including what is referred to as 'a fair return to producers,' the multinationals are in an ideal capital position — a guaranteed, stable return on investment. This is ensured not only through the price of oil itself but through 'fiscal incentives' such as 'superdepletion allowances' and royalty deductibility schemes. The interest of the oil companies is in the bottom line — the long-term profit margin. Thus far the margin has been very sweet and the state has been instrumental in keeping it that way.

As both a recipient of and base for foreign investment, the Canadian state is forced to 'play both sides of the fence.' It must maintain the legitimacy of foreign investment, since it sanctions a good deal of it in the rest of the world under the guise of Canadian investment abroad, while at the same time it must contend at home with the massive problems foreign investment causes.

As a result, there is no clear focus for the Canadian state. It is a state of confusion, since it contains within it contradictory interests and forces. It consequently is weak in its ability to deal with basic economic problems: trade, inflation, unemployment, development strategies and so on.

A recent example illustrates the point. The Canadian state was aware that the International Nickel Company (Inco) was about to expand its operations into Guatemala, regardless of what the Canadian state did. In response, it performed an illusion. It turned Inco into a Canadian company simply by changing its official classification. Suddenly there exists a 'Canadian' company that can operate in the world system and give Canada a presence. A further indication of the irrationality of the system is the fact that the Canadian state has exempted the company from normal taxation so that it can 'modernize' its Canadian operations, which means mechanization and automation, thus the elimination of jobs. In addition, the Canadian state provided a $78-million loan through the Export Development Corporation to Inco for its Guatemala operations. The net impact of such policies in Canada is the loss of about 4,000 jobs.

Another example of state policy wrought with contradictions is the Foreign Investment Review Agency (FIRA). The agency was established as an instrument of legitimation in response to nationalist pressures, both broadly based and from small Canadian businesses. It was, however, soon turned on its head by the powerful forces in support of dominant capital. Provinces cried out that they cannot be cut off from foreign investment. Politicians ran around the world saying it did not really make any difference. And the agency itself became a conduit for foreign investment by providing services for foreign capital and giving their investments legitimacy. Claude Bennett, the Ontario minister of industry, said, "We'll show them that it's not difficult to get through it, and we'll simplify the processing of their applications" (*Maclean's*, 1 November 1976:40). Since October 1975, FIRA has approved over 80 per cent of the takeover bids, certainly not a record that would suggest any attempt to reduce foreign control. Indeed, the government has been bending over backwards to attract even more. In 1978 the federal and Ontario governments offered Ford Motor Company a subsidy of $75 million to build an engine plant in Ontario rather than Ohio, just one in a series of subsidies to the 'big three' U.S. automakers, and not a dime toward building an indigenous automobile industry as exists in every other advanced industrial nation of the world.

In its rush to meet the increasing demands on its resources, the various branches of the Canadian state have found themselves running to the New York money markets. The costs of building a resource infrastructure and maintaining the false economy of branch-plant industry are enormous. In 1976 government borrowing was $8 billion, of which $3.5 billion was raised outside Canada. Compare this with the $7.6 billion borrowed by private business, only $400 million of which was raised outside (see *Weekend Magazine*, 18 December 1976:4). Canada is being made capital poor because of the costs of foreign ownership and the demands being placed on its revenues. The Canadian state is now in a position where it must borrow to repay the interest on its loans. According to Garth Stevenson, "By 1973 interest charges on all provincial debts amounted to nearly $1.2 billion, substantially more than the total of *all* provincial expenditures in 1950" (1977:84-85). By 1977 all levels of government were making interest payments of $8.94 billion annually. Ottawa alone paid over $225 million in interest in 1977 on *foreign* loans (see *Globe and Mail*, 7 April 1978:B1; 3 May 1978:1-2). It is not possible for the state to continue indefinitely in its giveaways and concessions.

The closeness of the capitalist class in Canada to the state makes it all the more difficult for the state to be autonomous. This is especially so when fractions of the capitalist class, at times in concert and at times in conflict, have very close relations with different branches and levels of the state (see the following paper, chapter 4). Since corporate power is political power, these interests become translated directly into contradictory state policies and behaviour. As the scope of these demands enlarge and call for increasing state action, the contradictions must become manifest.

Distortion in Canada's Class Formation
Most of the previous focus has been on the capitalist class and its various fractions, with only a few oblique references to the effect of uneven development on other classes. As with the state sector, it will only be possible here to sketch some ways uneven development has affected the class structure of Canada. The following should be regarded as a very preliminary outline, which subsequent papers begin to elaborate.

It was illustrated earlier that there is an unequal distribution of manufacturing capacity in Canada, with the industrial heartland residing in the golden triangle. Outside this area most productive workers are part of a 'resource proletariat' whose jobs are in activities like mining, minerals, pulp and paper, lumber, fishing or hydro. They tend to live in single-industry towns far from major urban centres, and their costs of living are high. Most important, they tend to work with non-renewable (or poorly managed) resources, and their livelihood is constantly threatened by exhaustion of these resources or fluctuations in world markets. Boom-bust cycles for Canada's resource proletariat are legion; there are constant fluctuations between labour shortages and labour surpluses in these industries because their fate depends so heavily on external demands.

Traditionally, many people working in staple industries were independent commodity producers. In fact, up to the Second World War, the petite bourgeoisie was the most powerful class outside the capitalist class and accounted for much of the political resistance to the dominant class. Increasingly they have been drawn into wage labour. In 1957, 79 per cent of the labour force were paid workers, and by 1976 this increased to 89 per cent, while the proportion working for themselves decreased from 12 per cent to 5 per cent. In numerical terms, this means an increase over ten years from 4,540,000 paid workers to 8,272,000 and a decrease of the self-employed with no employees from 667,000 to 512,000. It is important to note, however, that the decline of the traditional petite bourgeoisie of fishermen, farmers and small shopkeepers has not meant a proportionate increase in the traditional industrial working class. What has occurred instead, as will be argued shortly, is a dramatic rise in the number of state workers, thus resulting in a situation where a major part of the working class is employed by various branches of the state. It is from this new set of state workers that much of the militancy in the post-Second World War era has emanated and where much of the growth in unionization (particularly national or Canadian unions) has taken place. The militancy is particularly evident here because it is these employees' wage demands that the state can best control, and under periods of restraint the state attempts to hold down their wages.

It goes without saying that the state in Canada does not use class categories in its various information-gathering agencies. As a result, census and labour force surveys provide only approximations of classes, not classes

Table 3.6

Forms of Labour in Canada, 1957-76

(percentages)

	Paid	Own Account	Employers	Unpaid Family	Total
1976	89	5	4	2	100
1966	85	8	5	2	100
1957	79	12	6	4	100

Sources: Information Canada, *Perspective Canada: A Compendium of Social Statistics* (Ottawa, 1974), p. 124; Ministry of Supply and Services, *Perspective Canada II: A Compendium of Social Statistics* (Ottawa, 1977), p. 116.

themselves. Unfortunately, they are the only systematic data available that can be used over time, thus forcing the use of their categories for describing general class patterns. These data can tell us something about the patterns of class transformation but fall short of providing definite answers, and certainly explanations, for the dynamics of class. Sometimes the data are presented by industrial sectors but most often by occupations. They do not provide even sufficient information for the economic dimensions of class, no matter the political and cultural sides.

Table 3.7

Distribution of the Labour Force by Sector, 1901-78

(percentages)

	Primary	Secondary	Tertiary
1901	44.3	27.8	27.9
1921	36.4	25.8	37.8
1946	29.4	30.8	39.8
1955	19.8	32.5	47.7
1964	12.5	32.5	56.3
1970	9.3	28.7	62.0
1973	7.9	28.7	63.4
1978[a]	7.6	26.8	65.6

[a]As of October 1978.
Sources: Statistics Canada, *Canada Year Book 1962* (Ottawa, 1962), p. 711; Statistics Canada, *The Labour Force*, cat. #71-001, various issues.

The most basic kind of information about changes in the labour force concern broad sectoral shifts from primary to tertiary activities. The movements have been dramatic: the primary sector has declined from being the main location of the labour force at the turn of the century to now occupying a minor place. It has been replaced by the tertiary sector, while the secondary sector has not changed significantly throughout the twentieth century. The pattern of a declining primary sector and rising tertiary sector is not unusual;

what is unusual is the absence of a period when the secondary sector, which is mainly composed of manufacturing, has the dominant position. It began the period equal to the tertiary sector but is now well under half the size of this sector. Canada's secondary sector is proportionately smaller than that of other advanced capitalist societies. The major disparity is in manufacturing. Moreover, 40 per cent of Canada's manufacturing labour force in 1971 "worked in industries chiefly engaged in the transformation of raw materials of the land, sea, forests and mines."[1] Aside from general indications, these data tell us little about class transformations.

Table 3.8

Employment Changes by Sector in Canada, 1946 to 1978

	1946		1978[a]		
	(000's)	%	(000's)	%	Percentage Change
Production	3,187	68	4,404	43	38
Agriculture	1,185	25	520	5	-56
Other primary	187	4	275	3	47
Manufacturing	1,213	26	2,024	20	67
Construction	224	5	698	7	212
Transport./Util.[b]	378	8	887	9	135
Circulation	1,479	32	5,877	57	297
Trade	574	12	1,754	17	206
Commerce[c]	121	3	570	6	371
Service[d]	784	17	3,553	35	353
All	4,666	100	10,282	100	120

[a]As of October 1978.
[b]Includes transportation, communication and other utilities.
[c]Includes finance, insurance and real estate.
[d]Includes community, business and personal service, and public administration.
Sources: Statistics Canada, *Canada Year Book 1968* (Ottawa, 1968), p. 759; Statistics Canada, *The Labour Force*, cat. #71-001 monthly.

Another way of looking at similar kinds of data is to break the sectors into finer categories that tell us more about the actual activities within them. This arrangement of the data is somewhat different than for the traditional categories that distinguish between 'goods-producing' sectors and 'service-producing' sectors, since transportation/utilities are included in the sphere of production rather than circulation. Even with this rearrangement, it is clear that the sphere of circulation has overtaken that of production since the

---

[1]Statistics Canada, 1971 Census of Canada, *Profile Studies: The Industrial Structure of Canada's Labour Force*, cat. #97-715, vol. 5, pt. 2 (Bulletin 5.2-4) (February 1978), pp. 1-3. The comparison is with Australia, France, Germany, Japan and the United States.

Second World War. All the subsectors within circulation have grown faster than the overall labour force, while only construction and transportation/utilities have kept up in production. The most dramatic decline has been in agriculture and to some extent other primary industries, while manufacturing has declined significantly in its relative position as an employer. It is clear that a declining proportion of workers in production are being required to support a rapidly growing sphere of circulation. The single greatest contributing factor to the overall pattern since the turn of the century is the decline of agriculture. In 1881 nearly half (48 per cent) of the labour force was engaged in agricultural pursuits; this declined to two-fifths in 1901 and again to a third by 1921 and a quarter by 1941. Now this sector accounts for only one-twentieth of the labour force. The twenty-percentage-point drop in agriculture between 1946 and 1978 presented in Table 3.8 is sufficient to account for almost the entire increase in the circulation sector over the period, while the production sectors stagnated. Why has the shift in employment occurred in this way? The data themselves cannot tell us because they only describe, they do not explain; explanation lies at least partially in the uneven development of Canadian society.

Another traditional form of data distributes the labour force by occupational categories. One problem with occupational categories, such as those in Table 3.9, is that they tell us nothing about changes within them. For example, clerical workers today are very different from those at the turn of the century; the agricultural labour force masks farm labour, self-employed and employers under one category; professional and technical workers include doctors, engineers and lawyers, all of whom usually direct workers, along with the nurses and technicians who are directed. The managerial category includes capitalists, people managing large numbers of people, and others directing mainly themselves (as in corner stores). Traditionally, studies of class have sought to rank occupations and assumed mobility when someone moved from, say, agricultural to clerical work. There is no reason to assume, however, that the resulting loss of independence, skill or even income is 'upward.' Nor is it, as is often assumed, usually a matter of choice.

It is possible, nevertheless, to use occupational categories as rough approximations of some dimensions of class. Table 3.9 provides, to the extent possible, a meaningful organization of these categories since the turn of the century. The shift in agriculture already indicated is obviously one involving, as far as official statistics are concerned, a movement of men out of this activity, since the proportion of women recorded as working in agriculture has always been low. This, of course, reflects a bias in the treatment of men as the 'head of the household' in census data, thus usually not counting farm wives (or daughters) as even being in the labour force.

To some extent, as Table 3.10 indicates, the overall decline in the sphere of production and rise in the sphere of circulation is partially reflective of changes in the sexual composition of the labour force. Between 1931 and

Table 3.9

Labour Force Distribution in Canada, 1901-71, by Sex

(percentages)

	1901	1911	1921	1931	1941	1951	1961	1971
Men								
Managerial	5	5	8	7	7	9	10	11
Professional-technical	3	2	3	4	5	5	8	11
Commercial proletariat[a]	9	11	13	14	14	17	21	21
Resource proletariat[b]	5	6	4	4	6	5	4	3
Industrial proletariat[c]	28	31	27	32	31	35	35	34
Transport./Communication	5	6	6	6	6	7	8	7
Agriculture	46	39	38	34	32	19	12	7
Not stated	0	0	0	0	0	1	3	8
Total	100	100	99	101	101	98	101	102
Women								
Managerial	1	2	2	2	2	3	3	3
Professional-technical	15	13	19	18	16	14	15	16
Commercial proletariat[a]	50	53	54	59	60	58	59	55
Resource proletariat[b]	0	0	0	0	0	0	0	0
Industrial proletariat[c]	30	26	18	16	18	18	13	10
Transport./Communication	1	2	3	2	2	3	2	1
Agriculture	4	4	4	4	2	3	4	3
Not stated	0	0	0	0	0	1	2	12
Total	101	100	100	101	100	100	98	100

[a]Commercial proletariat includes clerical, commercial, financial, sales and service.
[b]Resource proletariat includes fishing, hunting and trapping, logging and mining, and quarrying.
[c]Industrial proletariat includes manufacturing, mechanical, construction and labourers.
Sources: 1901-21 — Sylvia Ostry and Muhamood Zaidi, *Labour Economics in Canada*, 2nd ed. (Toronto: Macmillan, 1972).
1931-71 — Statistics Canada, *Occupations: Historical for Canada and Provinces*, cat. #94-716, vol. 3, pt. 2 (June 1978).

1971 the proportion of women has risen by 346 per cent, while men only increased by 74 per cent. On the other hand, the proportion of men classified as industrial proletariat has remained fairly constant, while women have declined substantially. Women have dominated and continue to dominate the commercial proletariat, while they are virtually absent from the resource proletariat.

The increases for both sexes in managerial, professional-technical and commercial categories is apparent from Table 3.10, but again, without greater understanding of the actual content of the work grouped here, it is not possible to extrapolate the class implications. To what extent do the people in these occupations perform the functions of capital by organizing production and overseeing labour and to what extent do they perform the functions of labour by actually aiding in production? These questions are unanswered. The data do provide some information but not sufficient to permit an

Table 3.10

Labour Force Changes in Canada, 1931 to 1971, by Sex

(000's)

	1931	1971	Percentage Change
Men			
Managerial	211	594	182
Professional-technical	125	602	382
Commercial proletariat	450	1,171	160
Clerical	(153)	(368)	(141)
Sales	(162)	(320)	(98)
Service	(136)	(484)	(256)
Resource proletariat	142	140	−1
Loggers	(42)	(52)	(25)
Fishermen and trappers	(46)	(27)	(−43)
Miners	(54)	(62)	(15)
Industrial proletariat	1,035	1,911	85
Craft and production	(602)	(1,539)	(156)
Labourers	(433)	(373)	(−14)
Transport./Communications	187	392	110
Agriculture	1,094	400	−63
All Men	3,245	5,649	74
Women			
Managerial	11	86	709
Professional-technical	118	475	304
Commercial proletariat	390	1,627	317
Clerical	(119)	(903)	(658)
Sales	(47)	(208)	(345)
Service	(224)	(516)	(131)
Resource proletariat	—	—	—
Industrial proletariat	105	289	176
Craft and production	(93)	(254)	(173)
Labourers	(12)	(35)	(202)
Transport./Communications	16	40	148
Agriculture	24	100	318
All Women	664	2,960	346

Source: Statistics Canada, *Occupations: Historical for Canada and Provinces*, cat. #94-176, vol. 3, pt. 2 (June 1978).

analysis of class cleavages. This remains to be addressed in subsequent papers.

Hugh Armstrong has shown that the state sector has grown more rapidly than any other, accounting for more than a third of all new jobs since the Second World War. It has increased from 8.9 per cent in 1946 to at least 21.2 per cent of the labour force in 1974, with provincial employees increasing at a much faster rate than federal ones (1977:296). Because of the increasing pressure for legitimation of the state with the myriad of contradictions it must face, the state has grown to meet these demands. In addition, growing foreign investment since the Second World War has been highly capital intensive and concentrated, about four and a half times the size of Canadian non-financial corporations in terms of assets and over six times as large by equity and profits, thus requiring much less labour. Moreover, much of the value added in these industries occurs outside Canada, thus employing fewer people than would be the case if the manufacturing were done here. Consequently, the Canadian state is forced into a position of employing a larger share of the labour force and dealing with inordinantly high unemployment.

Alongside this is the general growth in the number of clerical workers. This is the result of two types of changes, those within factory offices and those through the growth of 'clerical industries.' The first process is reflected in the following figures for Canada: the proportion of administrative and office workers in Canadian manufacturing increased from 11 per cent in 1917 to 19 per cent in 1939 to 22 per cent in 1954 and 28 per cent in 1971. The second is the rise of 'paper empires,' such as companies in the commercial sector (banks, trust companies, life insurance, real estate, etc.), which are primarily clerical, and to some extent sales, in their work. Their main activity involves accounts, stocks, payrolls and so on.

The decline of the primary sector is not an uncommon phenomenon in industrialized nations. Typically, as suggested earlier, it results in a rise in the secondary sector and only much later an expansion of the tertiary sector. In Canada the decline in the primary sector is matched by a rise in the tertiary sector and a steady proportion in the secondary sector. Most of the change in the primary sector involves agricultural jobs. This is a result of the increasing mechanization and capitalization of farms. A large part of the demise of farmers is also accounted for by state policies regarding tariffs and the fact that processors of agricultural products have become highly concentrated and have fallen into the hands of U.S. capitalists who command the world markets (see Clement and Janzen, 1978). Almost the entire shift, in aggregate terms, has gone to 'white-collar' jobs, especially clerical, sales, and lower-level technical and professional occupations.

Another factor of importance is the weakness of Canada in terms of research and development, with much of it taking place under the command of parent corporations outside of Canada. Of related concern is the exporting of resources and importing of processed goods, which means that labour and skill-intensive jobs are also exported. As the studies by Pierre Bourgault have shown, "When we examine the nature of our imports and exports, we find that we export mainly raw materials and resource-based products while importing most manufactured goods, particularly those which have a high knowledge content," that is, those jobs involving advanced technology and skilled labour (1972:82). Little wonder Canada's employment rate runs at about 10 per cent *officially* — over a million people. Canada's uneven development affects not only the distribution of the labour force but also the number of jobs in the labour force itself. Even the rapid increase in state employment has not been able to meet the demand for jobs caused by the capital-intensive foreign control of Canada's productive sector and the decline of the traditional petite bourgeoisie.

The ability of Canadian labour to exercise its power is also strongly affected by the uneven development of the economy and the development of multinational corporations. The Canadian labour movement is highly fragmented, with divisions between national and international unions, between trade, industrial and public unions, between French- and English-speaking unions, and between organized and unorganized workers. Added to this is the flexibility capitalists have in dealing with labour as they become multinational in their operations. The recent layoffs in the mining and automotive industries reflect their ability to shift production outside the country and weaken the power of Canadian labour. An illustration that this is not unique to foreign-controlled multinationals is provided by Massey-Ferguson, a part of the Argus holdings. In 1968 Canadian workers at Massey-Ferguson were demanding wage parity with their U.S. counterparts in the same company. Massey-Ferguson threatened to withdraw its operations from Canada. Their threat was successful, resulting in a strike settlement without parity. Massey-Ferguson applied the same threat to the Canadian government over recommendations from the Carter Commission on Tax Reform and was successful in having the recommendations rejected.

The vulnerability of Canadian labour to the flexibility of multinational corporations and to the vagaries of a resource-based economy means that the working class must be constantly on guard for its jobs and standard of living. It is no longer possible, on a large scale, to escape wage labour by 'striking out on your own.' The traditional areas of small business, such as shopkeepers and farmers, have been thoroughly penetrated by capitalism. The capital requirements to enter either now pose an insurmountable barrier for virtually all workers, who must accumulate from deferred consumption (that is, out of personal savings). Those who escape wage labour do so mainly by entering into contractual relations with large corporations to manage concessions or chains in the fast food business or corner stores. There they have little more control over their lives than they did as wage labourers because the corporation sets the rules and regulations by which they must abide and shifts much of the risk onto the individual running the franchise.

It has not been possible in the space of this paper to develop a detailed analysis of transformations in Canada's class structure as affected by uneven development. The purpose has rather been to suggest that there are important implications of uneven development, not only for the capitalist class and the Canadian state, but also for the kind of work available for people in this country. The experiences of inflation, layoffs, unemployment and rising state expenditures are directly related to the kind of economy Canada has and to its relationship with broader continental and world forces.

Conclusion

Canada cannot be characterized as an independent capitalist society; nor can it be grouped with the various periphery nations often called the 'Third World,' although it shares some features with each. Rather, Canada is a politically independent nation state, enveloped by the economic spill-over of the most powerful capitalist society in the world. While Canada's economy is largely controlled and shaped by U.S. economic power centres, these external centres do not operate in a complete power vacuum in Canada. What has been forged over the past century is an unequal alliance between the leading elements of Canadian and U.S. capital, which mutually reinforces the power and advantage of each. The leading forces of capitalism in both Canada and the United States benefit by this alliance, while smaller Canadian capitalists and the Canadian populace experience its costs.

Not all Canadian capitalists are pleased with this continental power structure, particularly smaller capitalists in vulnerable manufacturing and trade activities, but the state in general and dominant capitalists in particular have been unable to see beyond their immediate economic gains arising from this method of 'nation building' and surplus extraction. Over the past century, the two economies have become so intertwined because of these dominant continental interests that it becomes difficult for many capitalists and members of Canada's ruling class to visualize the two economies apart from one another. Thus, the resource and market demands by U.S. capitalists and the internal opportunism of Canada's ruling class have created a continental political economy wherein U.S. capitalists dominate but some Canadian capitalists also benefit.

Although most of the means of production are foreign controlled in Canada, the relations of production remain capitalist. Ultimately, however, from the perspective of the metropolitan capitalist class, the interests of Canadian workers are secondary to even those in the United States. Canadian workers are often engaged in resource extraction and subject to the booms and busts of this industry, while many others are employed in manufacturing branch plants where the employment priorities are U.S. oriented. Canadian workers are particularly vulnerable, a fact which is reflected in the million unemployed and 10 per cent official unemployment rate. Capital is more mobile than labour, particularly with active state controls on the migration of labour, thus leaving labour especially vulnerable to shifts of capital both within the nation or internationally. A fragmented labour movement adds to the weakness of the Canadian workers, all the more so since it is dominated by international unions, which are subject to pressures and interests emanating from the United States.

It is not only the Canadian working class that is vulnerable. The Canadian state is also within a relatively dependent position within the system of U.S. hegemony. This is reflected in its international political and military role as 'mediator' between the interests of the United States and other nations. Internally, various branches and levels of the Canadian state struggle over foreign investment, further weakening and fragmenting resistance to domination. Self-determination for the people of Canada will necessarily mean resistance to foreign domination *and* the dominant fraction of the Canadian ruling class, which has mediated this dependence within the world system.

Chapter 4
The Corporate Elite, the Capitalist Class and the Canadian State

Originally published in 1977 in the collection The Canadian State, *this paper was written in the midst of the 'structuralist' versus 'instrumentalist' debate over the nature of the state in advanced capitalist societies. The paper attempts in a limited way to bridge that debate. The Canadian state, I would argue, has always been particularly instrumentalist in the sense that the capitalist class has enjoyed direct access both to state decision makers and key state positions. This is the empirical substance of the paper. On the other hand, and this is the theoretical substance of the paper, as a capitalist state it has been subject to the real structural constraint of overseeing a complex capitalist economy. It is not the contention of this paper that instrumental ties between the capitalist class and the state explain state politics and practices; rather the opposite. These ties exist because of the particular type of economy that has developed in Canada — a highly concentrated economy, one strongly dependent upon the export of natural resources and highly limited by the world capitalist economy. Instrumental ties reflect rather than cause the constraints on the state in Canada. The paper's main weakness, aside from documenting the actual development of state policy (an issue addressed in the next paper, chapter 5), is its focus on the federal state. Increasingly the provincial and even municipal levels have attained major importance, and these levels may correspond to different fractions of capital. I suspect, but this paper does not address the proposition, that structural explanations are more effective for understanding state policies and practices governing labour conditions (hours of work, health, safety, etc.) and social welfare measures (unemployment insurance, old age pensions, workmen's compensation, etc.), where class conflict is articulated by both labour and capital; whereas economic policies are determined in much more instrumentalist ways by directly* representing the interests of capital to the exclusion of other classes. In contrast to the first two papers, however, this one begins to integrate power and class analysis at least for the economic elite and the capitalist class, if not for the working class.

The corporate elite is the most powerful fraction of the capitalist class; it is the group of people who own, control and manage the *largest* corporations in Canada. The capitalist class includes the individuals and their families who own, control and manage (at a senior level) *all* corporations in Canada. In terms of an empirical analysis, it is practical to focus on the corporate elite for some purposes because they are more readily identifiable than the capitalist class as a whole; and, more significantly, they are the most powerful part of the capitalist class and control most of the privately owned capital in this country.

There are important fractions within the capitalist class and the corporate elite that require specification. The most important division is between corporations controlled indigenously by Canadians and those controlled by foreign capitalists through branch-plant operations. Related to this is the sector or activity of the economy the capitalists control — whether it is in finance, transportation, utilities or the mass media where the indigenous fraction dominates or whether it is in secondary manufacturing or resources where the foreign-controlled fraction dominates. This paper will analyse, in a variety of ways, the relationship between these fractions of the capitalist class and the state in Canada, between 'public' and 'private' power.

Before specific ties between various fractions of the capitalist class and the Canadian state are examined, the general character of this relationship merits some discussion. Initially, the structural relationship between the state and capitalism will be explored, followed by an empirical examination of connections between those who run the state and Canada's capitalists. The empirical material includes several levels on which this relationship is based: personal ties between state elites and the capitalist class, advisory boards established by the state, and a systematic analysis of previous and contemporary ties between members of the economic elite and the state system. Once this has been done, a number of different types of relations will be examined: state regulation of the economy, a case study of the recently established Royal Commission on Corporate Concentration, and the role of corporations in political party financing. The thesis of this paper is that the capitalist class and the state have enjoyed a very close association. In terms of fractions of the capitalist class, large foreign and Canadian capitalists have been effective in using the state apparatus to aggrandize their own power in their respective spheres of concentration, while smaller national capitalists have often been left to 'fend for themselves.'

Capitalism and the State
One of the essential roles of the state in capitalist society is to create and protect the 'rights' of private property. These 'rights' are the basis of capitalist society, for they sanction the claims of some classes to control others. Thus, the institution of private property is predicated on the protection afforded by the state. But the state itself has been shaped by private property in capitalist society. To change the economic function of private property would be to alter radically the fundamental role of the state.

Since it is the capitalist class whose continued privileges depend upon the state remaining capitalist, it follows that this class will take actions to ensure its continuing existence. This principle has long been acknowledged by political economists. Writing in *The Wealth of Nations*, Adam Smith argued: "It is only under the shelter of the civil magistrate that the owners of that valuable property, which is acquired by the labour of many years, or perhaps of many successive generations, can sleep a single night in security. . . . The acquisition of valuable and extensive property, therefore, necessarily requires the establishment of a civil government" (1869:561). While the state would protect property, Smith believed that the forces of the market, the "invisible hand" of many property holders, would protect the public from the power of property. This was an understandable argument, given Smith's role in the struggle against the state-granted monopolies of mercantilism in favour of laissez-faire capitalism; but it is no longer a reasonable assumption in the era of corporate capitalists where a few dominant corporations are the seats of enormous power, negating the forces of the market.

Adam Smith was looking back to the emancipation of the bourgeoisie from the constraints of feudal society, and thus lauding the capture of the state by capitalist interests. On the other hand, Karl Marx identified the major roles of this newly formed state. In *The German Ideology*, written in 1845 and 1846, he maintained:

> By the mere fact that it is a *class* and no longer an *estate*, the bourgeoisie is forced to organize itself no longer locally, but nationally, and to give a general form to its mean average interest. Through the emancipation of private property from the community, the State has become a separate entity, beside and outside civil society; but it is nothing more than the form of organisation which the bourgeois necessarily adopt both for internal and external purposes, for the mutual guarantee of their property and interests. [1970:80]

While the state in capitalist society is essentially a mechanism to ensure the 'rights' of capital and expedite its operation, there are a variety of ways this can be carried out, and indeed, the state can have many different roles in regulating the specific relations between various capitalists and between the capitalist class and other classes. The particular character of the state is variable in Marx's framework. Only through empirical analysis can these qualities be identified for different states and different capitalist societies. This task is particularly important today, since the size and scope of the state in all capitalist societies have expanded enormously. It is crucial to understanding the contemporary capitalist state to see that this expansion has not been undertaken at the expense of capitalism but rather to provide the conditions for its continued existence. Moreover, the state must take into account all the forces and movements in capitalist society if it is to maintain the stability required for the reproduction of capital.

At its most fundamental level, capitalist society is shaped by the process of surplus creation and extraction — hence the focus of Marxism on the point of production and the major classes associated with the capitalist mode of production. These are the underlying features of capitalist society that shape class relations and determine the role the state will have in reproducing these relations. Again in *The German Ideology* Marx wrote:

> The material life of individuals, which by no means depends merely on their 'will,' the mode of production and form of intercourse, which mutu-ally determine each other — this is the real basis of the State and remains so at all the stages at which division of labour and private property are still necessary, quite independently of the *will* of individuals. These actual relations are in no way created by the State power: on the contrary, they are the power creating it. . . . Their [individuals who rule] personal power is based on conditions of life which as they develop are common to many individuals, and the continuance of which they, as ruling individuals, have to maintain against others and, at the same time, maintain they hold good for all. [1970:106]

Thus, the actions of individuals and the role of the state are set by the material conditions of the society. The paradox of the state in capitalist society is that it must strive to maintain its legitimacy and with that the legitimacy of capital by portraying itself as representing the common inter-ests of all its citizens, while at the same time upholding the right of some to extract the surplus created by others. As C.B. Macpherson has argued:

> Political power, being power over others, is used in any unequal society to extract benefit from the ruled for the rulers. Focus on the *source* of political power puts out of the field of vision any perception of the necessary *purpose* of political power in any unequal society, which is to maintain the extractive power in any unequal society, which is to maintain the extractive power of the class or classes which have extractive power. [1973:47]

This is certainly contrary to the commonly held view presented by the state and by capitalist ideology, that the state acts simply as a 'sounding board' for all interests in society and that all citizens are responded to equally. In fact, if capitalists' rhetoric is to be accepted at face value, the state has become a threat to their 'free' operation.[1]

Given the dominant ideology in Canada of a state equally accessible to all and acting in the common interest, it remains an important task to analyse empirically the actual nature of the relationship between the capitalist class and the state. Even though theoretically it can be contended that the state must act to ensure the rights of capitalists in liberal democracies, it is by no means a widely accepted view among Canadians that this is the case. Consequentially, it remains an important task to destroy the dominant ideology that shrouds the role of Canada's state and to explore the real nature of that relationship. But, in doing this, it remains important to keep two things in mind: first, the purpose of the state in capitalist society is to create the conditions for the extraction of surplus by some classes for the aggrandizement of others; and second, one must avoid falling into the argument that the state acts simply as a front for capitalists. As Leo Panitch has pointed out, it is necessary "to distinguish between the state acting on *behalf* of the bourgeoisie from its acting on their *behest*" (1977). That is, the state does not act at the command of the capitalist class but for its interests or, more correctly, in its *general interest*. Since the capitalist class in Canada is a fractionalized one in terms of size and control, it is also important to understand the particular as well as the general interests being served. Moreover, in its attempt to provide the conditions for capital accumulation, the state is the major instrument for creating class harmony. Thus, a great deal of state policy is directed at moderating the glaring inequalities of capitalism towards this end, but it draws the line at the greatest inequality, that of the private power of property.

Personal Ties between the Corporate World and the State

The period of simultaneous direct participation in state offices and the corporate world is past (except for the dinosaur institution of the Senate). The increasing complexity of an industrial society has required a relatively autonomous state capable of responding to various capitalist class fractions and other demands of the society to provide necessary conditions for stability. However, this has not prevented other types of connections — career switching, kinship ties and advisory posts — all of which reflect an affinity and community of interest between the highest levels of the state and the economy in capitalist society.

These ties have been particularly intimate in Canada; an interesting exchange gives an unusual indication of this intimacy:

---

[1]See the views presented by nine of Canada's top capitalists in *A Case for the Enterprise System*, assembled by the Investors Group and published in September 1975. It was serialized in Canada's largest newspapers during this period in full-page advertisements.

A conversation last week about the issues raised when businessmen go into government and then have to deal with people from their former field eventually got around to Jack Austin. Mr. Austin, a mining promoter and lawyer, became deputy minister of Energy, Mines and Resources (before moving on to the Prime Minister's Office). When the subject of a possible conflict of interest came up, he was fond of saying that "you can't get virgins with experience." When this quote was tossed back to a senior civil servant working on the current problem he replied: "Yeah, but we don't want prostitutes with an air of innocence either." [*Globe and Mail*, 5 April 1976]

In these terms, there have been few 'virgins' (not to take the implication to the opposite extreme) in the highest state offices in Canada. A review of Canada's prime ministers from Robert Borden to Pierre Trudeau indicates the strength of business connections in this highest political office.[2] The most conspicuous links are with the dominant corporations in Canada.[3] Borden was a corporation lawyer, director of the Bank of Nova Scotia, and founder, with Sir Charles Tupper (an earlier Conservative prime minister), of the Crown Life Insurance Company before becoming prime minister from 1911 to 1920. After leaving politics, he became president of Barclay's Bank (Canada) and president of Crown Life. Borden was succeeded in office by Arthur Meighen, who was prime minister between 1920 and 1921 and again in 1926. Meighen was also a lawyer allied with the Toronto financial community and managed to hold numerous financial offices. William Lyon Mackenzie King, prime minister from 1921 to 1926, 1926 to 1930, and 1935 to 1948, a total of over twenty-one years, was a grandson of the 'rebel leader' William Lyon Mackenzie. Before entering electoral politics, he had become a wealthy man, largely through gifts and payments from corporations. Not the least of his sources of wealth was the Rockefeller family, with King serving as an advisor to John D. Rockefeller. He was deputy minister of labour and labour minister before becoming prime minister.[4] From 1930 to 1935 Richard Bedford Bennett was prime minister. He was a lawyer and financier before entering politics and later became president of Calgary Power, owner of the E.B. Eddy Match Company, and a director of Imperial Oil and the Royal Bank (the latter position he also held before entering politics). Louis Stephen St. Laurent was a corporation lawyer and before entering politics was a financier and director of Metropolitan Life and the Bank of Montreal. After acting as prime minister from 1948 to 1957, he became chairman of Rothmans of Pall Mall Canada and a director of IAC Limited.

---

[2]The following sketches are based in part on David Nock, 1976, chap. 4. Earlier prime ministers also had extensive business careers: see, for example, J.K. Johnson, 1976.

[3]For the criteria used to select the 113 dominant corporations, see Clement, 1975:125-32.

[4]For a detailed review of King's early career, see Ferns and Ostry, 1976.

Unlike the previous five prime ministers, John George Diefenbaker, in office from 1957 to 1963, Lester Bowles Pearson, in office from 1963 to 1968, and the current prime minister, Pierre Elliott Trudeau, did not have extensive corporate careers. Diefenbaker was a criminal lawyer without a business career and remained in politics until his death (thus not having a post-political business career). Pearson's early career was with the Department of External Affairs; he later acted as Canadian ambassador to Washington. His political career was financed by big capital, most notably by Walter Gordon, and his post-political career included a directorship on Crown Life (a dominant corporation). Trudeau's father made a fortune of $1.4 million in 1933 by selling his chain of gas stations and automobile association to Imperial Oil, thus leaving the present prime minister independently wealthy. Although marrying late, he married well. His father-in-law is James Sinclair, a former minister in the St. Laurent Cabinet, and currently deputy chairman of Canada Cement Lafarge and a director of Alcan Aluminum, Canadian Industry, Sun Life and the Bank of Montreal; all five are among Canada's largest 113 corporations. Apart from having surrounded themselves with Cabinets heavily laden with businessmen, there have been no shortages of direct and family links between Canada's prime ministers and its corporate elite. Indeed, four members of the current economic elite are directly related to these prime ministers (Meighen's and St. Laurent's sons, Borden's nephew, and Sinclair), between them holding no less than twenty dominant directorships!

David Nock has summarized the relationship between federal Cabinets and big business. For the Conservative Cabinet of the Bennett government, sixteen of the twenty-three members (70 per cent) "had a close relationship to some form of business," as did twenty-one of the thirty-four members (62 per cent) of the Diefenbaker Cabinet "either before or after their cabinet tenure." For the Liberal government between 1935 and 1957, thirty-seven of fifty-eight Cabinet members (64 per cent) "held some important business position before or after their tenure of office" (1976:227-28, 244). Using a different approach to this issue, Dennis Olsen's analysis of the political elite in Canada between 1961 and 1973 finds that "a minimum of 16 per cent of the *elected* members of this [political] elite were connected to substantial family wealth before they entered politics." Focusing on changes over time, Olsen finds that "about 27 per cent of the volume of circulation through the federal cabinet involves those who have had, or will have, business or corporate roles." This represents an increase from 18 per cent of those in the federal Cabinet between 1940 and 1960 who had prior business careers to 27 per cent of those in this office between 1960 and 1973. Of those leaving, 9 per cent during the earlier period and 19 per cent during the latter have left for full-time business careers (1977).

Within the Trudeau Cabinets the prominence of kinship ties to the current corporate elite are readily apparent: Jeanne Sauvé's husband, Maurice (himself a former minister in Pearson's government), is a vice-president of

Consolidated-Bathurst and a director of BP Canada; C.M. Drury's son, Chipman, is chairman of Montreal Life Insurance; James Richardson's brother, George Taylor, is president of James Richardson and Sons, governor of the Hudson's Bay Company, and a director of the Canadian Imperial Bank of Commerce, Hudson's Bay Gas and Oil, and the Interational Nickel Company of Canada. Moreover, some of the departed members of the Trudeau Cabinet quickly found their way into Canada's most powerful boardrooms. Before being recalled to head the Anti-Inflation Board, Jean-Luc Pépin was welcomed into the boardrooms of Bombardier, Canada Steamship Lines, Celanese Canada, Westinghouse Canada, and the biggest boardroom of all, Power Corporation. As if to upstage his former Department of Consumer and Corporate Affairs colleague, John Napier Turner, former minister of finance and Cabinet minister from 1965 to 1975, immediately became a partner in the Toronto law firm of McMillan, Binch and was recruited to the boards of Crown Life Insurance, Crédit Foncier, Marathon Realty, Canadian Investment Fund and, to round it off, Canadian Pacific (CP). This caused the *Globe and Mail* on 22 March 1976 to herald his "instant adoption into the corporate fraternity," noting that "Turner's knowledge of how a Cabinet is likely to approach a problem or how the civil service is likely to present it to its ministers will be of considerable value to CP or any other company with a major interface with government without one door being opened or one telephone call made." Still other members of the Trudeau Cabinets had their careers in dominant corporations before their political careers. Mitchell Sharp, for example, was closely associated with James Richardson and Sons before joining the Department of Finance and becoming deputy minister of industry, trade and commerce. Leaving this bureaucratic elite post after the Liberal defeat in 1958, he joined the corporate elite as vice-president of Brascan, where he stayed until 1962, after which time he served in Liberal Cabinets as minister of finance, industry, trade and commerce, and external affairs.

Intimacy is not a quality confined to Canada's political elite — Canada's bureaucratic elite has done quite well itself in the corporate world.[5] For example, Michael Pitfield, "one of Canada's most powerful civil servants — clerk of the Privy Council, secretary of the federal cabinet and key advisor to Prime Minister Pierre Trudeau" (*Toronto Star*, 19 June 1976; also *Financial Post*, 19 June 1976), is brother to Ward Chipman Pitfield, president of Pitfield, Mackay, Ross and a director of M. Loeb Limited and Husky Oil (and chairman of the Investors Dealers Association, "the national self-regulating body of the securities industry"), as well as being brother-in-law to Ross T. Clarkson, chairman of Caribonum (Canada) and a director of National Trust. Like politicians, many senior bureaucrats are "instantly adopted" by

---

[5]For a detailed listing of 'elite switchers,' see Clement, 1977:260-65.

the corporate world upon leaving. For example, Simon Reisman was immediately 'snatched up' by George Weston Limited and became a director of Burns Foods after leaving his post as deputy minister of finance, also setting up a consulting firm in Ottawa with James Gundy, who happens to be the former deputy minister of industry, trade and commerce.

Of course, the Senate — that institution established to directly represent business in the state — is rampant with connections to the economic world, but they would be too numerous to list. Suffice it to say that seventeen members of the current economic elite have enjoyed the privilege of Senate membership. This is a time-honoured tradition. For example, of the 308 senators between 1925 and 1962, 62.4 per cent were found to be from law, manufacturing, commerce or finance, while only 2 (0.6 per cent) represented labour (Kunz, 1967:66). Louis Giguere, the Liberal senator involved in the Sky Shops scandal, is reported to have said: "What's wrong with having a senator do a little business now and then? . . . Do Canadians expect senators to be drawn from the ranks of the Salvation Army or something?" (*Montreal Gazette*, 21 April 1976).

The importance of the close relationship between the Canadian state elite and the capitalist class is not that all positions in the state elite are snatched up by members of the capitalist class. Indeed, many capitalists expressly avoid the kind of public exposure that goes with any elected office. (But as will be shown, election is a prerequisite for only a small proportion of important state positions.) The important point is that an understanding of the ties between the economic elite and the state as a whole challenges the postulate that the state performs an unbiased role as manager of society for the benefit of all. The Canadian case illustrates that the highest levels of the state include many members who are directly from the corporate elite or are connected with them through close kinship ties. From this it would seem reasonable to deduce on empirical grounds alone that the state in Canada does not operate independently of the capitalist class.

Dennis Olsen's study (1977) deals with the relationship between the state and the economic world from the perspective of the state. The data here examine the relationship between those holding senior executive positions and directorships in Canadian dominant corporations (the economic elite) and various positions within the state system from the perspective of the economic elite. Table 4.1 demonstrates that one-third of the 1975 Canadian-born members of the economic elite held in the past, or continued to hold, positions directly within the state system. Moreover, 47 per cent either were themselves or had close kin who were in the state system at a senior level.

As the data illustrate, many members of the Canadian economic elite had operated directly within the state system and many still do. Thirty-seven members of the 1975 Canadian economic elite were recruited from political or bureaucratic elite posts, while seventeen had been or continued to be senators. As well, there were another seventy-five who had served in other

Table 4.1

The Economic Elite of 1975 and the State System

	Economic Elite with State Affiliations (current and past)	Cumulative[a]	
	N	N	%
Direct Personal Affiliations			
From political or bureaucratic elite	37	37	5
Senators	17	49	7
Wartime bureaucracy	53	88	13
Other political or bureaucratic posts	38	124	18
Crown corporations	45	160	23
Royal commissions	26	170	25
Boards or commissions	84	219	32
Party executive[b]	13	225	33
Kinship Ties[c]			
In political or bureaucratic elite	91	278	40
Senate	23	293	44
Member of Parliament	38	315	46
Lieutenant-Governor	12	318	47

Note: This table is based on an updated sample of the 1972 Canadian-born economic elite (N = 683): this revised sample represents an 84.4 per cent coverage as opposed to the 81.9 per cent used in *The Canadian Corporate Elite*, chaps. 5 and 6, pp. 259-63. In addition to the increased coverage, the quality of the data used in this table is better than that of the earlier sample because of the availability of additional material. See Clement, 1977.

[a] Does not include those already listed in prior affiliations.
[b] While party executive is not a position directly within the state system, it does provide a particularly close individual tie to the state apparatus.
[c] Includes fathers, fathers-in-law, brothers, grandfathers and, in a few cases, uncles.

political or bureaucratic posts for the state, bringing the total proportion who had served the state in a full-time capacity to 18 per cent of the economic elite. Besides full-time positions within the state, there was a series of part-time advisory and decision-making roles, such as on crown corporation boards, royal commissions and other boards and commissions all directly within the state system, which brings to one-third the proportion of the 1975 economic elite who had or continue to have direct positions within the state system. Of the over three hundred positions within the state system held by members of the economic elite, a mere handful have involved elections; the vast majority have been appointed positions.

The importance of these direct and kinship ties between the economic elite and the state system cannot be overstressed. They mean that this set of people, more than any other, is the one taken into account by the state. Indeed, the members of this group are very often those directly establishing policy on behalf of the state. In periods of crisis this has been particularly apparent. During the Second World War the senior ranks of the state bureaucracy swelled with members of the economic elite drawn upon to run the state machinery and guide the process of rapid industrialization. Within the current economic elite there are fifty-three members who held senior positions within the wartime bureaucracy. Not only did they control the state machinery during this period, they established important connections most useful for later business ventures. As Peter Newman has noted, "When the dollar-a-year men fanned out at the close of World War II to run the nation they had helped to create, the attitudes, the working methods, and the business ethic they took with them determined the country's economic and political course for the next three decades." Their experience forged them into an intimate set of people, well acquainted with one another and the operation of the state. Newman says, "They had come to Ottawa as individuals; they left as an elite" (1975:316).

Advisory Boards

When the state elite wants advice, it turns to the most powerful members of society. One of the formalized ways this occurs is through advisory boards to various ministers. For example, a *Financial Post* article, "The People Who Have Jamieson's Ear," says, "Industry, Trade & Commerce Minister Donald Jamieson has come to count heavily on his high-level Advisory Council." The article quoted Jamieson as follows: "World competition is getting tougher and tougher. But we in the government tend to use funds to help the faltering companies. It becomes more and more clear that we need to decide which of our industries — which sectors of industry — can do best in the world." With the state elite deciding which corporations it will be feeding through its loans and subsidies, it is important for members of the economic elite to be in touch to ensure that a share is directed their way. In the same article Clive Baxter says: "Jamieson appears delighted with the flow of information he is getting through the council — he says that some of it helped a lot in drafting parts of the federal budget last month" (19 June 1976).

Just who are the thirty-seven men who make up this advisory council to Industry, Trade and Commerce, have Jamieson's ear, and are involved in drafting federal budgets? It is clear that the economic elite has the greatest access to the board. Of the thirty-seven members, twenty (54 per cent) are directly from the economic elite, between them representing forty dominant corporations. What kind of dominant corporations are represented? The most heavily represented sector is finance, with sixteen of the forty dominant directorships from this sector, including nine from Canada's top five banks (all of which are represented), with four from the Bank of Montreal alone. Eight are from the transportation/utilities sector (including three from Canadian Pacific), eight from manufacturing, six from resource companies and two from trade. The dominant companies represented are mainly Canadian controlled (twenty-seven), followed by six from the United States, and only one each from the United Kingdom and elsewhere, while another five are joint Canada-United States consortia. Similarly, the elite members themselves are mainly indigenous Canadian capitalists (thirteen), with five U.S. compradors (that is, whose main affiliation is with a U.S.-controlled company), and one each are U.K. and other compradors. Besides the twenty members of the economic elite who clearly dominate this advisory board, there are another seventeen capitalists from smaller companies. They are even more likely to be indigenous Canadian capitalists and associated with Canadian companies. Of the seventeen, fourteen are from Canadian companies, two from U.S.-controlled ones, and one is associated with a U.K.-controlled company. Of all thirty-seven members, twenty-seven are indigenous Canadian capitalists, while the other ten owe their main power position to foreign capital.

Canada's capitalists are certainly given ample opportunity to have their wishes heard within the Canadian state, especially those from finance and transportation, which account for 60 per cent of all dominant directorships represented on the advisory council. It would be wrong, however, to think that their collective wish is to inhibit the entry of foreign capitalists. Rather, from the beginning of the Canadian state, Canada's capitalists have encouraged the state to stimulate the entry of foreign capital. The largest Canadian capitalists are not in conflict with foreign capitalists but in alliance, an issue to be returned to later.

Before leaving the subject of advisory boards, one further example illustrates economic elite dominance in these kinds of forums. It also indicates another bias of both the state and economic systems in Canada. Of all the advisory boards, the one most likely to provide an avenue for women's views in the corporate world would be the one on "the business community's progress of status of women issues" created by Marc Lalonde, the minister responsible for the status of women. Reflecting the lack of women in the economic elite — that set of people the state seems insistent on consulting — there is only one women on the eight-person board. Six of the eight are members of the economic elite, with one of the others a former president of the Canadian Broadcasting Corporation and the other a president of RCA Limited (Health and Welfare Canada, News Release, 5 May 1976). Half of the members of this advisory board hold directorships in one of Canada's dominant banks, but there is room made for only one woman. Quite a reflection on whom the state elite perceives as their most important constituency even when the issue is women in business!

State Regulation and Investigation

On another front, it is important to examine the increasing role of the state in regulating business. While it is certainly correct that there is increasing state regulation of business, it is important to be careful how this is interpreted and to note whose interests are being served. In a perceptive passage, columnist Geoffrey Stevens writes: "The prospect of greater use of regulatory powers ought, I submit, to cause real concern. But not concern on the part of ordinary workers and consumers who look to the 100-plus federal regulatory agencies to protect their interest and who are too often disappointed. Surely, it is time to explode the myth that government regulation is antithetical to the interest of business. With few exceptions (and the CRTC may be one of them), regulation operates mainly for the benefit of the industry which is regulated."[6]

Stevens goes on to examine the case of the Canadian Transport Commission (CTC) and its relationship with Bell Canada, which trades off its monopoly position for guaranteed profits through government regulation. Recently the CTC granted Bell Canada its full request for a $110.3 million rate increase. Bell has been known to spend upwards of $1 million on an application, which, ironically, is tax-deductible and actually calculated into the rates. Compared to Bell's army of accountants and lawyers, "there was only token public representation at the 26 days of CTC hearings and it was, in the Commission's judgment, too weak or too ill-informed to merit serious consideration."

But the problem runs deeper than this question of the unequal resources of all parties that appear before the regulatory boards. The basic assumption of the boards is a 'fair rate of return' on capital invested. The state gives the company a monopoly over a certain territory (in Bell's case most of Canada's industrial heartland), thus restricting the consumers' choice to either use Bell or go without a telephone. But, in return, Bell makes the 'sacrifice' of having its profit return guaranteed. Quite a sacrifice. Moreover, only part of its operation is regulated; the production end — through its subsidiary Northern Telecom, which supplies Bell's equipment — is able to make whatever it can selling to its parent.

Given this, it is little wonder, as Michael J. Trebilcock, chairman of the Consumers' Association of Canada's advocacy committee, notes, that "most of the extensively regulated industries, at least, prefer being regulated to competing and actively seek and sustain accommodating regulatory regimes." Trebilcock goes on to quote John Turner when he was minister of consumer and corporate affairs as saying, "I've looked at a lot of regulatory agencies, and the longer I'm around here, the more I believe that every one of these tends, in a period of time, to reflect the interests of the industry it is supposed to be regulating" (1975:13,14).

Turner's observations certainly fit for the Foreign Investment Review Agency. At least publicly, opposition to FIRA was recorded by the dominant capitalists in Canada (through the Bankers' Association of Canada, the Canadian Chamber of Commerce, the Canadian Manufacturers' Association and the Mining Association of Canada) when the scheme was first announced.

---

[6]*Globe and Mail*, 31 December 1975. As will be shown, it is doubtful whether the Canadian Radio-Television and Telecommunications Commission acts contrary to the benefit of dominant media complexes; indeed, it gives state-sanctioned media monopolies to a privileged few.

Thus there was a unified response by the dominant fractions of the comprador and indigenous capitalist class, both expressing concern over possible restrictions on the free movement of capital. They were concerned, in fact, that even the *appearance* of restriction would inhibit foreign investment. The state elites, however, were fully aware of the ideological value of such a review process and, in a minority government situation with pressure from the New Democratic Party, appeared to be following the interests of the Canadian Federation of Independent Business, which represents small Canadian capitalists — that is, those threatened by foreign takeovers and manipulated by the two dominant fractions of the capitalist class in Canada. It would not be correct to argue in this case that the state acted against the interests of the dominant fractions of the capitalist class; the state was simply looking after the 'common affairs' of the dominant class. It is not that the dominant capitalists were concerned about state intervention; they have frequently encouraged such interventions. Rather, they were concerned about how the controls would be used and by whom.

It is always important to look beyond the level of state policy to that of actual practice, and here the record of FIRA speaks for itself. As of mid-1976, it had approved 84 per cent of all the applications for takeovers and 94 per cent of new foreign businesses. Rather than a 'screen,' it has become a 'funnel' for foreign direct investment by steering this capital towards particular activities. There is an appearance of action, but FIRA is a lion without teeth, a giant public relations exercise to 'cool out' nationalist sentiment. Neither its purpose nor its practice is to prevent foreign control over the Canadian economy. This could be accomplished much more simply and effectively.

In areas where Canadian capitalists are strong, particularly in banking, life insurance, trust companies, transportation, utilities and the mass media, the state has provided strong protection against foreign control. In these areas, legislation prohibits foreign capitalists from owning sufficient stock to control or take over companies, thus protecting the 'turf' of Canadian capitalists. But legislation (as in FIRA) to 'protect' other areas, such as retail trade, manufacturing and resources, although recommended on several occasions, has only recently been enacted. Moreover, the Foreign Investment Review Agency simply reviews or examines proposed takeovers of Canadian companies in these sectors by foreign capitalists, and there are no across-the-board prohibitions (as in other areas) or any effect on the many companies that already exist. This difference between various sectors of the the economy reflects in legislation the historical development of these sectors under the command of either indigenous or foreign-controlled capitalists; that is, the law is a mirror of the economic power structure of Canadian society.

In terms of who is administering FIRA, the dominant fractions of the capitalist class have little to be concerned about. The head of FIRA since 1974 has been James Richard Murray, educated in McGill's undergraduate and law programs. His father is James Richard Murray, former chairman of the Canadian Wheat Board (and thus part of the bureaucratic elite) and director of such companies as Federal Grain and Buckerfields. The son was with the Foreign Service Office, Department of External Affairs, posted at the Canadian Embassy in Washington from 1945 to 1950. He then joined the Hudson's Bay Company and became its managing director, as well as a vice-chairman of the U.S.-controlled Hudson's Bay Gas and Oil Company and a director of the Canadian-controlled Royal Trust. He dropped these directorships and his other directorships on Air Canada and *Time* Canada before becoming head of the government's screening agency. He will have plenty of opportunity to discuss state policy with his corporate elite colleagues in the club rooms of such exclusive men's clubs as the Vancouver and the Mount Royal. He represents one of the few cases of movement from the economic elite to the bureaucratic elite in recent times, but his job, like that of Jean-Luc Pépin, who was also recalled from the corporate world to head the Anti-Inflation Board (AIB), warranted someone perceived as 'safe' by both the state and corporate elite and experienced in both. Pépin, as would be expected, turned out to be the right choice — at least for the corporate world. The record of the AIB illustrates its propinquity to control wages, while in the long run profits have only been enhanced (Panitch, 1976).

Another area related to state regulation is that of government investigations. The most recent example that some may perceive as a threat to dominant capitalists is the Royal Commission on Corporate Concentration. Once again, such a perception would be misplaced, ignoring the ideological value of such ventures and the adaptability of dominant capitalists to such situations. Why was this royal commission called? Prime Minister Trudeau's official reason was explained in his press release announcing it on 22 April 1975:

> With the current activities suggesting that further large-scale concentration of corporate power in Canada may be taking place, particularly in relation to conglomerate enterprises, the Government has decided that it is necessary at this time to inquire into whether, and to what extent such concentrations of corporate power confer sufficient social and economic benefit to Canadian society as to be in the public interest.

But this is no more than 'motherhood' — political rhetoric for public consumption. A more revealing reason appears in another not so well prepared comment by Trudeau in *Hansard* on the same day: "I would certainly agree that in the constitutional sense the government has the power to act [to curb corporations]. I do not agree that in a legal sense we have made laws which permit us to interfere with the rules of the game as they are now played legally by the corporate players." What does this more candid statement mean? It means that Trudeau and the other Liberals have been unable to have as much impact on Canada's economy — its inflation rates and unemployment, both volatile political issues — through the traditional fiscal mechanisms of the state as they would like, and they have decided to turn attention towards the real economy, the private economy, that directs this country. It has been decided that some of the political heat, particularly stimulated by Power Corporation's attempt to take over Argus Corporation, will be shoved off onto the nebulous 'business community' and buried in a royal commission. In other words, the focus will be off the Liberal government, at least for a while, leaving a public impression that 'something is being done.'

What does this mean? It does not mean, as Peter Newman has suggested, a showdown between business and government (1975:390). If that were the case, the commission members would be radically different from the ones Trudeau selected. Newman should have investigated who runs the commission and what interests are served — the interests of big business and giant corporations, the very institutions that are supposed to be investigated. Robert Bryce, head of the commission, was himself one of the most powerful civil servants during most of the 1960s, when, as Trudeau said, the laws were *not* made to interfere with the "rules of the game" of the "corporate players." Bryce's father was a member of the economic elite, as is another commissioner, Pierre Nadeau, currently president of Petrofina and a director of the Royal Bank. The third commissioner and chief research director have both made their careers servicing corporate giants (Lorimer, 1975). Not a likely lot for a showdown.

What, then, will the conclusions of the commission most likely be?[7] Even before the commission got under way, the research director, Donald Thompson, already gave a strong indication. "Big, big business is beautiful," according to a *Globe and Mail* profile which quotes Thompson as saying: "I hope the organization will tell us about the positive side of the social implications of large size. It could be that we will conclude, not that there's too much corporate concentration but that there's too little" (*Globe and Mail*, 4 October 1975). As if dominant corporations and the capitalists needed an invitation!

Following Mr. Thompson's obviously unbiased perspective, it is likely that the commission will find that Canada needs to develop some score of giant multinational companies that will be able to operate on a world scale to help strengthen Canada's economic position. This seems to be the theme hummed by the dominant capitalists and their spokesmen in the state system. Ontario Treasurer Darcy McKeough said before the Bryce Commission that "the size of the postal workers union is more of a problem than the size of Massey-Ferguson or Argus Corporation." That depends upon whose problems McKeough is talking about. His are quite obviously seen from a corporate perspective, as the following statement attributed to him also suggests: "Judged by international standards, any of our firms are of sub-optimal size"

---

[7]This was written in the midst of the Bryce Commission hearings, and no official reports had been released. See the following paper, chapter 5, for an assessment of the Bryce Commission report.

(*Globe and Mail*, 4 June 1976). A similar theme is taken up by Don McGilivray in the *Monetary Times* (9 May 1976), when he asks: "Are Canadian corporations becoming giants at home but pygmies abroad?" Although cast in more technocratic language, Robert Bryce's answer to this question indicates his internalization of the perspective of big business. He is reported to have said: "There are a lot of these oligopolies in Canada which aren't against the law and which, in fact, reflect the situation that we have a limited number of big companies that are able to compete internationally working in a reasonably moderate sized market in Canada" (*Globe and Mail*, 24 April 1976).

In addition to this major conclusion, or justification, the commission is likely to recommend some type of greater disclosure of information by corporations to the state (long overdue in Canada) and, along with this, a hope that corporations will work more closely with the state in determining economic policy. It clearly will not touch the fundamentals of the private exercise of power and private advantages accruing from this power. It will hardly find any necessity for corporations to become accountable to their workers or to consumers or for any real democratization or decentralization of the economy. But what about the 'social benefits' mentioned in the mandate? It is unlikely that the commission will ever even come to a real understanding of what this means. Here is what was reported about the research director's thoughts on the issue: "'That word, "social" has troubled everyone who's read it,' [Thompson] says. Most of the work on the social implications of large scale size has been done by sociologists rather than economists, and Mr. Thompson feels that sociological research is 'soft' and unreliable" (*Globe and Mail*, 4 October 1975). Research is unreliable, presumably, when its conclusions do not match the predisposition of the commissioners. The dice have been loaded well in advance to determine the outcome of such an inquiry.

All this aside, what does the government do with the massive reports it commissions? In other words, what differences do such inquiries really make (aside from their obvious ideological value)? The most recent example of a similar study is the *Senate Report on the Mass Media*, an impressive document in terms of its data if not its conclusions. In spite of its shortcomings, the report resulted in an antitrust action against the Irving media interests in New Brunswick, a commendable undertaking and the first of its kind in the highly concentrated media world. But, after some delay, the Irving interests had the court ruling overturned (both in New Brunswick and in the Supreme Court of Canada) and today roll happily along as before.

What has changed in the media since the report was filed? Quite a bit. The report found there to be enormous concentration within the media that was detrimental to everyone's interest except, of course, those few who controlled the media. It identified the largest media complexes in the country in 1970, but since then some interesting changes have been occurring. Telemedia Quebec, one of the largest fifteen, was acquired by Montreal Trust, itself a subsidiary of Power Corporation, adding to Power's already extensive newspaper holdings in Quebec, which had already put it among one of the original fifteen largest. Then Standard Broadcasting, itself a subsidiary of Argus Corporation, took over Bushnell Communications, another of the fifteen largest (Ottawa Journal, 29 April 1975). This takeover was accomplished with the approval of the Canadian Radio-Television and Telecommunications Commission (CRTC), which provided Standard with a telegram to that effect. Since the Senate report, in addition to a multitude of smaller newspapers being bought out by the largest chains, four of the fifteen largest entire complexes have been reduced to two, and if the Power-Argus deal eventually works out, these four would be reduced to one.[8]

But does this ownership of the media — or any economic corporation for that matter — make any difference? There is some strong evidence that it does. In a New York Times article of 6 April 1975 entitled "Paul Desmarais, An Aggressive French-Canadian," the following was reported:

> Three years ago, his largest newspaper, La Presse in Montreal, was closed by a long and bitter strike, with the employees seeking a greater measure of control. "Nobody is going to control this paper," Mr. Desmarais said. "It's my newspaper. If they want control, let them start their own newspaper." That strike represented a showdown with the Quebec separatists among editors and reporters. Mr. Desmarais won the battle.

It does matter who owns and controls media complexes and economic corporations, but the history of government investigations into such matters is one of inaction and inadequate response to the conditions uncovered. Only recommendations the government is predisposed towards are carried out, and the investigators themselves are carefully selected to work within the framework of capitalism for their solutions.

Political Party Financing

Political party financing has long been an obvious source of corporate influence on politicians. Even in a non-election year, the two major parties use about $2 million annually to keep their political machines lubricated. The grease is supplied by the dominant corporations, as Geoffrey Stevens has pointed out:

> The two major parties are heavily dependent on contributions from the corporate sector. The chartered banks are their ranking angels. In fiscal 1974-75, the Bank of Montreal gave the Liberals $25,000 plus another

---

[8]As of June 1976 Power Corporation held 428,082 common (25.2 per cent) and 4,053,038 class C participating non-voting shares (59.9 per cent) in Argus Corporation. However, 61 per cent of Argus voting shares are held by Ravelston Corporation, which is controlled by John A. McDougald (Globe and Mail, 9 June 1976). (Control of Argus later passed to the Black Brothers. See the following article, chapter 5.)

$25,000 in prepayment of its 1975-76 contribution; it gave the Conservatives one payment of $50,000. The Canadian Imperial Bank of Commerce donated $26,233.20 to the Liberals and $26,000 to the Tories. For the Toronto-Dominion Bank, $20,261.60 to the Liberals and $20,800 to the Conservatives, and for the Bank of Nova Scotia, $20,180 to the Liberals and $21,000 to the Tories.

Thus, between them, Canada's five dominant banks supplied $285,000 in contributions to the two dominant parties in one non-election year. They were not alone, however:

> Alberta Gas Trunk Line Co. Ltd., a member of the Foothills group which is seeking to build an all-Canadian gas pipeline up the Mackenzie River, contributed $15,270 to the Liberals then covered its bet with $15,000 to the Conservatives. . . . Following is a partial list of some of the larger contributions to the Liberal Party, with their donations to the Tories in parentheses. British Columbia Forest Products, $10,000 ($10,000); Crown Zellerbach, $5,000 ($5,000); Falconbridge Nickel, $4,000 ($4,000); International Nickel, $27,500 ($25,800); Noranda Mines, $15,000 ($15,983); Gulf Oil, $21,449.60 ($21,703); Southam Press, $10,000 ($10,000); London Life, $6,000 ($6,000); Dow Chemical, $10,840 ($10,109.80); Dominion Foundries and Steel, $25,000 ($25,183); IBM, $5,580 ($6,183); Moore Corp., $5,000 ($5,000); Molson Companies, $8,200 ($8,373.20); Weyerhauser Canada Ltd., $5,000 ($5,000). Even Denison Mines, whose chairman, Stephen Roman, ran unsuccessfully for the Tories in the 1974 election, proved even-handed in its 1974-75 donations — $25,000 to the Liberals and $26,000 to the Conservatives. . . . On the other side of the coin, department stores seem to prefer Conservatives. Eaton's of Canada gave the Tories $26,368 and the Liberals $15,000; for Simpsons-Sears, it was Conservatives $13,330, Liberals $700. [*Globe and Mail*, 11 February 1976]

Twenty-five of the top corporations operating in Canada gave a total of nearly $400,000 to each of the two dominant parties in 1975. There is little difference in party choice for foreign-controlled firms or those firms that are consortia of Canadian and U.S. capital; in fact, if there is any difference, it is a slight preference for the Conservatives, who received an average of $11,618 from the ten foreign-controlled or related firms examined, compared to an average of $10,384 for the Liberals.

This type of reliance for party funding will ultimately be expressed in the type of approach the state takes towards the corporate world. In his comprehensive analysis of this question, K.Z. Paltiel was led to conclude that "overdependence of parties on any single source or socio-economic group inevitably narrows the freedom of action of political decisionmakers. Such parties tend to become the spokesmen of narrow social interests losing the aggregative function attributed to parties in liberal-democratic thought" (1970:161). Even within the capitalist class there are few corporations like the Bank of Montreal that could manage to give the two major parties $100,000 between them without feeling the pinch.

The fact that Canada's top corporations give, and the two major political parties receive, such large donations reflects the ideological affinity between them. For the corporations, they are a form of insurance and leverage, enabling them to keep avenues of access open. For political parties and politicians, they defray the costs of campaigning. To 'bite the hand that feeds them' would certainly jeopardize their ability to be re-elected. Nevertheless, this must be perceived in the broadest sense. Specific corporations and specific capitalists may be rejected by state actions because their particular interests are in conflict with the general interest of the capitalist class and the state. Very seldom, however, are the general interests of labour taken into account at the expense of capital. The bias of the Canadian state is in favour of capital over labour, and big capital (whether Canadian or foreign) over small capital.

While the relationship between capitalists and the Canadian state cannot be fully revealed by examining personal ties, the state decision-making bodies, and political party financing, the exploration of these areas in this paper does at least serve to indicate the general affinity between the dominant class and the state. This general affinity means that the state in Canada is predisposed to ensure the general interests of capitalists and assure capitalists that the conditions necessary for the orderly extraction of economic surplus into their hands are provided. To understand the peculiarities of each individual transaction between the Canadian state and capitalists would require detailed case studies, but generally this type of information is carefully guarded. John Turner, former Liberal finance minister, summarized the problem of access to information when speaking to the Canadian Bar Association: "[In politics] there is a vested interest in presenting any policy or any decision in the most favourable light. This sometimes means selecting facts. It often means managing or manipulating information. It often involves orchestrating and timing. Full and immediate revelation of all the facts can be embarrassing, I know. I've been there" (Globe and Mail, 1 September 1976). Only after several decades does this type of detailed information emerge in Canada's archives.

Nevertheless, the various kinds of information presented here serve to substantiate the thesis that Canada's capitalists have enjoyed a close relationship with their state. The state has served as both an important recruiting ground for many members of the corporate elite, and in return many appointed positions within the state that are investigatory, regulatory, advisory, and policy setting in nature have a very high proportion of members from the Canadian corporate elite, the most powerful fraction of the capitalist class.

As was suggested, to understand the full implications of such an intimate relationship would require detailed case studies. This evidence, however, should make the reader closely examine state policies that *appear* to contradict the wishes of capital. For example, a policy such as the recent creation of

Petro-Canada, a crown corporation now operating in the oil industry, should be seen as what it is — a move by the Canadian state to look after the general interests of Canadian capitalists, not Canadians in general. As Maurice Strong, chairman and president of Petro-Canada has candidly admitted: "The time will come when it will be recognized that the private petroleum industry's survival in a large measure has been ensured by Petro-Canada's existence. . . . For one thing our presence relieves the pressure for the nationalization of the whole industry" (*Globe and Mail*, 21 January 1976). As the former vice-president of Dome Petroleum and president of Power Corporation knows well, Petro-Canada is mainly oriented toward explorations and is not intended to compete with the international oil cartels. Its task will be to socialize oil companies' risks, not their profits.

While the oil industry is not alone in its ability to pass its risks on to the state, Larry Pratt's analysis of Syncrude in *The Tar Sands* serves as an important illustration. By a capital strike, Syncrude threatened to withdraw from an oil sands project and brought the federal, Alberta and Ontario governments to their knees. As Pratt summarizes the Syncrude situation:

> The companies' conditions for development of the tar sands include much higher prices and returns, but they also want to transfer much of the risk and the heaviest costs involved to the public sector. Thus government must shoulder the enormous financial burden of building the massive infrastructure required to service and supply these remote projects, provide equity and debt financing, royalty holidays, guaranteed returns and prices, ensure labour stability, train a work force, underwrite environmental studies and costs — all of which carried a price tag in the billions. [1976:95]

The power of the Syncrude partners in forcing such a 'sweet deal' cannot be reduced to personal ties with the Canadian state (although there are enough of those). It must be seen in terms of the tremendous resources, technology, capital and market access they control. It is this power that gives them such enormous leverage in dealing with the Canadian state. It is power like this which explains ties between capitalists in Canada and the state.[9]

In the oil industry, it is the dominant comprador elite within Canada, supported by foreign-based capitalists controlling the multinational headquarters of these companies, who have determined Canada's oil policy. To a large extent this has been the case in all areas related to resource- and manufacturing-based companies, with the notable exceptions of the steel industry, food and beverages, and the pulp and paper industry, where dominant indigenous Canadian capitalists have had much more impact. On the other hand, state policy associated with most financial institutions, transportation, utilities and mass media has been in support of dominant

---

[9]A further example where the state has facilitated private interests in the oil and gas industry is provided by Dosman (1975). He analyses relations between the state and North America's largest energy companies in their exploitation of the North.

indigenous capitalists. This pattern suggests that there is not a basic conflict of interest between foreign-controlled capitalists, who control the major productive sectors of the Canadian economy, and the dominant indigenous Canadian capitalists, who thrive in the areas of circulation and service.

As is stressed in several papers in this collection, the Canadian state is a fragmentary one, consisting of a federal government, two territories and ten provinces. At the provincial level, the state is often forced to reconcile conflicting demands from foreign capital attracted to provide manufacturing capacity or resource extraction and from the dependent class of small service capitalists that emerges in conjunction with this foreign-led activity. This service capitalist class, in turn, particularly because it is vulnerable, turns to the provincial state.[10] The fact that both the foreign- and Canadian-based fractions of the economic elite have enjoyed such a close relationship with various branches of the Canadian state serves to reinforce their respective bases of power. Outside these two dominant fractions of the capitalist class, small capitalists and members of other classes do not have nearly as great an impact in determining federal state policy.

As long as the various branches of the Canadian state continue to be controlled by the two major political parties, there is little hope that the state will be used to alleviate problems associated with foreign control because it is not in the general interest of Canada's own leading capitalists to promote such a policy (Clement, 1977:289-302). As long as Canadian society continues to be shaped by the capitalist mode of production, the most powerful class will be the capitalist class. As long as capitalists control the means of production and circulation, they will use their power to ensure that the Canadian state will operate to their best advantage. And their best advantage does not represent the common interest of most Canadians.

---

[10]For a detailed discussion of emerging classes in Alberta, see Pratt, 1977, and for a broader view, Stevenson, 1977; also see Fournier, 1976.

Chapter 5

An Exercise in Legitimation: The Bryce Commission's Justification of Corporate Concentration

Publication of the Bryce Commission's report in 1978 occasioned two sources to ask me to examine two separate sections, one on ownership and control and another on foreign investment. Both investigations have been integrated into the following paper. As the previous paper indicated, it was possible to anticipate the commission's findings well before its results were released. These were determined largely by the personnel selected to run the commission and the assumptions of the commissioners. What is most interesting about the report is what it reveals about the Canadian economy and the Canadian state. Unlike the previous paper, the following one examines state policy formation in some detail by exploring the assumptions and findings of one of Canada's most important royal commissions. This investigation reveals many of the weaknesses of the Canadian state as it relates to the economy, and exposes the thinness of the justifications offered to defend the existing order. Should we laugh or cry? Were the stakes not so high, it would be preferable to dismiss the commission's report as mere buffoonery, but the issues are real and of importance.

All is right, just and proper in the world of Canadian business. Businessmen are looking after business; roll over and go back to sleep. This is the impression conveyed by a reading of the *Report of the Royal Commission on Corporate Concentration* (the Bryce Commission). Its conclusions are as expected, given the selection of commissioners and mobilization of resources by self-congratulatory capitalists. The conclusions also follow naturally from the *assumptions* under which the commission was conducted. Before specifically evaluating the report's conclusions, it is necessary to examine some of these assumptions and place them within the context of the nature of power in liberal democracies.

The Commission's Assumptions

The assumptions under which commissions are conducted determine in large part their outcomes. This can be illustrated by briefly contrasting two recent government inquiries: the Berger Commission (*Northern Frontier, Northern Homeland: The Report of the Mackenzie Valley Pipeline Inquiry*) and the Bryce Commission. Berger criticized the dominant assumptions about development, delved into social, political and cultural consequences of a form of corporate power and viewed as a major part of its constituency those most directly affected — the people who call the North their homeland. The Bryce Commission did none of these things. It chose, rather, to accept the dominant assumptions about Canadian society; that is, assumptions held by those in control of Canada's largest corporations. These assumptions were predetermined by the selection of those in charge (Clement, previous paper; Lorimer, 1975:7). It was dominated by lawyers and economists — both most comfortable in the service of capital — and by capitalists themselves. The commissioners are quite explicit about their values in the preface to their report:

> We shared a conviction regarding Canadian society. We believed that our political system, with its major role for governments as well as private business, and respect and safeguards for the freedom of individuals, was sound in its basic elements and structure and more appropriate for Canada than any other . . . our society and our economy should function both efficiently and equitably, without a basic rearrangement of roles and relationships. This we believe also to be the view of most Canadians and we have therefore looked for improvements and made recommendations concerning the working of our institutions within the existing structure of society. [xx][1]

This conviction, that Canada, as a liberal democracy and thus a capitalist society, is basically equitable and efficient and requires no fundamental overhaul, served to impose a selective perception and input on the commission. It meant, from the outset, that the commissioners were committed to legitimation of the prevailing order.

There is a great deal to question in this assumption. This society harbours some fundamental flaws. Inflation is high, hovering around 10 per cent, and threatening to remain so even when the United States rate is declining; Canada's balance-of-payments deficit is increasing annually, reaching $54 billion in 1977; the mainstay of the economy is exporting non-renewable resources; its dollar has fallen to less than 90¢ against the U.S dollar; the various levels of the Canadian government are so in debt that interest payments alone are over $9 billion annually; the productive cornerstones of

---

[1]Unidentified page numbers refer to the *Report of the Royal Commission on Corporate Concentration* (Ottawa: Supply and Services Canada, 1978).

the economy in manufacturing and resources are foreign controlled; over a million people, about 10 per cent of the labour force, are officially unemployed.[2] Is this efficient? Is this a sound economy?

And to assume that Canadian society is based on equality is to take a very limited and naive view of the world. It requires ignoring the fact that the bottom 40 per cent of income earners in 1973 received only 15 per cent of total income, while the top 40 per cent received 68 per cent, with the direction of change since 1951 toward greater inequality (Statistics Canada, 1977:161). It requires ignoring tremendous inequalities of class and power in capitalist societies. Indeed, it is reasonable to argue that the commission itself is one of the many weapons in the state's arsenal to legitimate these inequalities and the private accumulation of capital. What the commissioners failed to say is that Canada is a society with formal political equality but tremendous economic and social inequality because it requires the private accumulation of capital in the hands of one class and the appropriation of labour from another class.

Size or concentration of corporate power is an important variable in understanding the nature of a society, but it is secondary to ownership and control of that power. In Canada ownership and control are dominated by capitalists, operating under capitalist assumptions and capitalist motivations. This is a system of private property (which does not mean the property each of us owns for purposes of consumption, but money that is utilized to produce more capital). Also important is state property, which is also used primarily under capitalist assumptions ('in a business-like way') to fulfil the state's accumulation and legitimation functions. This, by the way, is something the commissioners acknowledge: "There are a number of tasks in our society that may be best undertaken by government (often in conjunction with private enterprise). Some projects may be too large or risky for private firms to undertake by themselves without government support. Others may be in the national interest but not sufficiently profitable to attract private capital" (3).

As C.B. Macpherson, the eminent Canadian political theorist, has so ably argued, both state and private property are based on "rights of exclusion," while a third form of property, radically different from the others, is common property based on a "right *not to be excluded from* the use or benefit of something which society or the state has proclaimed to be for common use. Society or the state may declare that some things — for example, common lands, public parks, city streets, highways — are for common use" (1973:124). This is a democratic form of property whereby people are able to make democratic demands that ensure that their collective wishes are respected. It requires a kind of democracy that is society-wide, encompassing people's

---

[2]By 1982 even these figures understate the depths of the structural decay, with unemployment over 12.5 per cent (officially) and an 80¢ dollar.

communities and workplaces, not merely a formal mechanism for selecting governments.[3]

Put another way, the ideological blinders of the commissioners prevent them from addressing the central question: What is the essence of the corporation? The essence is the reproduction of capitalism, made possible only by the dominant class's realization of surplus value created by the working class. They are thus unable to come to grips with the social side of the corporation: the unequal access to power and the implications this way of organizing society has for the working class and consumers.

The Commission's Arguments

The commission was struck ostensibly to address the implications of a possible merger between Power and Argus corporations, given the lack of state policy adequate to assess this prospect. Its mandate was posed in the broader terms of an inquiry into "the nature and role of major concentrations of corporate power in Canada." Originally the commissioners did not intend to investigate either foreign ownership or the banking system because the former had been studied by a series of government inquiries and the latter was under its regular ten-year Bank Act review. The commissioners did, however, include chapters on each of these areas in their report, although they did not do any substantial research on them. They were included because each is central to establishing the report's major line of argument — the justification of corporate concentration.

From the outset it was apparent that the commissioners defined their principal task as the justification of corporate concentration; early on it was also evident what the basis of this justification would be — Canada's position in the world system. Statements by Donald Thompson (the commission's research director), Darcy McKeough (Ontario's treasurer), Don McGilivray (the *Monetary Times*) and Robert Bryce himself provided initial clues to this line of argument. The same argument was articulated by Paul Desmarais, chairman of Power Corporation, before the commission: "We should have more and bigger Canadian companies, and the reason for it is that if we are going to compete in a world, we have to be big in Canada, and we have to be able to handle it, and the only way to do that today is to be big" (Royal Commission on Corporate Concentration transcript, 10 December 1975:163).

The report operates in a world of delusion. By arguing that Canadian

---

[3]See also C.B. Macpherson's *The Life and Times of Liberal Democracy*, where he argues that "a fully democratic society requires democratic political control over the uses to which the amassed capital and the remaining natural resources of the society are put" (1977:111), and "The Meaning of Property," in *Property: Mainstream and Critical Positions* (1978). These arguments are expanded in chapter 9.

companies are smaller than the largest ones in the United States, the commissioners pose what they call "a basic conundrum facing policymakers in Canada. That is, while average firm size in many Canadian industries is below 'world-scale,' policies to promote larger firm sizes may exacerbate the potential problems associated with already high domestic levels of industrial concentration" (12; also see 24, 63-64, 98, 177, 213 and 405). Put quite simply, Canada is not the United States; it is a dominated society in terms of the international economy, not a centre nation. If the policies of the commission were followed, however, Canada would be headed toward becoming part of the United States. The first step would be a free trade policy, advocated by the commission.

The commission's strategy, rather than develop a national industrial market and expand Canadian processing of natural resources in demand in the world, is to open the floodgates and provide incentives for the development of some Canadian-based multinational corporations that could play in the world of international giants. They argue that "efficiency in many industries could be improved by permitting or encouraging firms to expand their operations to more efficient size or to merge, but this might also result in higher industry concentration or, in some industries, absolute monopoly control" (213). The 'efficiency' (which is obviously measured in international rather than Canadian terms) would be ensured through new international competitors that would enter the Canadian market once the existing tariff barriers were withdrawn. There is no reason to believe, based on the experience in such industries as automobiles or petroleum, that consumers would benefit through lower prices. Indeed, it is likely that existing branch plants within Canada's manufacturing industry would gradually close down and supply the Canadian market from the United States or from other branches in nations with cheap labour.

The commissioners even anticipate this happening: "As tariffs are reduced and as foreign competition, especially from low-wage countries increases, there will be a greater pressure to rationalization." "Rationalization," of course, means eliminating smaller companies and reinforcing the position of dominant multinational corporations. This is their strategy for dealing with the problem of foreign control. As they go on to say, "Rather than buying back foreign-owned companies, it would be preferable to provide incentives for the merger of both foreign and domestically owned firms in an industry into larger, more efficient units and to use laws that will override any antitrust objections in the United States and other countries" (208). This is what they call "workable competition," whereby, "under a specialization agreement competitors in a market would be allowed to allocate production among themselves to achieve longer production runs and resulting economies" (215). In other words, they are advocating international monopolies where private corporations carve up markets, all with the best wishes of the Canadian government. As a final touch they then advocate a hands-off approach by the government: "The proportion of the Canadian government constrained by government regulation or ownership should be reviewed and possibly reduced" (216). Somehow the public is expected to gain through lower prices. The solution to foreign investment is an international economy, controlled by private multinational corporations that are to be granted monopolies in particular products.

The commissioners' proposal to resolve their dilemma of concentration versus 'world-scale' production is to opt for giant multinational corporations. They provide no mechanism to ensure that Canadians will benefit. The result will be to place Canadian consumers and workers even more at the mercy of a few dominant corporations directed by private interests and a self-selecting, self-perpetuating set of people, and the elimination of smaller Canadian manufacturers who serve local or regional markets. They have opted for free trade and a group of privately owned Canadian multinationals to 'fight for Canada' in the world market, along with the open entry of the Canadian market to foreign corporations. Even more than already exists, this would lead to an ever more specialized economy directed by ever fewer people who are increasingly less accountable to nation states, consumers or workers. This approach has got us where we are today, a society where manufacturing and resource extraction are dominated by U.S. corporations, an economy geared to supplying low-processed natural resources to other countries, and a highly concentrated economy, not to mention simultaneous high inflation and high unemployment. The commissioners propose more of the same.

The commissioners' position on the international system and foreign ownership is riddled with contradictions. At one point they argue:

> There was a strong direct correlation between the degree of foreign owner-
> ship and the degree of concentration and the presence of large firms. The
> degree of foreign ownership is very high in those industry segments where
> an oligopoly of three or four firms account for a high proportion of total
> sales in the industry. [192]

This is a sensible enough observation, as anyone who has purchased an automobile or gasoline to fuel it could attest. Escaping all reason, the commissioners conclude a few pages later that "foreign direct investment does not seem to have increased the concentration of industries in Canada" (194). The commissioners never allow evidence (even their own) to get in the way of a conclusion they are determined to make. In addition to the obvious concentration in areas dominated by foreign investment, there is additional concentration of control resulting from many branches of the same parent operating 'independently' in Canada, as will be argued shortly.

The commissioners are unable to escape the irrefutable conclusions drawn from many government inquiries on the distorting impact of foreign direct investment and even reproduce some of the findings:

It may atrophy or limit the ability of Canadian firms to develop indigenous research and development, entrepreneurial enterprise or export capacity, decrease the amount of upgrading of Canada's natural resources before export and cause a reverse flow of dividends, interest and capital. In addition to these potential economic problems, foreign ownership may not be compatible with Canadian political sovereignty. [182]

Repatriation of dividends and interest charges at the rate of $2.5 billion per year reduces the growth of domestic pools of capital. Because of their backing by their parent firms, multinational subsidiaries are often able to obtain capital in Canada on more favourable terms than domestic companies of the same size. [4]

Despite these observations, the commissioners nevertheless proceed to conclude: "There is no irreconcilable conflict between the desirability of foreign direct investment as a vehicle for prosperity and the impact of such investment on the social, economic and political milieux in Canada" (207). The evidence to support such a claim simply does not exist; instead, the commissioners offer the suggestion that "Canada must formulate policies to work with multinational corporations and the countries in which they operate to achieve an equitable distribution of the benefits they generate" (209). There is no reason to believe that even if the Canadian state did generate such policies they would work; moreover, there is no evidence that multinationals will work for a national interest. Their interests, as instilled in them by those who control them and necessitated by the capitalist system that creates them, are self interests to generate and accumulate as much private capital as possible. Such policies would simply draw Canada into a world system where it is already very vulnerable and where it has very limited strength.

Canada's vulnerability is illustrated by examining its foreign trade as a proportion of its Gross National Product. In 1960, 15.7 per cent of Canada's GNP was represented by foreign trade, and by 1972 this rose to 21.2 per cent. Compare this with the United States, which had 3.6 per cent in 1960 and 4.6 per cent in 1972 (Marfels, 1977:188). Moreover, what Canada exports are raw materials and what it imports are manufactured products, resulting in the export of potential jobs and capital. The 'trade' itself is in fact largely intracompany transfers of materials within multinational corporations that have branches in Canada for the purposes of extracting raw materials for shipment to their parents or for marketing manufactured goods produced abroad. Neither the so-called market nor the Canadian government exercises much control over this process.

Dealing with foreign direct investment is not simply a matter of a 'will' to gain the greatest possible benefits for Canada, as the naive proposals of the commissioners suggest. There are inherent within this form of investment distorting effects that will persist as long as these investments persist. To encourage their expansion will only exacerbate the distortions.

Even in those areas where Canada already has significant world-scale multinationals, such as in banking, there is little evidence that Canadians benefit or that the state has chosen to set policies to ensure this will occur. As of 1975, the five largest Canadian banks derived 25 per cent of their revenue from outside Canada, where they had 30 per cent of their assets. International expansion has proceeded much more rapidly than domestic expansion. Between 1966 and 1976 domestic assets of Canadian banks expanded by 394 per cent, but foreign ones by 667 per cent (238, 232). Thus, the international operations of Canadian banks have become central to their overall position. This is something the commissioners celebrate:

> One great advantage of the size and strength of the Canadian banking sector is seen in its ability to compete in international financial markets. The largest Canadian banks have also gained considerable expertise in the type of consortium financing necessary to develop the largest of our energy and resource projects during the rest of this century. [251]

The commissioners do not provide statistics on the disadvantages of present banking practices, such as the amount of capital loaned to foreign-controlled companies in Canada. The deficiencies of the report's chapter on banks are due in part to the commissioners' determination to justify concentration and multinational corporations but must also be partially attributed to the sources used to reach their conclusions. Briefs were received from four of the top five banks, plus the Canadian Bankers' Association, and they admit, "We have not contracted outside research studies on matters relating specifically to the banks" (219).

What has the Canadian government done to ensure that benefits of internationalization by banks accrue to Canadians? By the commission's own admission, virtually nothing: "International activities by Canadian banks are not closely monitored by Canadian authorities and are not specifically regulated under the Bank Act. Canadian banks do not have to hold cash or liquidity reserves against foreign-currency deposits" (232). It certainly appears that the multinationalization of Canadian banks has allowed them to escape the watchful eye of the Canadian state and has made them more independent than had they remained principally national corporations. This is what the Bryce Commission advocated for all sectors of the Canadian economy. Who would benefit? Certainly not those Canadians who work for these corporations or consume their products. The ones who would gain are dominant Canadian capitalists and their international allies.

The top banks in Canada serve as important coordinating institutions for the dominant fraction of the capitalist class, both indigenous and foreign. Their boardrooms are forums for the exchange of information among Canada's top capitalists, and their capital is important in financing national and international expansion by this class. They are ideal core institutions for the dominant class because of their concentrated control and stability. As the commissioners admit, "Banks have a built-in stabilizer, which produces profits in good times or bad while industrial corporations do not. . . . In a buoyant economy the banks make money on volume. In a declining or stagnant economy they make money on spread" (229). This is reflected in their levels of profitability. The top seven Canadian banks had an average after-tax return of 13.6 per cent for the period 1968-75. This can be compared to a return of 10.3 per cent for a sample of thirty large non-financial institutions in Canada and 12.6 per cent for the five largest U.S. banks during the same period (227).

Although the banks seek to camouflage the fact, their most important activities concern other top corporations. In 1977 their business-loan volume was $28.2 billion. Of this, loans over $1 million (6,400 of them) accounted for $16.6 billion of the total volume. While this represented only 2 per cent of the number of loans, it was 58 per cent of the volume (237). It is clear that the kind of corporations taking out loans averaging over $2.6 million each are not the smallest ones.

An illustration of the role of banks is provided by the Power bid to take over Argus. The sum of $148.5 million was committed to Power by the Royal Bank and the Canadian Imperial Bank of Commerce to finance the expenditure. As it turned out, Power used 'only' $70 million in its attempt and acquired this capital by selling income debentures to three banks (174). There are not many companies that would be able to command such an enormous line of credit. Just what is Power Corporation, and its quarry, Argus Corporation, that would give it access to this amount of money and make it the object of such attention?

Through a 75 per cent voting control of Gelco Enterprises Limited, and thus 53 per cent voting control of Power Corporation, Paul Desmarais has majority control over Laurentide Financial Corporation, Canada Steamship Lines, the Investors Group, Dominion Glass, Montreal Trust and the Great-West Life Assurance Company, and effective control (38 per cent) of Consolidated-Bathurst. Each is among the largest in its field. "The relationship between the companies in which it has interests (with the exception of Argus)," according to the commissioners, "is one of active and interested supervision over broad policy matters and of important activities such as the selection of a chief executive officer and board nominees" (171). Power is thus a complex of the many of Canada's largest corporations controlled by Paul Desmarais.

Argus Corporation operates somewhat differently. As of the end of 1977 John A. McDougald and his associates, through Ravelston Corporation, owned or controlled about 62 per cent of Argus. While in each case they have less than majority ownership in the giant companies of their empire, each is commanded through the executive committees. Table 5.1 illustrates Argus's control. The commissioners report that "Argus is careful to say that it does not 'control' these companies. It readily acknowledges, however, that it influences their affairs. The influence is such that no major transaction is undertaken by any of the companies without the approval of the Argus representatives on the boards." This is simply a matter of semantics; the commissioners point out that "as a practical matter, there is no important difference in the influence exercised by Power over its affiliates and that exercised by Argus over its associated companies" (173).

Table 5.1

Ownership and Control by the Argus Empire

	Total Board	Executive Committee	Ownership Percentage
Dominion Stores			
All directors	12	8	
Argus directors	6	6	24
Domtar			
All directors	14	8	
Argus directors	5	5	17
Hollinger Mines			
All directors	10	5	
Argus directors	5	4	21
Massey-Ferguson			
All directors	10	5	
Argus directors	5	4	16
Standard Broadcasting[a]			
All directors	11	n.a.	
Argus directors	6	n.a.	48

[a]Standard Broadcasting does not have an executive committee.
Source: Argus Corporation brief to the Royal Commission on Corporate Concentration, 15 December 1975, p. 10.

By now it is well known that Power did not gain control over Argus Corporation. While it holds 53 per cent of Argus's equity stock, this represents only 25 per cent of the votes. Control at Argus has, however, changed hands. Conrad Moffat Black and his brother, G. Montegu Black III, recently wrestled control from Maxwell Meighen, who had taken over after the death of John A. McDougald in March 1978. The coup occurred from the inside and resulted from a series of deaths. George M. Black, Jr., died in June 1976, leaving the Black brothers a 22.4 per cent interest in Ravelston Corporation. They added to this the estates of McDougald and Eric Phillips, thus gaining a 69 per cent interest in Ravelston (which in turn holds 62 per cent of Argus). Acting quickly, George Montegu Black III is now president of Ravelston, and Conrad Moffat Black, president of Argus (*Globe and Mail*, 7 July 1978:B1).

As far as the Bryce Commission is concerned, the important issue is its evaluation of a concentration of economic power the size of a merged Power-Argus. As might be anticipated, "Power has suggested that the take-over would be beneficial, since a combined Power-Argus would 'create a

Canadian company of size capable of operating more effectively on a world-scale.' [John A.] McDougald commented, regarding this statement, that 'Most of (our companies) are . . . fairly good on the world scale as it is and we don't need anyone to help us.'" While the commissioners doubt the extent to which this would have occurred, they continue to argue that "Canada certainly needs firms that can mobilize the capital and other resources required to do business in competition with foreign corporations" and if such a combination can produce this result, all the better (177).

Important in the consideration of a merger was the impact in the field of the mass media, as will be examined later. In commenting on media concentration, the commissioners said, "We see no advantage to the public interest in the common ownership of the Power-Argus communications interests, and there is a potential detriment to the public interest if enough important instruments of communication, in different media fields, are owned or controlled by one person or group" (179). They do not say what "enough" means. Indeed, they conclude: "In our view, the overall consequences of such a merger [Argus-Power] are relatively neutral . . . it would not thereby have significantly increased its market power in any industry" (177-80). If such a merger would not have increased their "market power," particularly in the media, then these standards mean that virtually any concentration of private economic power would be acceptable to the commissioners.

Concentration and Control
To assess the Bryce Commission's conclusions about corporate concentration, it is necessary to evaluate its findings. Besides failing to take into account joint ventures between dominant corporations, like those occurring in the forest products industry[4] or others like Syncrude in petroleum, the commissioners make several fundamental errors that distort the rates of concentration reported. This is of particular importance because of the significance they attach to their 'finding' that concentration has remained stable from 1965 to 1972. Since the following problems, like the growth of joint ventures, have compounded since 1965, it is fairly safe to conclude that the actual rate of concentration has grown.

First, the commission reports that "we have adopted as a convention the definition that a corporation is effectively controlled by another when the latter owns 50% or more of the voting shares of the former"(13). This decision eliminates companies like Argus Corporation, an object of its investigation, from representing corporate concentration. By this decision, Massey-Ferguson, Domtar and Dominion Stores are counted separately, and other

---

[4]Export Sales Company Limited markets newsprint exports to Southeast Asia for MacMillan-Bloedel, British Columbia Forest Products, and Crown Zellerbach and is jointly owned by them; MacMillan-Bloedel also markets much of British Columbia Forest Products' output under an agreement originally struck between H.R. MacMillan and E.P. Taylor.

components of Argus Corporation are not counted at all. Similarly, Consolidated-Bathurst is not included with Power Corporation. By any standards, those in control of Argus have power over the companies in its empire, and this represents concentration of corporate power. The commissioners' decision could lead to the absurd position of one company controlling all the 'Top 100' corporations in the country by less than majority ownership, and still giving the impression of low concentration because each corporation would be tabulated separately.

Second, the commission fails to take into account 'independent' branches of foreign corporations that are legally separate in Canada but owned by the same foreign parent. This is the case with companies like the Ford Motor Company of Canada and Ensite Limited, both subsidiaries of the Ford Motor Company of the United States but counted independently in concentration figures. The same holds for General Motors of Canada and G.M. Acceptance, two other top companies on the commission's list. Besides this, there are several other U.S. companies with multiple operations in Canada that are not consolidated in this country but would likely be of sufficient size to make the top list, such as the thirteen Canadian subsidiaries of W.R. Grace and twenty-six of Beatrice Foods (Clement, 1977b: 156-57, 162).

Third, the Bryce Commission separated financial and non-financial corporations into separate lists, so Power Corporation was measured separately from the Great-West Life Assurance Company, Montreal Trust, and the Investors Group, each of which is majority controlled by Power but counted individually, thus reducing aggregate concentration rates. In spite of its high-powered researchers and access to information not available to private researchers, the commission continues to accept the corporate mirage.

There are several related problems. The various companies in the Irving family complex have not been included along with Irving Oil Limited. Incredible as it may seem, the commission did not acquire the necessary information, saying, "Through their counsel the Irvings said that they would not provide us with the basic financial information needed for a study which would be made public" (333). Similarly, it was necessary for the commission to 'estimate' the sales, assets and net income of the T. Eaton Company. In both cases, there appears to be no justifiable reason for the failure to obtain information of this sort, given their powers of investigation. Finally, the commissioners showed no sensitivity to the differences between state and private property and included crown corporations alongside private companies. Their listing includes Canadian National Railways, Air Canada, Ontario Hydro, Hydro-Québec, Canada Development Corporation and British Columbia Hydro among the Top 100 without making a comparison of state and private ownership.

All of these problems with determining concentration make the commission's conclusions suspect and cause great concern, particularly given the theoretical importance placed on its results. These problems call for a serious re-evaluation of the claims the commissioners make and the policy recommendations they propose.

Another area central to the understanding of corporate concentration and power is the interlocking that occurs between the directors and executive members of corporations. This is of importance because it demonstrates that behind a veil of independent large companies runs a network of highly integrated decision-makers who serve to draw these companies together. In an earlier work, I demonstrated that there were 1,848 interlocked positions among the top 113 corporations in Canada (Clement, 1975:159-69). This represents a tremendous web that binds those in command of the largest corporations into a social group of interacting people. What did the commissioners have to say about this practice? They did not even find it significant enough to investigate:

> We have not endeavoured to count these interlocks or to interrelate them. We found no real evidence that individual interlocks are significant in themselves. Many large companies are looking for the same type of person as a director, and these individuals are apparently willing to serve on a number of boards.
>
> The significance of the phenomenon lies in the relatively limited group from which companies select directors, and the similarity of background and outlook that this frequently implies. [301]

They admit they did not do an analysis of interlocking, yet they conclude that there is "no real evidence" that it is "significant." The commissioners have chosen to ignore, because of their own intuitive feelings and the dismissal of the practice by dominant capitalists, an entire body of literature in Canada and the United States which demonstrates that large corporations are densely interlocked and that this practice serves to consolidate corporate power (for a review of the findings and literature, see Clement, 1977b:163-84, 328-29).

Equally amazing is the failure of the commission to make a study of individual stock ownership. The *least* that could be expected from the commission would be a systematic review of the various control structures, including institutional and individual shareholdings, for each of the top financial and non-financial corporations. This would have been a simple matter, given their mandate. They could have required each corporation to provide a listing of the top fifty individual and institutional shareholders and information on other control structures. From this a proper analysis of ownership and control could be made, but obviously the commissioners were not interested in addressing the real issue of corporate control. It would also have been possible, given the resources of the commission, to make a study from information on insider trading listed in the Bureau of Corporate Affairs *Bulletin*, the Ontario Securities Commission *Bulletin*, and the *Bulletin hebdomadaire* of the Commission des Valeurs Mobilières du Québec. As it is, they chose only to examine corporations controlling other corporations and to ignore individual and family control.

As a result of this serious failing, their discussion of types of corporate control is very weak. They list three types: "Absolute Control" (which accounts for twenty-two of the Top 100 industrials), where they discuss the wholly owned subsidiaries of foreign parents but not of families like the Eatons; "Majority Control," over 50 per cent ownership but less than total (which accounts for twenty-six of the Top 100), including companies like Power Corporation's subsidiaries; and "Minority Control" (no number indicated), with less than 50 per cent ownership but with a single identifiable control group, like Argus Corporation. This rather weak discussion misses the essence of corporate control through stock ownership. They do mention that there are other ways corporations may be controlled, such as "use of intricate capital structures, voting trust agreements, pooling agreements, shareholder agreements, loan agreements, supply contracts, complex debt instruments and other devices," but pay no systematic attention to them. A great opportunity to really understand the intricacies of corporate control, which is not likely to arise again in the foreseeable future, has been missed.

Not only is there no analysis of stock ownership in top corporations, there is no analysis of the distribution of stock ownership in the society. Available evidence indicates that only one-tenth of all income earners have as much as one share, and these people are concentrated among the highest-income earners. In spite of their paucity of evidence, the commissioners conclude: "Most shareholders apparently do not seem to want to participate more fully in 'corporate democracy'" (304). The latter term goes unexplained, and there is no evidence provided to support the statement.

As with so many important areas, the commissioners did very little research on the internal structure and control of corporations. They do admit that elections in corporations are predetermined affairs with little role for small shareholders (and it might be added, no role for employees or consumers). They say, "The outcome of the election [of directors] is invariably predetermined, because the process of nomination is in the hands of the incumbent management and board, as is the proxy machinery" (284). Generally, the Bryce Commission report leaves an impression of fairly rigid lines drawn between three important roles in the corporate world: stockholders, directors and senior officers. In fact, the commission does not examine the overlap among these roles, while the available evidence suggests that they are often held by the same people, with the senior officers of one company being large shareholders, often with a long-standing family interest in the company, as well as being outside directors on several other important boards. There is little evidence in the report to provide convincing statements about the activities of the people occupying any of these roles.

In its attempt to explain the way directors and senior officers are selected, the report becomes caught up in its own contortions: "In practice, the *directors* of most large Canadian companies are selected by senior management in consultation with the *board* (or by the controlling shareholder, where there is one), and the shareholders at the annual meeting almost invariably ratify that selection by electing those persons as directors" (emphasis added, 292). The "directors" and "board" are exactly the same, as in the board of directors. Inadvertently the commissioners are admitting that the directors select themselves, which, in fact, is what happens unless some other group manages to acquire controlling interest.

Although the commissioners chose not to do a study of the social characteristics of the directors or officers of the largest companies, they do suggest that these things are changing, all without evidence, of course: "Since the board of a corporation is very visible, some corporations, partly in their own self-interest and partly to broaden the sources of advice at the board level, are now taking steps to obtain more diversity of interests and backgrounds among the people serving on their boards" (293). The same supposition was made after John Porter did his study of the economic elite in Canada for 1951. When I did my study for 1972, the evidence was unmistakable: not only were the same exclusion practices with respect to ethnicity and sex operating, but there was a significant increase in recruitment of those with upper-class origins into the elite. The commissioners did not attempt to refute this finding, only to ignore it, despite the fact that a report by Donald P. Warwick and John G. Craig, done at the commission's request, said that the evidence on these facts was "solid" (1975:10-11).

When appearing before the Bryce Commission, the late John A. McDougald, then chairman of Argus Corporation, gave the commissioners a straightforward answer to how people get selected to Argus boards:

> The executive committee usually sifts out the names and we go over the people in various parts of the country . . . and try to pick out people who have the *calibre and character and we put more on character than we do on brilliance*, and who have standing in the community and who can make a contribution to the company.
>
> We finally come up with two or three names and then the executive committee submits these names to the board as to why we picked so-and-so from such-and-such a place, and the reasons, and if the board agrees, they are nominated. [Emphasis added, RCCC transcript, 15 December 1975, p. 1371]

In light of such objective criteria as "calibre and character" for board selection, what did the commissioners recommend be done to alter the existing exclusion practices? They "suggest" that companies "diversify" their boards "in terms of occupational backgrounds and viewpoints." They do not mention sex, ethnicity or age, and cannot bring themselves to refer to class origins. And as they are quick to point out, lest concern spread in the boardrooms, these "are not recommendations for legislation. We think the results will be better if these views are adopted voluntarily" (297).

In defence of their position against recommending public directors, it is argued that "it is *never* easy to identify the appropriate constituencies, and the appropriate institutional forms are never clearly definable. . . . There will, in addition, be as many potential constituencies striving for the right to participate in the election of a director as there are interpretations of what is truly in the 'public interest.'" They then proceed to scapegoat trade unions and reject the notion of elections and democracy within corporations, saying, "We conclude, however, that the only practical and equitable method of selecting directors is one whereby the shareholders (a group that most commentators agree should participate in corporate government) elect or ratify management's choice of directors" (299). It would be difficult to imagine a weaker defence. Trade union members elect their leaders — one person, one vote — and regular votes on important matters like collective agreements are held. In corporations, each stockholder votes their shares, be they one or a million, with the largest shareholders having the controlling vote. Of course, under capitalist assumptions it is impossible to imagine anything other than to allow private property its rights. Outside these assumptions it is not at all difficult to envision a system of government whereby those working in a corporation and those consuming the products or services have an equal voice in determining the corporation's direction. That would necessitate, of course, turning productive property into common property.

Corporations and the State

Corporations do not operate in a social or political vacuum. By necessity they create a paid labour force and consumers. Parts of these groups are organized, or become organized from time to time, but for the most part they confront corporations as individuals. In order to survive and continue to legitimize themselves, capitalists must respond to demands emanating from these groups. Often sets of capitalists do not find it in their interest to respond positively to those demands, thus causing groups to become politicized; often capitalists are not capable, alone, of responding to such society-wide problems as unemployment or inflation. This is where the state becomes crucial in a liberal democracy. It is responsible for the *common* affairs of the capitalist class. These include providing workers' compensation, unemployment insurance, pensions, health care, availability of education, and so forth. None of these costs could be borne by individual capitalists, yet they are demands which must be met. It may even appear they are met against the will of particular capitalists through the pressure exerted by labour or consumers' groups, and indeed, they are important gains fought for by these groups. Fundamentally, however, they are concessions that sustain the prevailing system and do not interfere with the rights of private property; moreover, experience illustrates that the very groups making the demands are ultimately required to pay for them, while the state assumes control over their administration — thus alienating the groups making the original demands from control over these services. Put differently, the state 'socializes' the costs of maintaining capitalism and becomes increasingly involved in providing these services.

In addition, the conditions necessary for the continuous private accumulation of capital are provided by the state. Not all the socialized costs are in response to labour and consumer groups. Many are demands of capitalists to provide the required infrastructure of capitalism, such as the necessary transportation systems (CNR, St. Lawrence Seaway, ports, etc.) or energy for industry (provincial electrical systems). Also central to the accumulation function of the state is the provision of a labour force capable of meeting the demands of capital, thus the active role of the state in education and immigration. This is not to say that the motives of state leaders are suspect. It is rather that the assumptions and constraints of capitalism condition their actions. Notions such as "the common good" or "the national interest" or, to use the commission's favoured phrase, "the public interest," are equated in the minds of capitalists, state leaders and, by diffusion, the public, with profitable corporations.

This perspective on the nature of the Canadian state differs radically from that of the Bryce Commission. Its perspective on the state is basically a pluralist justification of corporate power, contained by the constraints of other power centres: "Our society is one of offsetting power — business, government, labor and other." Also included is a smattering of interest group theory: "The 'publics' of a corporation include shareholders, creditors, employees, customers, suppliers, governments and local, national and even international communities" (8; see also 318). Their method is to set up straw men and shoot them down, making their views appear as moderate and reasoned:

> While corporate influence is described extensively in the literature, beliefs about its nature differ widely. At one extreme, the view is held that because of the nature of class power and the power of the purse, big business molds public opinion largely as it desires and controls government actions by some form of conspiracy with ruling members of the federal and provincial governments. At the other extreme, the view is expressed that lobbying does not exist in Canada, that the mass media are dominated by radical writers and broadcasters, that governments are so dependent for votes on popular measures that their economic and social policies are invariably antibusiness, and that this produces an economic environment in which private enterprise and investment cannot continue to provide growth and prosperity.
>
> Clearly, both extremes misrepresent the reality. This Commission has relied on information gathered from a wide variety of sources in reaching an opinion on the subject. [337]

In fact, the commission did very little research on this issue. They admit that "representatives of major corporations can and do have greater access to both politicians and public servants than do other individuals," but they then imply an equality of access by saying that this is also the case for "farm and labor groups and by many others with special interests" (338). They go on to say that "it is not surprising that there should be close contact between many businesses and governments," since they have a "common concern with a wide variety of economic and social problems and legislative and regulatory measures. . . . It is in the public interest that there should be consultation in these matters" (339). Their discussion turns briefly to the complexity and secrecy of decision making, concluding that "evidence is usually lacking on who really influenced a decision" (339). This slight of hand into the 'black box' of government ignores the structured inequality among those making demands on the state and the ideological predisposition of those holding state power.

One of the studies published by the commission that dealt with state-corporate relations was Khayyam Z. Paltiel's *Party, Candidate and Election Finance*. This background report does not provide, as might be expected, original research on the size, control (foreign or Canadian) or sector (industrial, financial, etc.) of corporate donations. In fact, there is scarcely any analysis at all; rather it provides a review of existing Canadian legislation and little evaluation of prevailing practices or their implications for relations between corporations and the state. There is also a brief summary of practices in seven other countries. The most significant part of the study, and the one ignored by the commissioners in their report, is the commentary based mainly on Paltiel's earlier book, *Political Party Financing in Canada*. Paltiel argues that the two dominant parties in Canada depend on the contributions they receive from large corporations:

> The main sources of funds needed to finance the activities of the dominant Liberal and Conservative parties are the centralized corporate industrial and financial firms headquartered in Toronto and Montreal. These business givers may be counted in the hundreds rather than in the thousands, and are identified with the largest firms in the financial and industrial sectors of the country. [1977:6]

In examining the motivations for political party financing by dominant corporations, Paltiel says:

> The financial history of Canadian parties, however, is singularly devoid of acts of altruism. All the evidence is to the contrary. Material gain, policy decisions, the choice of leaders and the general course of government activity have all been counters in the effort to provide funds for the parties. At the lowest level the price has been concessions, dispensations and specific acts of patronage; at a higher level the aim has been to 'stabilize the field for corporate activity.' In both cases contributions have assured access to the decision-making authorities in party and government. [1977:107]

It would be wrong to place too much emphasis on the importance of corporate political contributions or on scandals resulting from the revealing of dishonest practices, that is, on Paltiel's "lowest level." This is the level the commissioners seek to rectify, saying, "We think suspicions can be diminished and potential conflicts of interests revealed by requiring disclosure of contributions from organizations as well as individuals" (343). This will have no impact on the "higher level" Paltiel refers to, of a general affinity between the dominant parties and giant corporations. This level of funding acts as a kind of insurance policy to weaken third parties and maintain the legitimacy of the party system. It is not sufficient to view political party financing in isolation from other relations between corporations and the state, since it is but one strand in an intricate web of relations that serves to reinforce their mutual interests.

During the Bryce Commission hearings, the issue of the relationship between big business and the state was raised by Robert Bryce with the chairman of Power Corporation:

> CHAIRMAN (Robert Bryce): But you don't see any indications that the government is more conscious of its dependence on big business for employment, or exports or for other matters leading to a greater regard being given to their views?
>
> MR. PAUL DESMARAIS: I don't think so. I don't think that the concentration first of all of Power and Argus would be that great, that it would have that much of an effect, and I don't see something of size in this country that could affect the government that way. I think that the government and the people that are in Ottawa are there to look after the public interest, and I don't think that they would think about it. If they wanted to change the laws, they could do it. We always have to abide by the laws. [RCCC transcript, 10 December 1975, p. 150]

There is an element of truth to Desmarais's argument. Clearly, no single corporation, even a combined Argus and Power, could overwhelm the power of the state. But this misses the point. It is not one corporation, but a class of people in command of all corporations, that is at issue. Certainly it is the state that sanctions and legitimizes the rights of private property and provides the conditions necessary for its reproduction, but the state itself is a capitalist state predicated on maintaining these property relations and is thus limited by this basic commitment. The state is in a position to make laws to which capitalists must adhere (or shift their operations to another jurisdiction). The laws that have been made, however, are ones that facilitate private accumulation of capital, not threaten it.

The state in Canada clearly does do a great deal of regulation of the economy, and the commissioners provide an important discussion of this activity, albeit in an uncritical way. They distinguish between *qualitative regulations* (these "extend across all industries and, indeed, all of society. Health, sanitation and product-safety regulations, hours-of-work laws and zoning bylaws are a few examples") and *direct regulation* (a "framework of laws, agencies, including Crown corporations, that bear directly on pricing and resource allocation") (395). Unfortunately, the commissioners did not do research to evaluate the effectiveness of qualitative regulations. Nor did they do any investigation of direct regulation, although they do make an interesting distinction between regulatory boards, which "concern themselves primarily with prices, profits and the adequacy of service," and self-regulation, that is, areas such as "professions and much of agriculture [which] operate under legislative umbrellas that give these groups broad powers to control quality, supply and prices" (395-96). Regulatory practices by the state are of particular importance for corporate concentration and control, since, as the commissioners themselves admit, "direct regulation, indeed, is a sanctioned restrictive practice" (396). This means the state gives direct legitimation to monopolies, such as Bell Canada, that have guaranteed their rate of profit, or restricts competition, as in the broadcast media and the CRTC regulations. State regulation most often means the state's guarantee of profitability and high concentration.

Another area of state regulation is examined in some detail in R. Schwindt's background study of MacMillan Bloedel done for the commission. Timber is one of Canada's most valuable resources, especially in British Columbia where it covers 60 per cent of the area. Legal ownership of 94 per cent of this is held by the provincial government; rather than harvest the forest itself, the state has chosen to give up possession of the land for specified periods of time to private corporations. Thus, state policy in distributing access to its land determines in large part the structure of the forest industry. This is known as the 'tenure system,' which is a complex way of distributing rights of access. MacMillan Bloedel's dominant position in the industry, and in the province, is sustained because of its control over a quarter of the province's timber output. In addition, the many small operators in logging are dominated in the marketplace by the large integrated firms to whom they must sell. Their continued survival in the face of domination is permitted, Schwindt suggests, since "these smaller firms enjoy more flexibility in their relations with the work force . . . they can avoid training costs by hiring away from the larger firms, and . . . they are able to circumvent costly Forest Service regulations on logging practices" (48). The privileged position MacMillan Bloedel has been granted is illustrated in the following figures for 1972: "MacMillan Bloedel's share of stumpage and royalty payments to the British Columbia Forest Service amounted to only 5.9 per cent of total forest industry stumpage payments. Yet the company produced about 13.7 per cent of provincial log harvest" (Schwindt, 1977:178).

The explanation for MacMillan Bloedel's privileged position cannot be reduced to personal ties between the state and the company. These ties do exist and are important; for example, "three of six men who have served as Chairman of the Board of MacMillan Bloedel formerly held influential positions in the British Columbia government or judiciary" (Schwindt, 1977:217). They include H.R. MacMillan, who was chief forester of British

Columbia from 1912 to 1915 and "one of the architects of the British Columbia Royalty Act"; J.V. Clyne, who was justice of the Supreme Court of British Columbia from 1950 to 1957; and Robert W. Bonner, who was attorney-general of British Columbia from 1952 to 1968. Other directors include Clarence Wallace, who was lieutenant governor of British Columbia from 1950 to 1955, and F.H. Brown, who was deputy minister of the federal Department of Taxation and National Revenue. These ties should rather be seen as an outcome of the dominant position MacMillan Bloedel occupies within the province, generating about forty-eight thousand jobs that account for about 5 per cent of the labour force and over 10 per cent of the province's exports (Schwindt, 1977:178, 283). Although state policies allowed MacMillan Bloedel to reach its present size, it is now so large that the province depends upon the revenues it produces and the employment it provides. A capital strike by a firm this size could undermine the ability of a government to function and may lead to its being removed from office.

The Mass Media

CHAIRMAN (Robert Bryce): Do you see any growing danger in this concentration of [media] ownership?

MR. JOHN A. McDOUGALD: No. I think, Mr. Bryce, it boils down to individuals. When you talk about power it is a matter of who has the power, I think in the final analysis what it is and how they use it [RCCC transcript, 15 December 1975, pp. 1429-30].

Mr. McDougald reassured the commission that there is no danger in concentrated media ownership. After all, individuals have power and we should trust their "calibre and character." The media was an important aspect of the commission's mandate because a merger of Power and Argus would have meant further concentration within this industry. Under the control of Power Corporation and Paul Desmarais are five daily newspapers in Quebec, including *La Presse*, which represent over half the French-language daily circulation; in addition, Power has control over twelve radio and six television stations in the province. Argus Corporation, through Standard Broadcasting, controls the largest radio station in Canada (CFRB Toronto) and Quebec's largest English-language station (CJAD Montreal); in addition, Standard controls Bushnell Communications, including Ottawa's largest television station (CJOH-TV).

The commissioners argued that the CRTC would mediate the "public interest" in the media if Power and Argus merged. This is the same regulatory agency that earlier allowed the takeover of Bushnell by Standard and did not act during the takeover of Telemedia Quebec by Power Corporation. Even though the CRTC has a stated policy to prevent "undue concentration," their behaviour is to the contrary. In practice, the CRTC has supported the dominant position of media giants and reinforced their power. The one recommendation that the commission makes is to expand the jurisdiction of the CRTC into print media, but there is no reason to believe this would challenge the existing high levels of concentration the CRTC has come to accept, nor to believe this would have any impact whatsoever on the important issue of the overlap between economic and media corporations.

Two aspects of concentration are particularly important in the media: the development of newspaper chains and broadcasting complexes, and the ownership of media by dominant economic corporations. Both of these practices give excessive control to the owners of the media, thus reducing the variety of opinions the audiences receive and weakening the position of those working in the media. The Power Corporation submission to the commission provides an excellent example:

> It is doubtful, for instance, if an independent newspaper owner could have survived the protracted struggle which took place at La Presse in 1971 and which put the future of the paper in jeopardy. . . . The objective of Gesca [controlled through income debentures by Power Corporation and Paul Desmarais] as a newspaper owner has been to create a strong French-language press having the same degree of financial strength as the English-language chains in the rest of the country, thereby permitting the individual newspapers to better serve the public interest. [Power Corporation, 1975:14]

In this case the "public interest" is defined by Paul Desmarais, and because of the concentrated media that he controls and the financial base that Power Corporation provides, he is able to withstand internal resistance within his media from journalists and broadcasters, as in the case of the 1971 La Presse strike and the recent strikes in Quebec newspapers. The policy of La Presse has now been clearly defined for its employees. Power's submission includes an appendix, titled "La Presse Definition and Policy," signed by both Roger Lemelin (publisher and president) and Paul Desmarais, which reads, in part:

> The Constitution
> LA PRESSE believes in a strong Quebec within a Canadian confederation resilient enough to satisfy the legitimate aspirations of Canadians of French language and culture.

> Economic Affairs
> Basically, LA PRESSE believes that the future of a prosperous Quebec depends primarily on work, personal discipline, competence and a spirit of individual enterprise. LA PRESSE believes in free enterprise as practised and evolving in the world but approves a degree of state intervention and planning. LA PRESSE will maintain vigilant surveillance of any tendency that might induce those in government to exceed the limits of valid intervention. [Power Corporation, 1975:48]

Thus it is clear that reporters whose opinions may be at variance with federalism or free enterprise or who advocate state intervention that is not "valid" (whatever that means) run the risk of losing their jobs. It appears this policy means that anyone supporting the duly elected Parti Québécois government contravenes the *La Presse* policy.

As one of its background studies, the commission published Yvan Allaire, Roger-Emile Miller and Paul Dell'Aniello's study of *La Presse*, which they say "suggests little cause for concern, except that potential editorial bias is created by any kind of concentrated ownership" (350). This seems a fairly major exception. If concentrated ownership does indeed cause editorial bias (and I would maintain it does), this is indeed cause for more than a little concern, given the fact that the vast majority of Canada's media are highly concentrated and intimately bound to dominant economic corporations.

The study provides information on *La Presse* journalists in the pre- and post-takeover eras (1968) in terms of age, education and previous experience, but this tells us nothing about their ideological orientations. Comment on this is left to a few impressionistic remarks, based on unsystematic interviews, to the effect that many different viewpoints can be found among the journalists. There is no examination, for instance, of those who left *La Presse*, either by resigning or being fired, since its takeover. More importantly, there is no analysis of strikes and labour discontent among the journalists or the issues involved. There is an implication that a balance of power exists between the owner, management and the union, but no evidence that the union is able to countervail the power of the others is presented. Indeed, there is some indication that the journalists' union leaders believe that ideological discrimination does take place (81) but are powerless in having this changed.

Just as the commissioners restricted their researchers through their mandates and predetermined the outcome of these studies through their selection of researchers, so too do newspaper owners and publishers establish the ideological orientations of their media. Clearly there is no one-to-one correspondence between those in command of the newspaper and those working for it. What is clear, however, is that the owners, through rights of property, establish the limits of tolerance the reporters must adhere to or find themselves without a job. In terms of the editorial content of *La Presse*, the limits are clearly established:

> Editorial writers are compelled to adhere to the ideological orientation of *La Presse*. The management of the union informed us, with a touch of bitterness, that for editorial positions the News Department promotes only candidates acceptable to it and by the same token certain journalists are cast aside because of their separatist or socialist leanings or because they could not adhere to the newspaper's ideological orientation. [66]

While reporters are not so formally restricted, they too must work within the paper's limits of tolerance, since their continued employment depends upon it. Certainly a newspaper where the reporters selected their own superiors would project an ideology radically different from the ones owned by Paul Desmarais or he would not have struggled so hard to retain management's rights by locking out his workers when they demanded greater control. Mr. Desmarais's power to enforce his 'freedom of information' is obviously much greater than the collective power of those working for *La Presse*. As with all the fundamental issues of corporate power, the commissioners fail to confront the implications of the power of property and the costs it involves.

The commissioners demonstrate very little concern for the relationship between economic and media corporations. They acknowledge that "each year corporations spend large sums in Canada on advertising: about $800 million in 1976" (346), but they do not consider the possible impacts on private media dependent upon corporate advertising revenue. Nor do they question ownership interconnections between the media and economic corporations. They are willing to accept what now exists and shift off onto others any real evaluation of the importance of concentration in the media. More than any other area, this is one where the commissioners could (and should) have fulfilled their mandate to analyse the social implications of corporate concentration.

Conclusion

The Bryce Commission report brings to our attention some fundamental issues concerning the kind of society we live in and the kind of society we want. The commissioners have decided that they are pleased with things as they are: "We conclude that no radical changes in the laws governing corporate activity are necessary at this time to protect the public interest" (413). To come to this conclusion requires that they ignore the tremendous inequalities in this society; it means that they must present their analysis in such a way as to obscure its class nature and its concentrations of power.

As already suggested, one way was to present the state as an objective arbitrator of many interest groups in society vying for concessions. Somehow the pluralist arena is expected to produce democratic decisions, even though one of the participants — the capitalist class — controls the dominant productive instruments of the society. Another way class relations are obscured is by accepting corporations as real in and of themselves, outside property and class relations. This is illustrated in the slight of hand performed with the concept of markets:

> The allocation of resources through the market mechanism does not imply that firms are privately or publicly owned, *nor does it say anything about the degree of competition* among those enterprises. It implies only that economic units are largely autonomous with regard to the decisions they make and that they deal with one another chiefly through voluntary exchanges of goods and services. [Emphasis added, 69-70]

Markets, according to the commissioners, have nothing to do with competition. Corporations ("economic units") are reified and given the power to make their own decisions, independent of the class that controls them. And those controlling corporations are presented as "largely autonomous" from one another. These assertions simply fly in the face of reality. Corporations are legal fictions, the creatures of property relations endowed with the rights of capital. The important thing to examine is the class of people who actually activate and direct corporations and the implications for those subject to their power. Once this veil is broken, it is obvious that the people making decisions in Canada's largest corporations are an interlocking, interacting set of people who are part of a social class that benefits from the privileges accruing from the rights of capital.

The argument of "largely autonomous" corporate decisions falls apart even in the commissioners' own discussions: "To ensure any kind of industry stability and joint profit maximization, however, firms must make parallel decisions not only on price but on all major aspects of a transaction" (78). And in another context, the ideology of the legal fiction is again exposed as we get a look under the corporate skirts: "The art of accounting [which we might say is the heart of the corporation as a legal fiction], even when it is employed in the traditional sense, subsumes a great many assumptions, estimates and predictions, and one of its faults is that it creates an *illusion* of objectivity and precision" (emphasis added, 388). No one could say it better.

In a way, quite differently than the commissioners intend, it is true that corporations — or to be more precise, class relations — have a life greater than the individuals who occupy them. The mode of production, the basis for organizing corporations, is much greater than any set of individuals. Individuals act out assumptions and conditions imposed by the dominant mode of production; hence corporations and the system that produces them have 'a life of their own.' The critical human quality that provides hope is that people have the capacity to produce things and to change their mode of production. This is an essential human quality that can perceive alternate futures and take actions to achieve them. People are motivated to do so only when what they have, no longer appears as 'right, just and proper.' This is clearly not the goal of the Bryce Commission. Its crucial function is to serve the dominant class by heightening its consciousness and organizing specific strategies and justifications on behalf of the class as a whole. This means they must present the interests of the capitalist class as identical with the public interest. This is exactly what is done in their conclusion:

> The *public interest* on an issue such as conflict of duty will coincide with *private interests*. While *private and proprietary rights are chiefly involved here*, in the broadest sense there is an overriding public concern. It is in the public's interest that the internal activities of *our* major corporations, and our other major institutions, be conducted on an orderly and equitable basis, and as far as possible be seen so conducted. The public's perception of corporations influences its confidence in the working of our economic system and affects its willingness to invest. We think it desirable that the

interests of all concerned with corporations be, and be seen to be, fairly protected. [Emphasis added, 309]

This explains why the commissioners say, "We found the social area the most difficult part of our mandate" (373). Businessmen are not used to thinking in these terms. Their examples of the social implications illustrate the limitations capitalist assumptions impose on their thinking. They argue: "It would probably not be correct to conclude that a corporation manufacturing automobiles is responsible for traffic congestion if that corporation and others like it had not produced automobiles" (383). In this case the relationship between advertising and consumption of automobilies must be seen in terms of the capitalist drive for profits. The fact that so many resources are poured into the production of automobiles, together with the power of advertising, inhibits the development of alternative modes of travel, which would indeed reduce congestion.

The commissioners are careful not to build up too many hopes about the social responsibility of corporations: "The most we should realistically expect corporate social responsibility to mean is that corporations will consider the social as well as the economic consequences of their decisions. If they do this, the decisions they make will result in a balance of economic and social benefits and costs" (385-86). This, of course, does not follow. To "consider" something does not mean it is given equal weight. Ultimately it is the interests of the individual capitalist or of collective capitalists that will prevail, for they must accumulate to survive. What needs to be questioned is the right to make these decisions in the first place. The following two examples provided by the commissioners again illustrate their limits:

> In one case, a company made determined efforts to hire people belonging to minority groups, believing that they had been the victims of previous discriminatory personnel policies. When economic conditions required some reduction in the work force, the seniority principle (particularly since it was embodied in a collective agreement) operated to undo much of what had been achieved. In another case involving a layoff of staff, the trade union criticized the corporation for imposing on its employees the consequences of economic restraint while it continued to support charitable organizations with donations. [386]

In these cases we are expected to sympathize with the dilemma of those making decisions for the company and implicitly blame the labour unions. What is not asked is why the layoffs happen and who should have the right to make such important decisions or how they are to be implemented. Why should the workers be forced to suffer the consequences of decisions they had no part in making? It is clear that those making the decisions will not suffer the consequences as dearly as the workers, yet they are not even accountable for their actions. Their primary interest is the profitability of corporations, not the products the workers produce or the quality of life for people working there.

With corporate concentration there is the creation of a system of extremely powerful economic units controlled by a small class of people who impinge on our lives in a multitude of crucial ways — as employees, as consumers, as citizens, as people with rights to a reasonable use of resources and to access to a healthy environment. This system is too important to leave in the hands of a set of self-selecting men with limited accountability for their actions, and to whom a vast majority have no access. This is simply too much responsibility for too few, no matter how benevolent or well-meaning.

The danger is that by implying there is a fundamental flaw in the system of power one runs the risk of being identified as crazy, uncompromising or even subversive — and one fears the brunt of the forces of repression — either mentally or physically. For most, it is easier to simply accept what we have and make the best of it. Fighting causes pain and anguish. The trouble is, so does what we now have.

Chapter 6
Canadian Class Cleavages: An Assessment and Contribution

The following paper represents a transition out of a power framework into one based on class analysis. It is also a consolidation of the various traditions and studies of class in Canada. A fairly rich tradition exists of studies of specific classes or fractions of classes (such as unionized workers), but less attention has been devoted to class relations. Classes as representative of inequalities follows from the social democratic tradition identified within the paper, while the relationship between classes (and class fractions) follows from the Marxist tradition of class analysis. This paper examines the former tradition but concentrates on the extent to which it is useful for developing the latter. As a survey of existing studies of Canada's class structure, this paper attempts to portray the development of the three major classes — capitalists, workers and petite bourgeoisie. Its major limitation, as with the studies it surveys, is its treatment of relationships between these classes and the dynamics of class struggle. It seeks to indicate various levels and sources of struggle, but it does not take this as its central proposition. Latter papers in this collection do concentrate more on this central tenet of class analysis, but this aspect remains a central weakness. If this paper serves no other purpose than to stimulate discussion, debate and — most significantly — research on class relations, it will have served well. There is an important base upon which to build, but Canadian political economy has far from met the challenge posed by the potential of class analysis.

A rich explanation of Canada's political economy can be derived from an analysis of class cleavages, using the classical divisions of working, petite bourgeoisie and capitalist classes, including various fractions within each class. It will be argued that the relations within and between these classes can account for the central dynamics of Canadian society. To carry out this task it is necessary to assess and evaluate various existing studies of class structure and relations in Canada. The literature in this field is richer than may have been thought, but there remain obvious and significant gaps, debates and disagreements. The aim in exploring this literature is to illustrate the explanatory power of class analysis and indicate some key areas of debate. Indications from research in progress suggest this field promises great vitality in the near future. To contribute to these blossoming developments, this assessment of existing explanations of class will be presented within the context of a substantive analysis of developing class cleavages in Canada.

Writing in 1965, S.R. Mealing noted the weakness of class analysis in Canadian history, arguing that "no important attempt has been made to base an analysis of our history on class, nor is there any weight of research to suggest that such an analysis is possible." He adds, "Our shortcoming has been to ignore rather than to deny the class structure of society" (1965:212, 214-15). Mealing himself ignores (as does Carl Berger in his historiography *The Writing of Canadian History*) the work of C.B. Macpherson, Gustavus Myers, H. Clare Pentland and Stanley Ryerson, but of course, these were not 'mainstream' scholars. Mealing was only partially correct. Besides the authors noted, he ignored the more subtle way traditional Canadian scholars have revealed the class formation. H.A. Innis and Donald Creighton, for example, both provide important evidence of the distortions in Canada's capitalist class.

There are two developed traditions of class analysis in Canada: the social democratic and the Marxist. The social democratic tradition begins with the League for Social Reconstruction (LSR), marked by the publication in 1935 of *Social Planning for Canada* on the inauguration of the Co-operative Commonwealth Federation (CCF) in 1935, and traces its roots through the publication in 1961 of *Social Purpose for Canada* on the eve of the formation of the New Democratic Party (NDP). This tradition's most-renowned expression is John Porter's classic study, *The Vertical Mosaic*, published in 1965, a book which dominated debate in the field for the next ten years. Developed around an analysis of nominally defined classes and plural elites, it was Canada's first *systematic* treatment of inequality. Its framework and orientation is social democratic, following the British tradition of Harold Laski and R.H. Tawney.

The Marxist tradition traces its roots to the neglected works of Macpherson, Myers, Pentland and Ryerson. Its revival is marked by numerous publications in the 1970s, beginning with *Close the 49th Parallel, etc.* The major analytical cleavage was national, but the book also examined some consequences for class formation. *Capitalism and the National Question*, following in 1972, was somewhat more diverse. Its major contributions were in the areas of the historical development of dependency, the development of Canada's class formation, the implications of international unions, and the relationship between class and nation in Quebec. It was also more pointed in terms of its explicitly Marxist perspective. The next year *(Canada) Ltd.* was published and in 1977, *The Canadian State*. The first concentrated on the dual questions of class and nation, while the second focused on the nature of the state in Canada as it contends with class cleavages. Other recent contributions will be examined in some detail shortly but first a brief mention of four important Canadian political economists.

Although all have had some impact, Harold Adams Innis, C.B. Macpherson, H. Clare Pentland and Stanley Ryerson have not received the readership within Canada their works merit. Each is widely read today by those in the political economy tradition and have made great contributions to Canadian scholarship, but there has been surprisingly little research stemming directly from their influence. Innis has been more influential in Canada but this has been somewhat restricted, possibly because of his primarily empirical contribution and lack of theoretical development.[1] Macpherson's influence, on the other hand, may have been muted precisely because he became oriented more to the development of theory than an analysis of Canada after his study *Democracy in Alberta*. Pentland's neglect is more understandable. Of his two major studies, "Labour and the Development of Industrial Capitalism in Canada" (his Ph.D. thesis, 1961) was not published until 1981 (as *Labour and Capital in Canada, 1650-1860*), and "A Study of the Social, Economic and Political Background of Canadian Systems of Industrial Relations" (prepared for the Task Force on Labour Relations, 1968) remains unpublished.[2] Ryerson's neglect, however, appears more politically motivated. His classic studies, *The Founding of Canada* and *Unequal Union*, have seldom found their way onto university curriculae, and Ryerson himself was kept out of academe for many years because of his political affiliation. The relative neglect of these authors has been a detriment to Canadian political economy. It remains the outstanding task of contemporary Canadian scholars to critically extend the work of Innis, Pentland and Ryerson and apply the theories of Macpherson. There must be developed and refined a tradition of Canadian scholarship. First, however, the wealth of existing knowledge should be acknowledged.

After a brief review of the key traditions in the class analysis of Canada, the bulk of this paper will be devoted to a portrayal of Canada's three major classes. First will be the capitalist class, with particular emphasis on the debates over its commercial and industrial origins and its relationship with foreign capital. This will be followed by an analysis of the working class, with a focus on its conflicts with capital and on the fragmented labour movement. Part of the reason for the political weakness of the working class in Canada is the important role the petite bourgeoisie has had in Canadian politics, particularly in the West, Atlantic Canada and in Quebec. The paper addresses

---

[1]See the following paper, "Transformations in Mining: A Critique of H.A. Innis."
[2]For a complete listing of Pentland's writings, see Paul Phillips, 1979b: 45-51.

this issue, concluding with a brief examination of various class fractions in Quebec. In the course of presenting an analysis of these three classes, the key works on class within Canada's political economy perspective will be utilized.

Two Traditions of Class Analysis
The Social Democratic Tradition
Although others had written in the social democratic tradition earlier, the LSR's *Social Planning for Canada* marked the consolidation of this work and a movement into the political domain with the formation of the CCF. The book is divided into two parts, "Survey and Analysis" and "Socialist Planning." The analysis covers areas such as income distribution; corporate concentration (mergers, stock ownerships and director interlocks), using concepts like 'monopoly capitalism'; capitalist culture; and a historical analysis of Canada's external dependence, staple production and staple rigidities, including the first detailed examination of foreign ownership. Also included, as might be expected, is an analysis of farm debt and the decline of agricultural prices (including the rising practice of tenant farming), along with a critique of the rival Social Credit party. While the fragmented labour movement and the state's cozy relationship with capital and control over labour are discussed, there is no analysis of class resistance on the part of the working class. In part this is attributable to the low ebb of working-class struggle during this period, since this class was experiencing the repression of political and economic forces more severely than at any other time; but in the main the reasons lay with the essentially petty bourgeois orientation of the book. Despite its shortcomings, *Social Planning* was a thorough, articulate analysis and program for Canada — likely the most systematic alternative program ever offered. Its theory of class was not developed; it offered mainly a critique of monopoly capitalism and a political party program designed to achieve parliamentary power. There was more reliance on farmers than industrial workers or trade unions as agents of change. In spite of these shortcomings, it makes much subsequent work in Canada look puny by comparison.

At the inaugural meeting of the LSR for the writing of *Social Planning* in April 1933, many outstanding Canadian academics were present; "even the sceptical Harold Innis attended briefly and gave his advice though not his adherence." Innis was later to call the book "a pretentious political document" (1975:xvi-xvii). It is interesting to note John Porter's comment on Innis's politics: "No one played a more important role in the depoliticizing of the higher learning in Canada than Harold Adams Innis." He went on to add on the general condition that "it would probably be difficult to find another modern political system with such a paucity of participation from its scholars" (1965:503). Porter was closely involved in the second landmark of the social democratic tradition, contributing two articles to *Social Purpose for Canada*.

In his editor's preface to *Social Purpose*, Michael Oliver discussed the relationship with the earlier book:

> One comparison kept recurring to us as the book took shape. In 1935, the League for Social Reconstruction brought out *Social Planning for Canada*. Among its authors was Professor F.R. Scott who has been intimately connected with this book, both as a most active member of its editorial committee and as a contributor. The sense of continuity from the thirties to the present [1961] must have been strongest in him, but it was shared by all of us to some degree. We could not have escaped the influence of the democratic socialists who wrote *Social Planning for Canada* if we had wanted to, and in spite of striking differences sometimes between the remedies (and to a lesser extent the diagnoses) proposed in the two books, their common purpose is unmistakable. [1961:vi-vii]

Oliver goes on to discuss another parallel. As mentioned, *Social Planning* was closely related to the CCF. J.S. Woodsworth wrote the original foreword, and the LSR was the intellectual source of the party's ideology. The fact that the NDP was created in the same year as *Social Purpose* was less related. "Rather," as Oliver says, "both are products of a revival in social and political concern. . . . The ideas contained in this book will, we hope, influence not only the New Party but all political parties in Canada" (vii). Oliver did, however, go on to become national president of the NDP.

The dominant conception of class used in *Social Purpose* is a rather loose notion of gradient inequalities, based on income, education and occupation. It is used descriptively, not as an explanatory factor. Class is perceived as a barrier to equality of opportunity (particularly in Porter's two articles) and the rational allocation of human resources, not as a structural problem for society inherent in capitalist social relations. Three articles illustrate this point: Stuart Jamieson's article is concerned primarily with the effects of labour unions on the distribution of costs and benefits, not with providing a class analysis of conflict between capital and organized labour; Meyer Brownstone's article on agriculture, unlike *Social Planning*, does not analyse in a sustained way the conflict between independent commodity producers and capitalism; George Grant provides an analysis of Canada's continentalist ruling class but detaches it from other classes by using the concept of "mass society," which he attributes to forces of organization and technology and reduces to problems of individualism, consumerism and impersonal relations. Each article is useful, some are even brilliant, but all are flawed by the weakness of their class analysis. This weakness becomes most evident in the landmark work of John Porter published four years later.

The fundamental flaw of *The Vertical Mosaic* is the *lack* of connection between the two sections of the book — the one on class and the other on power. To the extent these concepts are related in the book, it is on the broad issue of inequality, but both sections concentrate on inequality of opportunity (distributive) rather than inequality of condition (structural) (see Clement,

1975:5ff). Analysis occurs, for the most part, within the realm of individual characteristics rather than classes.

Writing some years later in a reflection of *The Vertical Mosaic*, Porter wrote that "obviously Marx could not be ignored, particularly since we were still in the period before ideology had ended[!] and when Marxian and neo-Marxian interpretations were in vogue," but he chose to reject so-called "economic determinism." Instead, "I decided that for theoretical orientation, I would be eclectic" (1970:157). In his book, classes are presented as "barriers"; that is, privileges to be overcome in order to grant opportunity, since they were impediments to the free development of skills and talents. He describes his personal values as "equality of opportunity" and the need for "the creative role of politics" as the means to improve "life chances" (1965:xii). The technique he chose was to dispel the "Canadian Middle Class Image." In Part I on "The Structure of Class," he argued that there is no class resistance or struggle, no agents of change in the working class, since we are now in a "post-Marxian industrial world." For him, class is a ranking of occupations, income and education; it is a "spectrum" of socio-economic status led by a wealthy and powerful elite. Indeed, classes are merely "artificially constructed statistical groups" with no real life or meaning of their own. This conception of class is very much a product of the dominant social sciences in the 1960s, as Porter was later to admit.

Porter's classes are not quite as simple as his anti-Marxist polemic suggests. As he argues: "If in reducing classes to artificial constructions we have argued them out of existence, it is necessary to bring them back. Social images about the lack of a class structure to the contrary, there is little doubt that class is something which is experienced in everyday life and hence becomes real" (11). In his explanations of social events, rather than in his descriptions, Porter does use class in a real sense (although most often using occupational categories as proxies for class). For example, he says, "French Canada has a class structure perhaps unique in North America for its similarities with older European class structures," going on to add that "a combination of historical factors destined the French-Canadian habitant to the role of forming an industrial proletariat" (93,95). He then proceeds to apply at length Hubert Guindon's "remarkable essay" on the "emergence of a new middle class" in the church and government of Quebec, as distinct from private industry which is in the hands of "'foreign' entrepreneurs." Elsewhere he treats farmers in class terms and suggests they have a consciousness of themselves as such.[3]

The Vertical Mosaic is the most comprehensive modern compilation of data on inequality in Canada, much of which can be read as informing analysis of class cleavages, but most of which is not analysed in this way.

---

[3]See Porter, 1965:109, 139; also see Porter's analysis of wealth and stock ownership (1965:118) and discussion of changing class structures (154).

The chapter on "Class, Mobility, and Migration," for example, can be read as the making of a working class through detachment from the land and particular immigration policies, but primarily it is an analysis of imported skills and education creating a "mobility trap" for native-born Canadians and an ethnically stratified society. Instead of class, Porter uses the concept of elite as a substitute, saying, "What we have instead of a class of capitalists is a small and probably more cohesive group — an elite within the private sector of the economy."[4] This obviously leaves a major analytical gap for all those outside the elite, particularly the working class and petite bourgeoisie but also smaller capitalists. Unlike the first part of the book, Part II on "The Structure of Power" deals with conscious, interacting sets of people. He says: "Elites are more than statistical classes. Common educational backgrounds, kinship links, present and former partnerships, common membership in clubs, trade associations, positions on advisory bodies and philanthropic groups, all help to produce a social homogeneity of men in positions of power" (230). The 'class' quality of the elite does not, however, resolve the problem of classes as forces of change. This requires an analysis of class dynamics.

Returning to Porter's reflections on *The Vertical Mosaic*, we find part of an explanation for the lack of relationship between the two parts of the book:

> In my original plan, there was to be a chapter which I called "The Emergence of the Canadian Class Structure," which was to provide an essentially historical perspective. Canada was a relatively new nation without a class structure with long historical roots. As my original notes said:
>
> > I would try to locate factors in the economic and social development of Canada which created a particular class system. The fur trade, railway building and early industrial activity are seen as the foundations of wealth. At the same time, an ethnically-heterogeneous labour force accompanied capital investment and eventually became sorted and sifted into a class system. [1970:172-73]

This chapter was never written. Had it been, Porter may have been forced to account for transformations in class structures and identify the forces and agents of change. Earlier, Mealing was quoted to the effect that such studies had not been carried out and that the tendency has been to "ignore rather than to deny" classes. Porter chose not to ignore classes but to deny them.

After *The Vertical Mosaic*, Porter went on to undertake two massive quantitative surveys, one on educational aspirations and another on intergenerational mobility. Each reflects the direction of class analysis already

---

[4]Porter, 1965:23; I argue to the contrary that the corporate elite is a fraction of the capitalist class and is a heuristic device for analysing part of the capitalist class, not a substitute for class analysis. For a more detailed critique of Porter, see Clement, 1980b.

evident in his book. Later, however, there was something of a recanting.[5] In his comments on Harry Braverman's influential *Labor and Monopoly Capital*, which made the opposite points Porter had made earlier about class, he said:

> The book was an articulate reminder of facts we did know but were prepared to overlook, and I use 'we' here in the sense of the whole gamut of followers of conventional social science, of the post-Second World War period. I think we were prepared to overlook this evidence because of our over concern for economic growth as the raison-d'être of industrialization. . . . Certainly social scientists accepted growth and upgrading of the labour force as basic to modernism, and I think the best illustration of that is found in every intergenerational mobility matrix where one compares the marginals of fathers and sons, and takes the difference as representative of progress because overall the sons have done better than their fathers . . . the basic assumption underlying analyses of these father-son occupational data, on which I have been engaged myself, is that the overall effects of industrialization have been beneficial and progressive. Social scientists, of course, bear this burden of oversight, or guilt, depending on how severe one considers the offence to be. [1978:23-24]

This summarizes the poverty of the socio-economic studies of statistical classes. Porter, along with many observers of industrialization, had assumed an increasing demand for and level of skills with 'post-industrialism.' Great promise was placed on the decline of unskilled and rise of semiskilled and skilled workers. They equated the decline of backbreaking labour with greater skill but failed to examine the content of the rising semiskilled category and changes among the skilled. It is now obvious that advanced capitalism brings along with it a great deal of deskilling and decreasing worker autonomy, affecting both clerical and industrial workers.

The social democratic tradition has overlooked the most important developments of advanced capitalist societies; it has failed to understand the processes of class transformation because it has been ahistorical; and its assumptions about the decline of real classes have been proven wrong. The point is not to dwell on its failings; it is more important to shift our attention to a Canadian tradition that has been richer in its explanations, if not its details.

The Marxist Tradition

Several recent key works in the Marxist tradition will be outlined, but their major impact will be most evident in the core of the section outlining class cleavages as they have developed in Canada. As mentioned, the revival of

---

[5]In his introductory comments on "Power and Freedom" in his *The Measure of Canadian Society*, written shortly before his death, Porter said, "I would probably want also to modify my views about how the changing occupational structure which has come with industrialism really provides upward mobility" (1979:209).

this tradition began in 1970 with *Close the 49th Parallel, etc.*, which had a strong focus on the social and cultural aspects of foreign control (Warnock and Dexter) and emphasized the issue of nationalism. Class analysis had a less prominent part, although there were several important pieces on the capitalist class (Drache, Bliss, Gonick and Resnick) and labour (Abella). Also included were articles on science (Wood, Rotstein and Tranor) and the universities (Steele, Mathews, Watkins, Laxer, Lumsden and Martell). Generally, however, each article was a brief overview of a limited field. The book, as a whole, offered only tentative support for the NDP. Caplan and Laxer argued, for example, that "the NDP is the most important institutional expression of the Canadian left" but qualified this support, maintaining the party is "timid" and "retreating further and further from any fundamental criticisms of capitalism" (1970:314-15). Their strategy at the time was to reform the NDP from within.

While *Close the 49th Parallel, etc.* demonstrated the need to reformulate the prevailing perspectives in the social sciences (hence the focus on universities), it was *Capitalism and the National Question* with its detailed focus on alternative formulations that strongly marked the turn toward a class analysis. It set the tone of debate in Canadian political economy for the 1970s. The main issues were the nature of the capitalist class, of the union movement, class formation and the relationship between class and nation in Quebec, all in an international and continental context. This book demonstrated that the strength of Canadian Marxism was its ability to situate Canada's dependency within the world system and the power of this to account for internal developments. Several articles offered critiques of social democratic parties, thus marking a clear break from the social democratic position.

Canada's dependence became the explicit theme of *(Canada) Ltd*. It picked up on the theme of providing a historical perspective to Canada's external dependence, both for the capitalist class and the labour movement. It was the first formulation of the de-industrialization thesis, arguing that Canada's dependent position would lead to the withdrawal of production as world economic conditions contracted. This has subsequently been borne out by various Science Council of Canada studies (see Britton and Gilmour, 1978). Other articles offered an analysis of the state in Canada and a critique of the NDP (the Waffle having been expelled from the Ontario NDP in June 1972). There was also one of the first analyses of women in the class structure (by Christina Maria Hill) and a specific rejection of Porter's approach to class (by John Hutcheson). The book also offered a program for change, based on an independent socialist Canada, by Mel Watkins. Watkins contributed two other pieces to the collection, one on the continentalization and fragmentation of the labour movement in Canada and the other containing an important analysis of the implications of staples production, particularly the new industrial staples.

The most recent addition to this literature is *The Canadian State*, which has as its touchstone an emerging class analysis, focusing on how class struggles become manifest in the state. The strength of the book is its analysis of factions of the capitalist class and the state; its weakness is the less central position afforded the working and petty bourgeois classes (although they are mentioned in most articles).

These four collections are only the most obvious signs of a revival of the Marxist approach to class. Others will be examined shortly. There should not be, however, an underestimation of the work remaining to be done. The state of the art of class analysis in Canadian social sciences is not well developed; it is only at a formative stage. What is needed, besides an assessment of what studies presently exist, is an analytical framework that will push forward by consolidating the present strengths and suggesting new areas of exploration.[6] In a *very* preliminary way, that is the purpose of this paper. Class will be used in the sense of social relations of production, rather than in the descriptive sense of an agglomeration of income, education and prestige, as it has most often been used in traditional social science. The focus here is on class cleavages or the relations within and between classes as they explicate the dynamics of social change rather than simply reflecting vague inequalities.

At a minimum, class analysis must identify the interplay between classes and the dynamics of class action as they are manifest in the development of capitalism. This includes the relationship between the two primary classes of capitalism: capitalists, who own the means of production and employ the labour power of others; and workers, who are compelled to sell their labour power because they lack control over the means of production. It also includes the declining fortunes of the petite bourgeoisie, who own their own means of production but employ mainly their own labour power and that of their families. Each of these classes has important functions, with distinct political and ideological expressions that can only be understood in the context of the development of the broad political economy of a nation. Canadians can learn a great deal from analyses of class elsewhere, but it is imperative that studies ultimately be situated in the context of each country. There are peculiarities to Canada's pattern of development manifest in a unique pattern of relationships which need to be understood. Some of these peculiarities were identified in 1962 by Stanley Ryerson as being essential elements of the formative stages of class in Canada:

(a) Conditions of colonial settlement in what was to become 'English Canada'—with attendant popular struggles against land-monopoly and colonial restrictions. . . .

(b) Beginnings of native *industrial capitalist development* in both English and French Canada. . . .

---

[6] I have identified fifteen distinctive features of Canadian society that are integral to such an analysis in *A Practical Guide to Canadian Political Economy* (1978:iv-vi).

(c) The *national struggle* in French Canada, which posed the issue (after the 1837-38 defeats) of industrial development in Quebec. . . .

(d) Political and economic dependency, with capitalist industry developing as an extension of that of the British metropolis, was reflected in dominant influence of British economic and political thought, later to be joined by influence from the U.S.A. [1962:47]

Besides the work of Ryerson, the writings of Myers, Macpherson, Pentland and Langdon, along with Naylor, provide the raw material for delineating Canada's class cleavages.

Canadian Class Cleavages
The Capitalist Class

The intellectual mentor of two leading scholars of the Canadian capitalist class is Gustavus Myers, author of the 1914 classic *A History of Canadian Wealth*. Both Stanley Ryerson,[7] who wrote the introduction to the book's reissuing (for the first time in Canada) in 1975, and Tom Naylor suggest that Myers inspired their own works. As the title indicates, its main focus was the capitalist class, but as Ryerson points out, "it provided for the first time — despite its limitations — a popular introduction to socioeconomic history in terms of a dynamic of class structure" (1975:xiv). Within the capitalist class Myers concentrated on the "mercantile and shipping merchants" (69) as the dominant faction, underplaying, as Ryerson justifiably laments, "the role of *production*, of productive labour as the well-spring of wealth" (xvi). Myers covers the period from European contact to the end of the nineteenth century. One of its highlights is an early study of the 1837-38 uprisings as an aborted bourgeois revolution for free trade — what he calls "the very quintessence of rising capitalism" (98). He also deals in some detail with the exploitation of native peoples and the process of colonization, although he ignores the relationship between French and English Canada. His major strength is his sustained analysis of what he calls "The Landed and Mercantile Oligarchy," where he concentrates on the capitalist class engaged in staples extraction, trade, finance and railway building.

Myers has been ignored or dismissed by most historians. Innis, for example, dismissed *A History of Canadian Wealth* as having "treated Canadian history as an evolution of the predatory culture" (1956:12). With the revival of the Marxist tradition in Canada, Myers has been salvaged from

---

[7] In *The Founding of Canada: Beginnings to 1815*, Stanley Ryerson writes, "The first major step towards a Marxist interpretation of Canadian development was Gustavus Myers' *History of Canadian Wealth*. It constitutes a landmark; I owe much to it, both in getting my initial bearings on this field over a quarter century ago, and in projecting some of the lines of search pursued in the present study" (1960:332). Besides the similarity of title, Tom Naylor writes in his preface that *The History of Canadian Business* is "intended in some measure as a contribution to the task begun by Gustavus Myers over half a century ago" (1975:xvii).

obscurity. But, as in so many aspects of Canadian analysis, it was Stanley Ryerson who led the way by using Myers's work long before its rebirth in the 1970s. It is Ryerson, for his detailed analysis and clear insights into class struggles, who deserves the mantle of the real intellectual mentor of the revival.

Whereas many of the analysts of Canada's capitalist class have stressed the mercantile and then commercial orientation of that class, Ryerson strongly emphasizes the importance of understanding industrial capitalists. It is not because they have been more powerful than the mercantile/commercial capitalists — indeed, he argues their development was retarded by this more powerful fraction — but because industrial capitalism is the cornerstone of capitalist production; it is the counterpoint of the development of an industrial proletariat. The Canadas before the 1840s, Ryerson argues, were characterized by small-scale manufacturing — mainly in sawmills, shipbuilding, rope-yards and iron forges. Three currents of industrialization were to be found. One resulted from the timber trade and involved "sawmills and shipyards"; the second was small "manufactories and machine shops" (building, for example, ships' engines); the third, and weakest, was "small-scale consumer goods enterprises" producing for local markets (1963:39). Industrialists clearly were not in command:

> All three of these currents of incipient industrialism were subject to the restrictive conditions of a colonial-mercantile environment. Power in the colony was in the hands of a triple alliance of class forces, none of which was particularly interested in the growth of a native industry as such. Imperial advantage and imperial trade were what concerned the British officials and the English-Canadian merchant-landowners; while their collaborators, the French-Canadian higher clergy and seigneurs, were committed to uphold the policies of the other two — the dominant — ruling groups. [40-41]

Ryerson stresses the conflict between the emerging industrialists and the ruling fraction of the dominant class.

Evidence of a class struggle against this domination is provided by the Rebellions of 1837-38, which Ryerson contends, following Myers, were a "national-democratic revolution" by a rising industrial bourgeoisie. Their defeat indicated a lack of maturity, but "these two Canadas were not the end but rather the beginning of the process of establishing a capitalist democracy in British North America" (84).

The changing fate of these nascent industrialists was also due, in part, to changes in British imperial policy resulting from the victory of British manufacturers over merchant-landowners and the repeal of the Corn Laws in 1846. This weakened the position in the Canadas of the mercantile oligopoly. The real boost came, according to Ryerson, with the railway-building boom, which peaked in the early 1850s. Indicative of the level of industrialization is the fact that 18 per cent of the labour force in Upper Canada and 13 per cent in Lower Canada were employed in industrial occupations (including artisans) by 1851 (see Table 6.1, p. 160).

The situation in the Maritimes was similar to the Canadas, with small-scale industry (for example, the 1,144 sawmills in Nova Scotia in 1871 averaged between two and three people each) and a ruling class that "was an amalgam of colonial-military officialdom with a closely-knit group of merchant-bankers possessing strong ties with London commercial houses" (194). In all areas of the colonies the main activity was the supplying of raw materials for export and, in turn, the importing of manufactured goods. To facilitate this activity, railways were built, but, Ryerson contends, an unintended consequence was to speed industrialization. While Ryerson argues the intent was commercial, building the railway at the same time fostered resistance by Canadian industrialists, who had a different vision. Demands for tariffs were made by W.H. Merritt in 1855; Isaac Buchanan organized the Society for the Development of Canadian Industry; and again, in 1858, A.T. Galt supported protective tariffs, all spurred on by the industrialization of the railway (see 239-40, 242-43). It was this double-edged quality that Ryerson stresses:

> Railways in British North America served both as an instrument of colonialism — extracting raw materials and semi-processed products required by the metropolis — and as engines of industrialization, stimulating the growth of local manufacturers and of a home market. . . . The 'chief interests' *were* in staples; but that is not where the mainspring of change, however small its proportions, was located. [258, 268]

Ryerson is obviously attempting to counter the staples interpretation of Canadian history offered by Innis by stressing not only the development of industrial capitalism but, as will be seen, an industrial proletariat.

Even up to Confederation, which is where Ryerson's major works conclude, he continues to identify commercial interests as the ruling fraction of capital but also notes the importance of the rising industrialists.

> Its dominant group, embracing first and foremost the men of the Grand Trunk and of the Bank of Montreal, was centred in Montreal. In Toronto and Hamilton there was a second cluster, divided roughly into three subgroups, with somewhat divergent interests. One was connected with extractive industries (milling, lumbering and shipping) and its members had close ties with their opposite numbers or with markets in the United States. The up-and-coming financial apparatus in opposition to the Montreal banks, were interested in government assistance in the form of protective tariffs against both the British and United States manufacturers. A third group, not entirely distinct from the second, was part of the railway-government crowd, with interests both similar to and conflicting with those of the Montreal group, whose financial power they had good reason to respect. [277]

Canadian industrial capitalists were retarded as a result of extended colonization, but, according to Ryerson, they became an essential ingredient in
Canada's class configuration. In the next section we will see why, but first it is
important to examine some other views of the capitalist class in its formative
stages.

Another writer who follows Ryerson's general view of industrialization
is Stephen Langdon.[8] His identification of industrial capitalists for the period
(early 1870s) differs only slightly. They emerged, he argues, along three
paths:

> First, some transferred capital made from other kinds of entrepreneurship
> into large-scale industrial activity, making a complete switch in their
> enterprise (as opposed to the merchants who undertook industrial produc-
> tion, but remained primarily merchants). . . . A second group of industrial-
> ists was, in a sense, self-generating. They began as small-scale craftsmen
> and gradually developed large enterprises, by plowing their earnings heav-
> ily back into their firms. This pattern seemed particularly common in the
> metalworking sector. . . . Finally, there was a third path. A substantial
> number of industrial capitalists in central Canada were transferring either
> entrepreneurial or technical experience from abroad. . . a quite remarkable
> number of new Canadian industrialists had simply migrated directly from
> the United States. [1972:158-61]

By this time, Langdon maintains, industrialists had formed into "a conscious
class, with its own ideology of industrialism" (185). Moreover, the merchants
who were beginning to invest in industry were following the ideology of the
industrialists, particularly with respect to protective tariffs (see 187-88).

Ryerson and Langdon have identified the emergence of an industrial
capitalist class in Canada in the 1870s, a period that encouraged its development because of the weakened position of the commercial capitalists, with the
decline of the British imperial system, and the industrial opportunities offered
as a result of the Civil War in the United States. They have not examined in
any detail its fate following this period. Tom Naylor, among others, has
traced the demise of industrialists in confrontation with financial capitalists
over the period 1867-1914 in *The History of Canadian Business*. During this
period two major developments affected industrial capitalists in Canada: one
was the growth of foreign-controlled branch plants operating behind tariff
walls, particularly after the National Policy of 1879, and the resulting
sell-outs by vulnerable industrialists; the other was a wave of consolidations
in industry led by central Canadian financial capitalists. Canadian financial
capitalists were instrumental in consolidating many primary manufacturing
industries, an outstanding example being the forging of many rolling mills
into the Steel Company of Canada (Stelco) and the concentration of production in central Canada. The second wave of industrialization, particularly

---

[8]Stephen Langdon is also following the early work of H.C. Pentland, 1950.

within the scientifically oriented industries in secondary manufacturing, was led by U.S. industrialists, outstanding examples being the electronics and automobile industries.

Naylor stresses the "colonial" quality of the Canadian economy, oriented to staples extraction for metropolitan markets and the receiving of foreign-produced manufactured goods. As a result, "Canada's commercial and financial system grew up geared to the international movement of staples, rather than to abetting secondary processing for domestic markets" (1975:I:4). Industrialization was retarded and the necessary capital remained tied to commercial activities. He says the "so-called 'manufacturing'" of the Canadas in 1850 amounted to only 18 per cent of the Gross National Product (GNP), with over half that amount in saw and grist mills basically producing staples. The National Policy of 1879 did stimulate new manufacturing, Naylor concedes, but its effects were undermined by the long depression lasting until 1896, taking its toll on these nascent industries and causing shutdowns, layoffs and losses. Here Naylor is in disagreement with Langdon, arguing that "much of the pressure for protection came not from secondary manufacturing, but from the mercantile community and some major primary producers" (I:37). Paul Phillips, following Pentland, contends that the National Policy suited the interests of both commercial-financial and industrial capital, arguing the intent "was to create a new resource frontier *within Canadian control* which would provide profitable investment opportunities" for one and "a captive market" for the products of the other (1979a:6). Thus, the strategy was principally a "regional policy" whereby the West's wheat production would serve the mercantile interests of central Canadian financial capital, and the West would be a captive market for central Canadian manufacturers (7).[9]

Naylor's argument about industrialization is that there are two possible paths with radically different consequences:

> Manufacturing industry can grow up 'naturally' by a process of capital accumulating in a small-scale unit of production, perhaps even artisanal in character, the profits of which are reinvested in the enterprise to finance its growth from within. A second path implies direct development into large-scale enterprise, often with direct state assistance, and with capital from outside the enterprise, be it commercial capital, state subsidies, or foreign investment, being invested in it to facilitate its expansion. The first path, if successfully followed, leads to the emergence of a flourishing, independent national entrepreneurial class. The second may or may not. The second

---

[9]Craven and Traves have provided a broader class analysis of the National Policy, arguing "Canadian workers, not surprisingly, resisted the competition of imported labour as strongly as manufacturers did the competition of imported commodities" (1979:18). As will be examined later, they also contend the petite bourgeoisie had a central role in the policy's formation and implementation.

path may simply reproduce the conservatism of commercial capitalism in a
new guise, and lead to the development of an inefficient, non-innovative,
and backward industrial structure. [1975, I:38]

Prior to the National Policy, both paths were followed; but Naylor argues it
was the second path that prevailed and the result was a structure of dependence on commercial capital, the state and foreign control. The commercial
class entered the industrial sector as promoters of mergers and watered-stock
schemes; they biased the pattern of industrial development and laid the
conditions for the influx of foreign investment. This becomes most evident in
his analysis of patents, foreign technology and an "imported second industrial
revolution" (II:57). The dominant class remained commercially oriented
toward the movement of staples for export; their failure to finance industrialization by Canadian manufacturers set the pattern for a distorted economy.

Some support for Naylor's argument is provided by the work of T.W.
Acheson. He also identifies the period between 1870 and the First World War
as the critical juncture for Canadian industrialization. "The leading industrial
firms of 1880 had, for the most part, been small family or partnership
concerns. . . . By 1910 the joint stock company had become the dominant
industrial form" (1973:184). Over the period there was a shift from
"manufacturers by vocation" to those by "avocation" whose base was in
commercial activities outside manufacturing.

Greater support for Naylor's view is offered by the later work of H.C.
Pentland, who argues that Canadian capitalists'

> attitudes have been predominantly commercial rather than industrial.
> There is, to be sure, variation. Hamilton, in particular, and southern
> Ontario cities generally, have had much more than the usual industrial
> context and outlook. Montreal, on the other hand, has had and still has a
> commercial outlook, notwithstanding considerable industrial growth. Prairie
> cities, and the main Atlantic urban centres, exhibit almost untainted
> commercialism. Vancouver is somewhere in between. [1968:24-25]

Canadian manufacturing at the turn of the century was undercapitalized, had
little advanced technology and was reliant upon skilled labour rather than
machinery. It was oriented to limited home markets and effectively protected
only by high transportation costs. Major changes did not appear until the
second decade of the century:

> In manufacturing, the major changes in structure centred on the rise of
> three industries: pulp and paper, automobiles, and electrical apparatus.
> While all have earlier beginnings, all experienced an extremely rapid growth
> between 1910 and 1920 and a more massive absolute growth (though a
> smaller relative one) in the 1920s. Industries related to these rose at the
> same time: rubber, automobile parts, industrial machinery. . . . All have
> exhibited the further concentration of many establishments in each firm
> characteristic of corporate or financial capitalism. [45]

Concomitant with these changes, Pentland argues, were the related movements toward increased centralization and U.S. direct investment. The only manufacturing areas retained by Canadian capitalists were older industries, like food and beverage processing where "profit rates were not high and steady enough to attract strong investment," and others where "exclusive access to markets is difficult to establish: examples are found in construction, some forms of merchandising, and agriculture" (50). Otherwise the manufacturing of the second industrial revolution fell to foreign control.

The role of Canadian financial capitalists in the movement toward concentrated industry has been documented by Lloyd G. Reynolds:

> Most Canadian mergers seem to have been promoted by men with financial rather than industrial experience, and promoters' profits seem to have been the largest single incentive to combination. This view is supported by the fact that the two bursts of merger activity occurred during periods of exceptional prosperity, when fresh stock issues were quickly absorbed by optimistic investors. [1940:173-74]

Canadian capitalists were often an integral part of the concentration of industry resulting from internal forces, profiting as they bought, sold and consolidated small manufacturers into corporate firms. They were also frequently involved in selling off these firms to foreign, particularly U.S., industrialists, who spread their market control into Canada.

The later history of Canadian capitalists is primarily one of their consolidating control in finance, transportation and utilities and of the capturing of manufacturing and resource activities by foreign capital. The evidence for this absorption into a concentrated, continental economy is extensive (see Clement, 1975, 1977, 1978). There continues to be an emphasis on resource extraction for export, although this has now shifted to the new industrial staples of pulp and paper, minerals and energy. The manufacturing sector is a miniature replica of the U.S. parent companies, and there is evidence, as mentioned earlier, of de-industrialization occurring in the late 1970s. At minimum, there is an unevenly developed economy with an underdeveloped industrial capacity and an overdeveloped resource extraction sector, both largely under foreign control (either through direct ownership or market control). Canadian capitalists in their areas of traditional strength (such as banks and life insurance) are powerful at home and abroad. All of these patterns were established in the formative stage of Canadian capitalism around the turn of the century. The direction could have been changed since then, but the dominant capitalists in Canada benefited from their unequal alliance with foreign capitalists and continued to direct the economy toward its present structure (Clement, 1977).

One of the reasons for the differences between the types of analysis of the capitalist class offered by Ryerson and Naylor is that they studied different periods, but this does not wholly account for it. The major difference between them is in the type of class analysis each performed. Naylor was concerned with accounting for the most powerful capitalists who were in command of the economy and caused economic distortions. Ryerson, along with Pentland, was concerned about class relations; that is, the relationship between the capitalist and working classes. As a result, they focused on the emergence of industrial capitalists and the formation of a working class. Although weaker than commercial capitalists, industrial capitalists were the counterpoint of an industrial proletariat. Pentland and Ryerson's analyses are not only the history of capital; they are also the history of labour. It is to this working class that attention will now be directed.

The Working Class

Having earlier examined capital formation in Canada (1950, 1953; also see Aitken, 1952), H.C. Pentland presented a penetrating analysis of the formation of a working class in Canada in "The Development of a Capitalistic Labour Market in Canada" (1959:450-61). Beginning with the formation of a capitalist labour market, he argued:

> The actions of workers and employers are governed and linked by impersonal considerations of immediate pecuniary advantage. In this market, the employer is confident that workers will be available whenever he wants them; so he feels free to hire them on a short-term basis, and to dismiss them whenever there is a monetary advantage in doing so. Hence, the employer takes no responsibility for the workers' overhead costs. . . . When the demand and supply conditions of labour are dependable enough to permit this pooling, the overhead costs of labour can be transferred from individual employers to the market, that is, to the workers themselves and to the community at large. The essential historical aspect of the capitalistic labour market, then, is the development of the supply and demand conditions that will support it. Two questions are especially critical: How are workers induced to flow into the labour market pool? And how are they prevented from flowing out again? [450]

These two fundamental questions pose the critical concerns for an analysis of the formation of a working class in Canada and of the destruction of petty bourgeois forms of organization, while at the same time implying an enlarged role for the state in capitalist society — to be responsible for the "overhead" costs of the reproduction of labour.

Pentland argues that the conditions for a capitalist labour market did not prevail until the 1830s, and not until the 1850s was the "essential structure" in place, operating with "some sophistication" in the 1870s (455). Before these conditions were met, a "quasi-feudal" structure[10] prevailed, since workers were scarce and there were few wage employers, creating a mutual dependence based on custom and contract in craft industries and the fur trade (see

---

[10]Pentland later changed this concept to "personal labour" to reflect the economic (labour market) aspect of this labour rather than the political connotation of "feudal" (1981:xxv, xxxi).

453-55). Three factors, he contends, accounted for the emergence and maintenance of a capitalist labour market. First was the "regular demand for
labour" provided by transportation construction, particularly the canals and
railways, and a home market for manufactured goods. He maintains "early
manufactures depended heavily on craftsmanship, but factory production
based on machinery and unskilled labour and mass demand was a feature
of the 1860s" (457). Second was availability of the "sources of labour
supply," made problematic by the draw of the land for native people, French
Canadians and immigrants. It was the immigrant Irish who provided the
source of construction labour, after access to land was cut off by the application of Wakefield's policies of barriers to landownership as a strategy to
create labour detached from its own means of production.[11] The third factor
was keeping workers within the labour market once they had entered it.
This was achieved — besides by limiting access to land — by importing wage
labour prepared to remain in the labour market, particularly Irish unskilled
labour and British artisans.

Accepting Pentland's periodization, Stephen Langdon (1972; 1975) provides an analysis of the formation of workers' movements that, he argues,
coincide with the emergence of industrial capitalism, particularly in the cities
of central Canada. The motivations for such movements were an undermining
of job security that went with a capitalist labour market and a decline in the
power of craftsmen, with the introduction of mechanization. The craft resistance of the early 1850s was transformed into a working-class movement by
the 1870s. Unions at this stage were "small and vulnerable," all with fewer
than a hundred members (see 1975:11). Not until the 1870s did the movement coalesce and take shape:

> First, existing locals grew larger. Second, further central Canadian and
> international links developed among employees in particular sectors. Third,
> city workingmen's assemblies emerged in central Canada. Fourth, union-
> ism consequently spread much more widely, including among semi-skilled
> and unskilled workers. And fifth, links were formed among all central
> Canadian working people. [12]

Langdon demonstrates that the number of strikes in Canada West and
Canada East rose dramatically in the 1870-74 period (see 1972), but he seems
to overstate the power of the workers' movement. By the end of the 1870s the
movement was on the defensive, struggling to maintain its gains in the face of
severe cutbacks in wages and jobs. There was established, nevertheless, an
important working-class tradition of resistance during this period. Langdon
offers an important qualification to this argument: "Almost all the [union]
institutions we have highlighted . . . [the Canadian Labour Union, the

---

[11]On the Wakefield policies, see Gary Teeple, 1972:44-45. He argues that the abuses of land
policy by the ruling class also caused a great deal of out migration and limited the development
of a home market.

Toronto Trades Assembly and the Workman] had disbanded before the end of the decade. And certainly the working-class movement we have described was not a mature, confident force capable of transforming Canadian society in the collective, egalitarian image it sometimes expressed" (1975:336).

In a later work Pentland extends the period of his coverage in what must be considered the most thorough (though unpublished) account of the working class in Canada to date, "A Study of the Changing Social, Economic and Political Background of the Canadian System of Industrial Relations," covering 1900 to 1967 (1968). As suggested earlier, the first manufacturing in Canada was small scale and mainly by craftsmen, such as blacksmiths, carpenters, shoemakers, silversmiths and tailors in small shops. Their trades were geared to local conditions and closely tied to small centres serving relatively large agricultural populations. The development of factory-scale manufacturing was also initially tied to agriculture through grist, rolling and saw mills, tanneries, breweries and distilleries, but as was seen, these were amenable to the forces of concentration led by financial capitalists. Pentland identifies the most notable transformation in the labour force as a shift out of agriculture, declining from 40 per cent in 1901 to 34 per cent in 1911, "despite the expansion of agricultural settlement in Western Canada." What is most surprising, according to Pentland, is that these losses did not flow into manufacturing, which in fact fell during the decade from 17 to 14 per cent. Gains were instead "in construction, transportation and communication, and clerical employment, and to a lesser extent in trade and finance and mining" (1968:38-40). During the next decade agriculture managed to hold its own but manufacturing continued to decline.

In a much neglected article — by far his most impressive statement on labour — Innis draws the connection between a staples economy and the creation of a particularly Canadian labour force:

> The supply of labour and the opportunities for its employment have been largely conditioned by the development of the Canadian economy upon the basis of a succession of staples products for export. Technological changes, particularly in transport, have to a great extent determined what these staples should be, the character of the industrial superstructure built up around them, and hence the part played by labour in the economy. [Innis and Ratz, 1940:353]

According to Innis, technology, particularly expressed in transportation, determines the nature and action of labour. The dynamic between capital and labour is absent, but he does provide an important analysis of forms of labour, systematically tracing these through a succession of staples and into industrial capitalism. He argues, for example, that "scarcity of labour inherent in an economy based on the fur trade contributed to the development of an indenture system, by which immigrants paid for their passage by working for a definite period, and of systems designed to bind the employee to the employer" (353). This condition was attributable, however, to the relations of production developed in the fur trade, with relations of trade between petty commodity producers and mercantile capitalists, thus leaving the producers with control over their own means of production and not requiring them to enter into wage relations. Imported indentured labour was therefore required outside fur trading. Not until capitalists were able to enforce their claims to the land and its products could petty commodity production be contained and wage labour created. Similar processes prevailed in the fishing and forest products industries, as well as in mining (see the following two papers, chapters 7 and 8). Innis enumerates these transformations but does not explain them, except by resorting to "the character of the staple":

> Labour has gradually shifted in the main from an individualistic basis to a share system prevalent in the early stages of development of basic industries, shown in the fishing industry, the fur trade, the lumber industry, placer gold mining (the lay system), and in agriculture (share farming), and to a wage system, the trend varying with the importance of capital equipment. Skilled labour, as in the railways, the building trades, and the crafts, has conserved modifications of the apprenticeship system, and strengthened its position in a period of expanding industrialism, but with severe strains accompanying the increasing periods of unemployment, and slackening the rate of expansion, craft organization has retreated. [1940:363]

The capitalization of resource and manufacturing industries with the onset of corporate capitalism had a dramatic effect on the working class. Capitalists first penetrated petty commodity relations by drawing together under one roof or on one plot of land individuals who had previously worked independently. This was followed by providing these artisans with powered equipment to increase productivity. It did this, but it also destroyed the basis for their earlier craft power.

This important development is documented by Pentland: "'Unskilled' employments (those with indefinite skill requirements and a heavy emphasis on physical effort) expanded in the first four decades of the century" (65). Whereas the skilled proportion increased in the building trades from 28 to 56 per cent between 1881 and 1921, in the manufacture of iron and steel it decreased from 87 to 65 per cent. Between 1891 and 1921 employment in the manufacture of leather and rubber goods declined in skill from 98 to 65 per cent. "The expanding transportation sector required a large number of indefinitely-skilled workers, the same was true of expanding extractive industries, and it is notorious that the rise of large-scale mechanized manufacturing entailed a diminished reliance on craftsmen and a much greater use of quickly-trained 'operators'"(65, 67). The working class was obviously undergoing an important transformation both in terms of the lower skill content of the work performed and the fewer number of workers required by more capital-intensive factory operations.

This development was not passively accepted by the working class. In an excellent study of the period 1901-14 for southern Ontario, Craig Heron and Bryan Palmer report that over two hundred strikes took place involving control over the workplace. They discuss in detail two forms of worker resistance to deskilling crafts and to the imposition of the discipline of the factory system. The first was "restrictive control," which limited the output and number of apprentices allowed in trades. The second was "shop control," which institutionalized union rules and regulations to establish committees, hours of work and work practices (1977:442-43). For the most part, however, much of this resistance was successfully challenged by capital through mechanization and the use of scientific management techniques.

Resistance also took place outside the factory. As Martin Robin has argued, workers began actively seeking changes in their condition through legislative means once they were granted formal political democracy. The prevailing party system was a major mechanism for containing their struggles, and one particularly capable of absorbing union leaders. "Just as the new factory system required a docile and disciplined working class to work at full capacity, so did the political system, which made the laws of the land and guaranteed the hegemony of the capitalist in the enterprise, require an electoral mass subject to the discipline of the party machine and candidate" (1967-68:333). At the turn of the century skilled artisans through their unions began to articulate their demands for various reforms, such as the nine-hour day and union recognition, but this was largely attempted through the existing parties by pressure groups, either directly or by means of public agitation.

One significant product of the working-class action was a revival of the union movement. As Pentland indicates, "Nearly three-quarters of all the local unions existing in 1902 for which a date of origin was known had been formed since the beginning of 1898, and when the first extraordinary wave was spent, by the end of 1903, about 60% of the 1395 locals reported had been established in the previous five years." Still, only about a hundred thousand workers belonged to unions (10 per cent of the non-agricultural labour force). These unions were concentrated in railroads and mining, with much lower rates in manufacturing (except for clothing, footwear, printing and metal trades). They were also concentrated in the four western provinces, the West accounting for 20 per cent of union membership in 1903 and 35 per cent in 1912, compared to only 11 and 24 per cent of the population during these years.[12]

---

[12]Pentland, 1968:70; see also pp. 110, 114. Innis and Ratz account for some of the western conflict by the nature of its industry: "The relatively weak development of secondary industries in British Columbia and the importance of capital equipment in the basic industries of mining, lumbering and fishing implied a weak development of craft unions and an emphasis on industrial unionism" (1940:359-60).

In western Canada the labour movement flourished, particularly in single-industry mining, forest products and railway towns. Pentland argues:

> What really distinguished the western labour scene, however, was that here a real possibility existed of organizing non-craft workers into viable unions. The workers were alert, hardy, somewhat reckless, and certainly not overawed. Conditions of employment often build up solidarity among them, while isolating them from other society. The frequent shortage of labour made unionism of the unskilled and semiskilled much more practical than it was in areas overflowing with cheap and timid labour. [1979:61-62]

Until the First World War, conditions favouring a politically active labour movement existed in the West. Thereafter both political and economic conditions deteriorated for the working class as massive immigration eliminated labour shortages and railway construction ended, thus reducing demand, and the forces of repression quashed their resistance (as in the famous Winnipeg General Strike of 1919).

The union movement "fell into chronic inter-union strife" after 1902, mainly as a result of the capture of the Trades and Labour Congress of Canada by the American Federation of Labor (Pentland, 1968:129). The ramifications for the labour movement were many. The most important was the shift in the locus of control, following the trend in manufacturing discussed earlier; as Eugene Forsey has commented, "With the advent of international unions, the centre of gravity of Canadian unionism shifted to central Canada. Till 1853, all the unions were purely local" (1974:4). Control was also frequently shifted out of Canada. International unions since the turn of the century have accounted for at least three-fifths of union membership until the mid-1970s.[13] This has aggravated the traditional structural weakness of unions in terms of splits between craft and industrial unions and fragmented the Canadian labour movement throughout its entire history.

Labour unions have received a good deal of attention by Canadian scholars;[14] until recently, however, the working class itself has received considerably less attention. Signs of change are reflected in numerous recent studies. For example, *Essays in Canadian Working Class History*, edited by Greg Kealey and Peter Warrian, represents the beginnings of a social history

---

[13]On international unions, see Robert Babcock, 1974; Roger Howard and Jack Scott, 1972; Charles Lipton, 1972; Robert Laxer, 1976.

[14]The most extensive review of institutionalized conflict between capital and labour is Stuart Jamieson, 1968. It documents the long and violent history of class conflict in Canada during the twentieth century. There are also key studies of labour resistance in *On Strike: Six Key Labour Struggles in Canada 1919-1949*, ed. Irving Abella, 1975. On the politics of unions, see Gad Horowitz, *Canadian Labour Politics*, 1968; Irving Abella, *Nationalism, Communism and Canadian Labour: The CIO, the Communist Party, and the Canadian Congress of Labour, 1935-1956*, 1973.

aimed at informing us of the working class in its various economic, cultural, ideological and political dimensions. Its contributors help us to recover our past, lost by most historians, who ignored workers and artisans. The essays illustrated the vitality and value of this type of analysis. Although lacking an articulated theory of class, they clearly demonstrate that history is not simply the stories of politicians and businessmen, or even of strikes, but also the history of the working people (see Kealey, 1974; Abella and Millar, 1978; Cross, 1974). A further illustration of this revival is the annual publication *Labour/Le Travailleur*, established in 1976 and devoted to an interdisciplinary approach to labour history. Of particular note are two recent studies: *A Culture in Conflict: Skilled Workers and Industrial Capitalism in Hamilton, Ontario, 1860-1914* by Bryan Palmer and *Toronto Workers Respond to Industrial Capitalism, 1867-1892* by Gregory Kealey — and, as well, a review essay by Kealey (1981).

Writing in the tradition of E.P. Thompson, Palmer stresses the experience of class: "Class is thus defined by men and women as they live through the historical experience. It is class struggle and culture, not class itself, as an analytical category, that are the primary concepts upon which classes themselves arise and assume importance" (1979:xvi). The "life" breathed into class *relations* by such an approach seeks to demonstrate, as Kealey argues, "that the working class was not just 'made' but rather the result of a dialectical interplay of class forces in which it was one of the actors" (1979:xviii). The concern exhibited in these studies for the dynamics of class adds a fresh and welcome dimension to what has all too often been a single-class approach. The fundamental notion that workers (and the petite bourgeoisie) resist the strategies of capitalists to dominate production requires a much more prominent place in Canadian political economy than it has had to date.

Until the Second World War, working-class movements in Canada struggled against repressive political, military and economic conditions, which took their toll. For example, "in 1935 there were fewer union members — about 275,000 — in Canada than there had been at any time since the First World War" (Abella, 1975:18). The greatest period of gain for organized labour since the turn of the century occurred in the 1940s when the proportion of the unionized civilian labour force doubled from 10 to 20 per cent. Pentland attributes this mainly to the effects of the Second World War, which doubled manufacturing employment between 1939 and 1942 by shifting people from other sectors, particularly agriculture:

> There was, therefore, a shrinkage of employment in sectors little affected by industrial clashes and a massive growth in the manufacturing sector in which the conflicting attitudes of employers and workers over the issue of collective bargaining were at their sharpest. Following from this and from labour discontent was a rapid rise in union membership, which was more than 50% above the 1939 figure (359,000) by 1942 (578,000), and more than 100% above it by 1944 (724,000). Discontent fed both on the backlog

of grievances from the 1930's and an ample current supply, and a tight labour market invited its expression. [1968:204]

Since then, the gains have been less spectacular. Following the war, capitalists used the strategy of capitalization through the introduction of extensive amounts of new technology, thus reducing the demand for labour in the factory and in resource industries, but increasing the amount in clerical and professional-technical work. Not until the late 1960s did workers in these growing sectors begin to organize, particularly in the growing state sector once collective-bargaining rights were attained. These workers had experienced a relatively favoured position until the late 1960s, thereafter discovering a contracting market for their skills and increased job insecurity.

Between 1967 and 1972 unionized state workers dramatically increased from 125,000 (about 30 per cent of public employees, mainly at municipal and provincial levels) to 348,000 (about 66 per cent of public employees, 44 per cent at the federal level).[15] The two largest unions in Canada are now the Canadian Union of Public Employees and the Public Service Alliance of Canada. As a result, much of the class conflict currently occurring is between state employees and the state, as the state seeks to use its own employees to curb inflation and reduce deficits. The major development requiring analysis is the relationship between state and private workers and whether these workers will be fragmented in their struggles or form alliances.

One final dimension of the working class requires comment. The proportion of women in the paid labour force has been increasing much more rapidly than that of men. Between 1953 and 1973 women increased their proportion of the labour force from 22 to 34 per cent, and their participation rate rose over the same period from 23 to 39 per cent. Studies of women in Canada's class structure have been slow to emerge. There have, however, been several excellent studies of the relationship between women and class. For example, Wayne Roberts's *Honest Womanhood: Feminism, Femininity and Class Consciousness among Toronto Working Women, 1893 to 1914* analyses in some detail the development of 'women's work' in service jobs (servants, laundry workers and waitresses), in production jobs (in the printing and garment industry) and in teaching and clerical jobs (also see Acton, 1974). In so doing, he presents an 'ecology' of working women, placing them within their ideological, cultural and economic situation (see also Trofimenkoff and Prentice, 1977). Roberts places the entry of women into the paid labour force in the context of other working-class developments at the turn of the century, arguing that women

> had been denied the work and life experience characteristic of the nineteenth century artisanal workman. Artisans exerted considerable power in the workplace based on a relative monopoly of skill, corresponding to a

---

[15]On the growth of state workers, see Hugh Armstrong, 1978.

relatively underdeveloped level of standardized machine manufacture. This artisanal tradition was common to most workers who formed strong unions in the early twentieth century. These workers not only entered the twentieth century with strong unions; most had retained some sense of craft integrity and some forms of social solidarity that buttressed their union strength considerably.

Women were denied this experience as a matter of course. Their entry into an occupation was the death knell of an artisanal trade. More, they were levers which destroyed its norms, habits and strengths. Their work lives typified the antithesis of artisanal modes. [1976:47-48]

A declining proportion of women are part of the industrial proletariat, even though at the turn of the century a greater proportion of women were employed in this activity than were men. The main location of women throughout the twentieth century has been the commercial proletariat, always accounting for at least half the women in the paid labour force.

The occupational segregation of women, which has been reinforced rather than eroded over time, has allowed capitalists to use the labour of women differently than that of men by creating 'female ghettos' with low pay and little chance for advancement, thus segmenting the working class into its male and female fractions. Over two-thirds of the women in the labour force in 1971 worked in the tertiary sector, accounting for over half the workers in the community, business and personnel service industries (58 per cent) and in finance, insurance and real estate (52 per cent). In manufacturing in 1971, women were concentrated in a few labour-intensive industries where they accounted for over half the work force: clothing industries (71 per cent), knitting mills (64 per cent) and leather industries (50 per cent) (Statistics Canada, 1978a:11-17). Even in industries where women are numerically prominent, men dominate supervisory occupations (42-43, 53). This is reinforced and maintained by discriminatory hiring and promotion practices (see Hill, 1973; Stephenson, 1977). The most recent study of this form of class fragmentation in Canada is *The Double Ghetto: Canadian Women and Their Segregated Work* by Pat and Hugh Armstrong. There is, however, a continuing need to understand the political and ideological dimensions of the relationship between sexual divisions and class cleavages, particularly for the working class.

The main characteristic that emerges for the Canadian working class is its fragmentation. Economically, this fragmentation is a product of the uneven development of capitalism with its emphasis on resource extraction and its failure to develop a strong manufacturing sector. Both activities are capital intensive as a result of importing more highly developed techniques from outside the country. There has resulted an overdeveloped commercial proletariat and a relatively weak (although active) industrial and resource proletariat. Politically, the working class has been continually fragmented by struggles within the union movement between national and international unions, where internationals have shown their greatest strength in industry, while national unions have developed their strength by organizing state employees. Ideologically, there have been numerous splits weakening the labour movement. The most basic of these have been the slowness to organize women and other poorly paid workers in the labour force, regional tensions within and between unions, and tensions that have existed between French- and English-language unions. Capitalists have also caused many of the structural weaknesses of the Canadian economy that underlie the fragmented labour movement through the shaping of the economy. A further crucial factor explaining the political weakness of the working class is the traditional strength of the petite bourgeoisie. The persistence of the petite bourgeoisie as an important political class has tended to deflect and mute the main struggle of capitalism between capital and labour. It is to this class that attention will now be directed.

The Petite Bourgeoisie
At the turn of the century 65 per cent of Canada's population was rural, declining to 53 per cent by 1921 but still at 44 per cent by 1941; the rural population dropped to 30 per cent in 1961 and to 24 per cent by 1971. This rural population has been composed in large part of the traditional petite bourgeoisie who own their own means of production and rely upon their own labour power and that of their families. Most of this class has traditionally been agrarian but included other small producers often also tied to small-scale agrarian production. The situation before the turn of the century was clearly one where agriculture dominated numerically, as Table 6.1 illustrates. Until 1941, agriculture remained the largest sector of the Canadian labour force, overtaken in 1951 by manufacturing and in 1961 by clerical and service workers. As late as 1926, 57 per cent of immigrants to Canada were 'farm immigrants' but by 1952 this had fallen to 10 per cent and by 1975 to less than 2 per cent.

Table 6.1
Agricultural and Industrial Labour Forces
in Upper and Lower Canada, 1851 to 1891
(percentages)

	1851	1861	1871	1881	1891
Agriculture					
Upper Canada	35	40	49	48	46
Lower Canada	39	43	47	47	46
Industry					
Upper Canada	18	18	20	21	21
Lower Canada	13	18	19	19	20

Sources: H. Clare Pentland, "Labour and the Development of Industrial Capitalism in Canada" (Ph.D. thesis, University of Toronto, 1960), pp. 286-87; also 1981:132-33.

With the decline in agriculture there has also been a reorganization of production within this sector. There has been a decreasing reliance on unpaid family workers and an increase in the proportion of employers and paid workers. Within agriculture, the unpaid family members were mainly women; in 1946, 174,000 of the 200,000 women in agriculture were unpaid, and 34,000 of the 46,000 in 1960. Even in 1971 two-thirds of the women in agriculture were unpaid family workers. Outside agriculture, unpaid family labour has a very minor place and nearly the entire labour force is engaged in paid labour (Urquhart and Buckley, 1965:63).

Although agriculture was the stronghold of the petite bourgeoisie, it was not alone. Petty bourgeois relations also characterized at various times manufacturing (e.g., blacksmiths), mining (e.g., placer gold), retailing (e.g., shopkeepers), construction and fishing. At different rates, each sector was penetrated and dominated by capitalist relations of production. In 1971, for example, only 10 per cent of the labour force in retail trade was self-employed, as was 11 per cent in construction, and 8 per cent in forestry. Complete destruction of the self-employed has occurred in manufacturing and mining, which have only 1 per cent each. In contrast, agriculture with 49 per cent and fishing and trapping with 56 per cent remain the preserves of petty commodity production (Statistics Canada, 1978a:20). The decline of the non-agricultural petite bourgeoisie has been neglected in the studies of class. Besides those already mentioned, there is a shortage of studies of real estate agents, insurance brokers or even independent professionals like doctors, lawyers, dentists, engineers and architects.[16] Although collectively not a large part of the class structure, this stratum, like its counterpart in agriculture, has been a powerful force in the politics of class relations. Similarly, the quasi-professionals, such as teachers and nurses, have not been adequately located in class terms, nor sufficiently researched.

The focus of this section on the petite bourgeoisie will be on the decline of agriculture, since it represents the greatest volume of class transformation in Canada and has had the greatest impact on relations between capital and labour. The decline of agriculture began in the Atlantic region in the period 1901-11, but overall there was agricultural expansion in the West and British Columbia until after the Second World War. Ontario had 43 per cent of all the agricultural population in 1900, while only 13 per cent was in the West; by 1941, 43 per cent was in the West (see Haythorne, 1941). This westward expansion must be seen in its relationship to eastern commercial and industrial

[16]One attempt, flawed by inadequate data and confusing conceptualization, is Leo Johnson's distinction between "independent commodity producers" ("farmers, fishermen and crafts-workers") and "small bourgeois businessmen" ("retailers, independent salesmen and rentier") as two groups within the petite bourgeoisie (1972:145-53). Johnson also discusses but does not clearly locate "the elite professions such as doctors, dentists and lawyers" as well as "engineers and architects" (167-68). Much of the confusion arises out of the use of occupations (as identified in the census) that themselves are distributed among all three major classes.

interests. As C.B. Macpherson has maintained, "The prairies, peopled by producers of grain and other primary products, were developed as an area for the profitable investment of capital, as a market for manufactured goods, and as a source of merchandising and carrying profits" (1953:7). This follows V.C. Fowke's assessment: "The clearest and most significant uniformity regarding Canadian agriculture for more than three hundred years has been its deliberate and consistent use as a basis for economic and political empire" (1946:3). Stressing the importance of the petite bourgeoisie in Canadian class politics, Craven and Traves argue:

> The tariff issue [of the National Policy] arose out of the programme of capitalist industrialism implicit in the National Policy, but in the context of Canadian economic development industrialism brought with it as well the reproduction of an agrarian petite bourgeoisie at the margin. . . . A triadic class structure has a unique complexity resulting from the possibility of cooperation in conflict, the more so since there seemed on practically every issue of significance to be grounds to unite class interests as well as divide them. [1979:37]

Two crucial issues are raised by these comments. The first is the complexity of class struggles in politics following from a structure where there is an active and persistent petite bourgeoisie, and the second is the unevenness of class development arising from Canada's peculiar form of regional domination.

From the outset, western farms were the product of a homestead policy directed by central Canada that created individual family holdings. In Alberta half the population were still on farms until 1941, although there was a relative decline from 1936 onwards. Owner-operated firms declined from 80 per cent in 1921 to 64 per cent in 1946, while the proportion of tenant farmers increased from 10 to 15 per cent (Macpherson, 1953:7). Farmers were forced off the land by the Depression of the 1930s and by a combination of pressures from central Canada. As Meyer Brownstone has argued:

> Confronted by well-disciplined and powerful market forces on both the farm supply and farm marketing sides of his operation, the Canadian farmer has been and is subject to severe exploitation. He has sought to counteract these pressures through the building of cooperative organizations and through the establishment of producer and government marketing boards. Neither the cooperatives nor producer boards have been sufficiently effective in a bargaining sense to achieve the requisite power in the market. [1961:334]

Petty bourgeois resistance to external domination has led, in spite of its failure, to the most important class-based politics in Canadian history.

What often passes for regionalism in Canada is in fact the expression of petty bourgeois politics manifest in 'third' parties, such as the Social Credit and CCF (besides Macpherson, 1953, see also Smart, 1973; Naylor and Teeple, 1972; Conway, 1978). The major class implication of these political expressions is that until the Second World War the agrarian petite bourgeoisie was the most powerful political class outside the capitalist class, thus weakening the development of working-class politics in Canada. Just because this class was ultimately defeated does not mean that it failed to have a major impact on political and economic institutions in Canada. One of the most persistent gains of this class has been the cooperative movement, strongest in the Prairies and Quebec, where populist parties have held power.

Writing in 1920, William Irvine identified why the class position of farmers leads them to form cooperatives. Referring to the conflict between capital and labour, he says: "The farmer in reality, combines in his own profession, the two antagonists. He is both capitalist and labourer. He knows that production is not furthered when war is going on between the two. . . and is thus led to the discovery of cooperation as the synthesis" (1976:101-2). It is this position that Macpherson, in his classic study, focuses upon:

> The independent commodity producer's double relation to the market
> — that is, his independence of the labour market either as a seller or buyer
> and his dependence on the price system which is ruled as a whole by the rate
> of profit of the productive employment of wage labour — tends to give him,
> as a fundamental part of his outlook, an illusion of independence. [1953:223]

Populist movements, rooted in agrarian petty bourgeois production, have a long history in Canada. The Rebellions of 1837-38 were based in both Canadas on class conflict between allied agriculture and emergent industrial interests against commercial domination. Politically, these interests were represented by reformers versus the "Chateau Clique" and "Family Compact." As Whitaker has pointed out, "Very specific class issues as perceived by small farmers were featured in the manifestos and political programmes of the rebels," concentrating on the issues of credit, produce prices and the costs of distributing products (1976:ix). Other expressions of the populist movements were the election of fourteen members of the Patrons of Industry to the Ontario legislature in 1894; the United Farmers of Ontario forming the government in Ontario between 1919 and 1923; the United Farmers of Alberta regime from 1921 to 1935, being replaced by the Social Credit; and the federal election of sixty-five Progressive party members in 1921 (see Smart, 1973:200).

The heyday of the petite bourgeoisie in politics was the first quarter of the twentieth century. Its back was broken in the 1930s, but it had peaks of power from 1907 to 1911 and early in the 1920s. Macpherson's eulogy summarizes the transformation: "After 1930 the western farmers were reduced to asking for relief instead of reform" (1953:9). In the economic domain their strength peaked during the same period, establishing provincial wheat pools in Alberta (1923), Saskatchewan (1924), Manitoba (1924) and Ontario (1926), coordinated by the Canadian Co-operative Wheat Producers' Company, which sold the grain. By 1920 these pools had some 140,000 members,

1,640 elevators and handled over half the West's wheat (see Griezic, 1975). After 1930 the price of wheat dropped drastically, and by 1931 the once prosperous pools faced bankruptcy. They were replaced, under farmer pressure, by the Canadian Wheat Board in 1935 when the state was forced to regularize marketing, limit production and subsidize prices. After 1949 the Wheat Board became the sole marketing agency, although subsequent developments have led to parallel private marketing companies. Once the state became involved in wheat marketing, the farmers lost control of the cooperative structure they had created and once again became subject to a form of external domination.

Macpherson analysed the "political radicalism" of the agrarian petite bourgeoisie as an attempt "to resist encroachments on the people's standard of living and independence" by external political and economic forces. Their reaction was limited, however, by the inherently vulnerable position of this class (1953:215-16). Moreover, their class position did not "permit them to depart from the basic assumptions of the existing property structure." The leaders of both the United Farmers of Alberta and Social Credit "were prepared to fight against the quasi-colonial economic subordination of their people, but not to do anything which would undermine the sanctity of property rights" (220). They struggled against the grain trader, railway owners and finance companies that continually threatened their independence, but the dominant economy, built on capitalist relations of production, ultimately undermined petty bourgeois relations, which occupied what Macpherson called an "increasingly anomalous position in the economy" (226). This transitory class was able, because of its numerical importance at particular historical junctures, to successfully organize politically to promote its interests, but its struggle was one destined to collapse. The family farm, the core institution of populist ideology, was undercut by the forces of capitalism, thus draining the strength of the agrarian movement.

Once destroyed politically, farmers formed interest groups like the Canadian Chamber of Agriculture in 1935, later renamed the Canadian Federation of Agriculture (CFA). It was no longer a political movement but a pressure group, with some 350,000 members in 1972. Another social movement of farmers has since arisen in opposition to the CFA. The National Farmers' Union (NFU), based in Saskatchewan, was formed in 1960 and now has between 30,000 and 75,000 members (see Griezic, 1975:xix). The NFU has shown signs of attempting to align with labour unions and promote a system of collective bargaining for farmers. It appears that the NFU sees today's farmers — obviously not the corporate farms but the remaining 'independents' — in a relationship to capital similar to that of the working class. Other evidence also suggests this is the case, as will be examined in the final paper of this collection.

Two recent books challenged conventional wisdom about politics and class in Canada, particularly as conceptualized from a central Canadian perspective. Both focus on the "middle classes" as social forces in shaping the politics of the West and Atlantic Canada. Two equally important investigations, although having somewhat divergent theoretical roots, *Prairie Capitalism* by John Richards and Larry Pratt and *Underdevelopment and Social Movements in Atlantic Canada* edited by Robert Brym and James Sacouman, are books about the struggles engaged in by the traditional and new middle classes, particularly as they respond to domination by central Canadian capital. The latter collection stresses the unevenness of class formation, the variety of fractions, and particularly the relationship between economic, ideological and political movements of class. Grounded in a wealth of knowledge about Atlantic Canada, this collection moves freely between the specific and general, the concrete and the abstract, simultaneously presenting several levels of analysis. One example is an article by Sacouman that argues against a "one-class" analysis of primary producers, examining the "variegated processes and structures of capitalist underdevelopment" in the Prairies and Atlantic Canada (1979:52). His major distinction is underdevelopment of two types: *direct*, based on relations of *production*; and *indirect*, based on relations of *distribution*. The former tends to produce resistance in the form of unions (e.g., for miners and fishermen); while the latter, cooperative associations (e.g., for farmers). He calls for a closer examination of the relations producers have with capital in resource extraction as the means to uncover the ideological and political actions of the "middle classes."

Richards and Pratt echo the end of "single-class analysis," bouncing their critique off the work of Macpherson. They offer the emergence of "a nascent regional bourgeoisie of substance and considerable power" as their explanation for the rise of power of the "New West." This new ruling class is said to include "the owners and managers of Alberta-based corporations, urban upper-income professionals with a stake in the continued growth of the regional economy, and senior provincial Conservative politicians and government bureaucrats" (1979:11). Although they return to the argument several times, it is never clear exactly what this "new bourgeoisie" denotes: mixed concepts such as "urban middle class," "alliance of business and professional elites," and "ruling families" appear side by side (148-49). The class analysis of Richards and Pratt is an advance in many ways over the justifiably criticized "one-class" analysis of "commodity producers" provided by Macpherson, but one is left with a mumbo-jumbo of either many names for one class or many ill-specified classes.

More important than precision in identification of classes (and their relationship to production, each other and property) is the social basis for their arrival. The Richards-Pratt answer is most unsatisfactory; their explanation is "mentality," either that of "rentier" during the early period or "entrepreneur" more recently. The core argument boils down to a change of attitudes (155-59) without an adequate explanation of where attitudes originate. It is important to note, however, that their study is a welcome break from earlier class analyses and introduces important political considerations and dynamics that were previously absent.

Class Dynamics in Quebec

The class structure of Quebec has always differed from the rest of Canada. The colonizers of New France represented an alliance of mercantile interests and the Catholic church, and original settlement was based on a form of "indentured bond-servants (engagés)," numbering some eighteen thousand at the beginning of the eighteenth century, who used the land to support about ninety seigneurs (see Ryerson, 1960). Many aspects of this quasi-feudal tenure remained intact even after the British Conquest in 1760, but this eventually gave way to traditional petty bourgeois holdings in agriculture. Since the Conquest, British, English Canadian and U.S. capitalists have dominated the private economy of Quebec, with indigenous elements in control of the state.

John McCallum argues that the major factor accounting for the differences in agriculture between Ontario (Upper Canada) and Quebec (Lower Canada) and their divergent paths of economic development was the absence of a market for Lower Canada's agricultural products. Whereas Upper Canadian farmers in the mid-nineteenth century were able to concentrate on wheat production, which accounted for three-quarters of their cash income and over half Upper Canada's exports until the 1860s, wheat production failed in Lower Canada (even to the extent that it had to import wheat for its own consumption by the 1830s). As a result, commercial agriculture, which served as the basis for Ontario's industrialization, was absent in Quebec (1980: 4). Primarily at issue was the cash available to farmers from the two provinces, thus the income necessary to fuel industrialization:

> In 1850 the average Ontario farmer had a value of cash sales at least five times that of his Quebec counterpart, and this ratio never fell below three in the years before Confederation. Such enormous differences in a sector comprising between one-half and two-thirds of the working population had profound and lasting effects on the patterns of development in the other sectors of the two provincial economies. [5]

Industry in Quebec, McCallum argues, was not based on internal markets as it was in Ontario but rather was owned by outsiders and produced for external markets: "Hence, the agricultural population, which constituted a growing market in Ontario, was little more than a reservoir of cheap labour in Quebec" (7). Ontario was able, after Confederation, to diversify its base in wheat and extend its industrial dominance westward; Quebec lacked such a market, either internally or within Canada.

Since 1860, the mainstay of agriculture in Quebec has been dairy farming. According to Bernard Bernier, this has left Quebec agriculture particularly susceptible to external control. Dairy farming requires extensive supplies of machinery, feed, fertilizer and insecticide, all under capitalist control; this was also the case for the outlets of dairy products, such as butter and cheese factories (1976:426-27). These pressures have resulted in the number of farms in Quebec being cut in half over the past century, while their average size doubled. Unlike the Prairie experience, in Quebec the Depression in the 1930s actually meant a return to the land for subsistence agriculture. Between 1941 and 1971 the general trend returned, and there was a decrease in the number of farms from 150,000 to 60,000 and a drop by over 50 per cent in farm population. Bernier reports that farm debts in Quebec almost match the total value of the farm: "In 1968, the average debt per farm was $33,000, for an average total value (including land, buildings and machinery) of $42,000 per farm" (429).[17]

While dairy farmers continue as 'independent' producers, other forms of agriculture have experienced direct penetration by capitalism. This is particularly the case with poultry, eggs and pigs. According to Bernier, "Feed producers (Purina, Master, etc.) through their local agent provide the buildings, equipment, animals and feed. The farmer provides the land (a minimum is all that is needed) and labour . . . he loses the ownership of the means of production. He controls his work process, but he is paid a certain amount per unit product. In fact, the farmer has become almost a wage labourer" (431). Although differently than in Alberta and the rest of Canada, Quebec farmers also experience proletarianization.

Traditionally the agrarian petite bourgeoisie has been a powerful political force in Quebec, particularly through its support for the Union Nationale party, but another fraction of this same class has also been of political consequence. In their analysis of class struggles in Quebec, Gilles Bourque and Nicole Laurin-Frenette identify the main historical conflicts as "the struggle between the administration of the English Canadian bourgeoisie from 1760 to 1800; the struggle of the petite bourgeoisie against the seigneurs and clergy from 1800 to 1840; the struggle between the urban and rural factions of the French Canadian petite bourgeoisie from 1840 to 1960" (1972:192). Superimposed on these struggles have been those between the "urban faction of the French Canadian petite bourgeoisie and English Canadian bourgeoisie from 1840 to today . . . [and the] French Canadian working class v. English Canadian bourgeoisie from 1945 to 1970" (192).

The major dynamic of Quebec's class struggle, Bourque and Laurin-Frenette maintain, has turned in large part on struggles among fractions of the petite bourgeoisie. The traditional petite bourgeoisie, based in agriculture and independent activities, such as small shopkeepers and non-salaried professions, "has consistently held an ideology of judicial-cultural nationalism of preservation" based on "a reactionary and economic-social plan" (194).

---

[17]Bernier appears to overstate the debt ratio for Quebec farmers. According to A.S. Brunst, the aggregate farm debt in Quebec for 1971 was $551 million to $2,200 million farm investment, a ratio of 25 per cent. This was, however, the highest provincial ratio in Canada (1978:3).

In contrast, since the 1950s, an urban petite bourgeoisie has emerged. "Its rise was due to the rapid industrialization which took place in Quebec during this period. Consequently, it came into existence in a capitalist economic context of monopolies and large public and private organizations, overwhelmingly dominated by foreign capital (American and Canadian)" (195). The Quiet Revolution marked the collapse of the traditional petite bourgeoisie and the ascendance of an urban petite bourgeoisie represented politically by the Liberal party, a party also supported by English capitalists.

This urban petite bourgeoisie is further divided into two fractions. One Bourque and Laurin-Frenette call "technocratic," which has increased numerically and is located in "management, administration, organization and planning of production and consumption of material and symbolic goods." Its strength is in the public sector (including the civil service and crown corporations), educational institutions and trade unions. The second fraction they call "neo-capitalist," which is located in private corporations where it performs the functions of management, such as planning and overseeing labour (196-97). This neo-capitalist fraction is allied with foreign capital, although it pressures for increased nationalist measures in terms of language and job opportunities, drawing back when "the technocratic faction of the French-speaking petite bourgeoisie makes its bid for political-ideological hegemony" (197). The Parti Québécois, since the late 1960s, has become the political expression of the technocratic fraction.

Recently an important debate about the nature of the bourgeoisie in Quebec and the class basis of the Parti Québécois has enlivened interest. Most analysts agree that at least until the 1960s the French Canadian bourgeoisie was insignificant. After this period, however, the significance of this class has become the subject of debate. Jorge Niosi contends that Bourque and Laurin-Frenette grossly understated this class's power. He argues that "the post-war period has seen the development of a French-Canadian (not uniquely Québécois) big bourgeoisie with trans-Canadian and transnational markets," stressing the rapid growth of the dynamic quality of the class (1979:119). "This francophone bourgeoisie," according to Niosi, "is nothing other than the French-Canadian section of the Canadian capitalist class" (148). Within this argument the francophone bourgeoisie "may lean on the Quebec state (which it has helped to build), but it has no interest in the separation of Quebec" (148). Rather, separatism is the expression of the petite bourgeoisie and its political arm, the Parti Québécois.

A radically different position has been taken by Gilles Bourque, who contends the Quebec bourgeoisie is "timid and splintered" and "lacks the necessary degree of economic coherence, characteristic of a true national bourgeoisie" (1979:142). His argument concerning the class base of the Parti Québécois is that "the PQ supports regional capital. But its politics must internalize U.S. and, to a certain extent, Canadian monopolistic interests" (154). The most sustained critique of Niosi comes from Pierre Fournier, who rejects Niosi's idea of a francophone bourgeoisie and assertion that it is merely a wing of the Canadian bourgeoisie. For Fournier, it is necessary to distinguish between a Québécois bourgeoisie and a francophone one. In a sophisticated analysis of class forces, he contends that "the Canadian and Quebec bourgeoisies are in conflict, and that the PQ is to a large extent the expression of a power struggle between the two fractions" (1980:68). He agrees that the Quebec bourgeoisie has grown stronger since the 1960s but says that this strength has been both "inside and outside the state," thus creating a complex dynamic between public and private capital, Québécois and external capitalists. These tensions are in turn manifest in the policies and practices of the Parti Québécois government. The debate is not resolved, and will not likely be until the present forces develop, but it does provide intriguing insights into class alliances and the nature of class politics.

Conclusion

To a greater extent than most of the writing on the capitalist and working classes, research on the petite bourgeoisie, whether in Quebec or the rest of Canada, has tended not only to incorporate an analysis of the economic position of class, but also to situate it politically and in its cultural/ideological context. As a result, these studies have concentrated more on the dynamics of class and have presented a richer understanding of the relationship between classes. They have also clearly demonstrated the presence of class-based politics in Canada and have made the subsidiary point that these struggles have most often been championed by the petite bourgeoisie rather than the working class.

The traditional petite bourgeoisie were commodity producers who entered into market relations with capitalists by selling their products or selling directly to consumers. They operated in a mode of production outside or alongside the relationship between capital and labour. They owned their own means of production and worked for themselves. Few people remain in this position today. The strongholds of this class were farming and retail trade, but these have been invaded and dominated by capitalist relations. Most members of this class have been displaced. In their place within the class structure has grown a large clerical-administrative stratum. This stratum has a wage relationship with capital and stands directly between capital and labour. To understand its political and ideological/cultural relationship with the two main classes of capitalism, it is necessary to study its degree of control over labour power — both its own and others. The critical characteristic is the amount of control they have over the use of their own labour and, related to this, the extent of their control over the disposal of the labour power of others (see chapter 9). Both major classes seek its political and ideological/cultural support. Ideologically, this stratum has traditionally placed a great deal of emphasis on the 'mental-manual' distinction with production workers, although this often flies in the face of the reality of their actual political and economic location. Politically, parts of this stratum perform the supervisory functions of capital, although in practice most are themselves closely supervised. Economically, they find their incomes declining below those of organized fractions of production workers. These conditions make this stratum the most volatile class fraction in advanced capitalist societies, particularly in Canada where its scale and political importance has grown dramatically. Often it is found floating between capitalists and production workers in its alliances. This stratum represents the greatest potential for unionization, although as a class its members often resist this for political and ideological/cultural reasons — and even when they officially unionize, they may act more like professional associations than traditional unions. There is some evidence, however, that traditional barriers are being broken as members of this stratum experience proletarianization by loss of control over their own labour power.

It is apparent that understanding the dynamics of this clerical administrative stratum — or as it has variously been called, the 'new working class,' the 'new middle class,' or 'urban petite bourgeoisie' — represents a major challenge to studies of class cleavages in Canada. There are other pressing issues remaining to be resolved. There is the difference between Pentland, Ryerson and Langdon contrasted with Naylor over the nature of the capitalist class, although some of these anomalies have been clarified here. The main difference in their approaches is between a focus on labour by the former and on capital by the latter. The society looks different at its peaks than it does at its base, but the critical point of analysis must be where they meet — in class struggle. To some extent there is also a difference in the period covered, whether pre- or post-Confederation. The classical historical work on the labour force has concentrated on the industrial proletariat and, as such, puts industrial capitalists into relief. The classical work on capital has focused on those in command, particularly the financial mechanisms of control, and, as such, places financial capitalists in relief. Each has tended, except in Quebec, to overlook the existence of a very large and powerful petite bourgeoisie, the resource rather than industrial cornerstones of the Canadian economy, and the dynamics of relations among the working class, petite bourgeoisie and capitalist class. The merit of both types of analyses is their situating Canada within the world system, both in its relationship to Europe and the United States, and developing the implications of these external relations for internal class formations.

There are other areas requiring more-detailed research. An outstanding example is the effect of regionalism on Canada's class formation. For reasons already discussed, the country is unevenly developed and has regional concentrations of particular fractions of classes, causing some of the most important class struggles to be fought at the provincial level and between the provincial and federal levels (see Cuneo, 1978). Another area, only briefly mentioned, is the relationship between class and gender cleavages. This is of particular importance because of the increased participation of women in the paid labour force but especially because of the critical position of the clerical-administrative stratum where women dominate numerically. Generally, the entire area of the new middle class and the traditional urban middle class has been underresearched and weakly conceptualized. Also in need of more study is the relationship between organized and unorganized workers. Given that only about one-third of the labour force is unionized, this raises an important issue, as does the increasingly important and related issue of the relationship between union leaders and membership, particularly as the leaders experience strong pressure from the state to restrain members in the face of wage controls.

Much remains to be done. Crucial to keep in mind, however, is just how much is already done. The revival of the Marxist tradition of political economy has given new life to a once static mode of analysis. Class cleavages can, better than any other distinction, explain the dynamics of Canadian society.

Chapter 7
Transformations in Mining: A Critique of H.A. Innis

One of the major approaches competing with a class analysis within Canadian political economy is the staples tradition. This paper seeks to directly address this controversy by demonstrating the greater explanatory power of class analysis. It does this, however, not by rejecting the staples tradition (as some have advocated) but by drawing upon its insights and integrating them into a class analysis. It is not a marriage of equals. In the following paper, the staples tradition provides the raw material; class, the explanation. A similar exercise could have been undertaken for the fisheries, agriculture, timber trade, railways or any of the other aspects of Canadian society the staples tradition has so richly explored. Mining was selected because of its juncture between commercial and industrial staples. As the next paper, chapter 8, will argue in some detail, mining is a particularly interesting subject because it is significant during two modes of production and encompasses both staple extraction and refining. If one is attempting — as I am — to build a comprehensive understanding of class in Canada, one cannot afford to ignore the rich staples tradition and its wealth of information. Its authors have been the most prolific chroniclers of Canadian political economy. But it is not simply that they have done so much work. As the following paper seeks to demonstrate, they have also provided valuable insights into the peculiarities of Canada's development and thus merit careful consideration.

Unlike most of Innis's work, his writings on mining have been much neglected, even though they include a major book (1936), an article (1956a), several reviews (1930, 1939, 1945) and a foreword (1941). In some ways this is understandable; most are obscure, laborious examinations of the most minute details of the industry, requiring a great deal of culling to yield much of theoretical importance. One reviewer of his *Settlement and the Mining Frontier* commented, "The general reader may be pardoned if he sometimes

172

wishes the author's command of the facts was a little less terrifyingly complete" (Knox, 1936:582). Nevertheless, running throughout his work are some brilliant insights into the formative stages of Canadian mining. As Abraham Rotstein has suggested, these insights are common in much of his writing: "Innis was not overly self-conscious about his style or method. But he did make tantalizing suggestions about a new economics that was needed for a non-European milieu where new settlement took place" (1977:6).

For purposes of developing an understanding of mining in Canada and generally situating it within a theoretical context, some of Innis's important observations will be abstracted from his work, while at the same time a critique and elaboration of his contribution will be offered. Staples approaches have generally lacked a concern for class relations and have made the 'character of the staple' the motor force of their analyses. An important exception to this, and one which demonstrates the value of introducing an analysis of modes of production where class relations become the motor force in transforming staples, is Mel Watkins's essay on the Déné (1977). This will be examined later, but for now it is sufficient to state that Innis has a great deal to say about the forces of production in mining — capitalization, markets and technology — as they are conditioned by various minerals. He has much less to say about the social and political relations of production, particularly how the forces of production condition relations between classes.

Recently Ian Parker has argued that "Marx's principal contributions to the reformulation and extension of Innis' approach will be found in the central role Marx ascribed to class antagonisms and class struggle in the development of economic systems" (1977:561). We would be on firmer ground by concentrating concretely on the way staples have conditioned the forces of production and in turn analysing their impact on relations of production, including class struggles. It should be acknowledged that this approach was foreign to Innis. His method was to work through the details of particular staples and accept what *appeared* to be the determinant factors inherent in the staples themselves. In contrast, it is important to bring the categories associated with transformations within and between modes of production to the empirical level so that they will assist in giving meaning to the mountains of information gathered by Innis. The purpose of this paper is thus twofold: to summarize and reintroduce some of Innis's valuable findings on mining and to offer an alternative explanation of these findings.

Theoretical Considerations

The staples thesis, as presented by Innis, is a statement about distortions caused in marginal societies by a concentration on extracting natural resources for metropolitan markets. As he argues in the conclusion to *The Fur Trade*, "Agriculture, industry, transportation, trade, finance and governmental activities tend to become subordinate to the production of the staple for a more highly specialized manufacturing community" (1956b:385). Within this, it is the character of the staple that for Innis determines the necessary techniques for exploiting the staple, such as the kind of capital structure, demands for types of labour, transportation systems and production methods. Contrary to Innis's contention, it will be the argument of this paper that capital formation and the resulting class relations offer greater explanatory power than does the physical quality of the mineral being extracted.

It is not necessary here to retrace the succession of staples, but it is important to establish that central to the staples thesis is the historical relationship between staples. Innis writes that "each staple has its own peculiar developments and its peculiar relations with other staples" (1956c:138). He argues, for example, that mineral production was "in some sense a by-product of wheat production. Railways built to produce and transport wheat were responsible for the discovery and development of minerals" (1956d:88). Mineral production, he maintains, helped defer the costs of railways and stimulated agricultural production to feed their labour force. These interrelations provide the focal point of his mining study. As Innis said, the purpose of his study was "to outline the effects of mining on railways and on the Canadian economy generally, and to suggest determining factors including overhead costs, hydro-electric power, technology and the character of ore bodies" (1936:171). This is one of the great strengths of Innis's work and the staples thesis generally: its insistence that each 'case' be integrated with a multitude of other factors and not be viewed in isolation. Indeed, the insistence that Canadian development cannot be understood without examining its capital, technological and market relationships with metropolitan nations has become the common link between the original and contemporary analysis of staples. Disagreement about how these factors relate to one another, however, becomes central. For example, Innis argues that "with a high degree of mobility of labour, finance and technique the character of the ore body assumed a dominant position" (1936:402). But the problem must surely be to explain how and why labour, capital and technology become mobilized; that is, to understand the social relations between these factors.

In another work Innis demonstrates an awareness of the plight of labour in a staples economy:

> Producers of staple exports subject to wide fluctuation are penalized by the increasing rigidities which accompany the increasing importance of the United States. Unorganized groups of labor in the industrial areas are squeezed between the depressed income of exporters of raw material and rigidity of prices as the evidence of unemployment, and sweated labor has shown. [1937: xxix; also see Innis and Ratz, 1940:353-64]

But this is not really the point. The question is not one of Innis's sympathies but of his mode of analysis. The relationships between labour and capital and between various modes of production do not have a significant part to play in his explanation of Canadian development. This is not to say that his work cannot be read with this in mind and used to advance such an analysis.

An excellent illustration of such an exercise is provided in *The Fur Trade*. There Innis argues that "as old cultural traits fell gradually into disuse and old ways of getting a livelihood were forgotten, the Indian became increasingly dependent on the products of the specialized equipment of Europe and increasingly dependent upon his supply of furs" (1956b:18). The fur trade also developed among the native people a class of "quasi-merchants," whereby the Iroquois and Huron became "middlemen [who] were able to exercise greater bargaining power over more remote tribes with the use of European weapons" (21). In the terms being used in this paper, this describes the destruction of a mode of production — subsistence hunting and gathering — and its replacement with an exchange economy, which turned some native people into commodity producers for trade. It is thus the class relations, not the staple per se, that account for social change. A contemporary illustration of such an analysis is provided by Watkins, who argues:

> The prosecution of the fur trade depended, at least initially in each region into which the fur trade expanded, on the Indian as fur-gatherer. As such the Indian was a commodity producer, not a wage-earner, and the fur trade was literally a trade, or a commercial activity. . . . he did not have to make two critical and traumatic adjustments that result from imposed industrialization. Firstly, he did not have to become a wage-earner, and secondly, which is really the opposite side of the coin, he did not have to yield up his ownership of the land. . . . Now mineral production (including petroleum) is an industry not a trade, and it needs both rights to the use of land and people who will work for a wage. [1977:87-88]

It is evident that the fur trade can be understood in terms of transformations in modes of production from hunting and gathering subsistence, through independent commodity production for trade, to its demise when in conflict with industrial capitalism. Moreover, this type of analysis provides greater explanatory ability than does the character of the staple.

On another level, differences between dominant modes of production explain changes in the types of staples. Mining, along with the forest products industry, marked a critical break in Canada's staple production. Fish, fur and wheat were *commercial commodities* geared to consumption and were gathered and produced by independent commodity producers who were dominated in the market through trading relations by merchant capitalists who in turn sold these commodities in Europe. Mining and forest products mark the development of *industrial raw materials* and penetration by industrial capitalists. The early stages of both these industries were characterized by independent commodity production — the gathering of gold in mining and the square-timber trade in forest products — but each was rapidly transformed as the products of the mines and forests became integrated into industrial production.

There resulted a destruction of independent commodity producers and the creation of wage labourers, although some traditional practices from earlier modes of production, such as the contract system, persist.

As should be evident by now, the argument here is that a more fruitful approach to the subject of staples is provided by an analysis of transformation in modes of production. It is not necessary to turn Innis into a Marxist; indeed, to attempt to do so would be to distort both perspectives. It is useful to ask, nonetheless, What does Innis have to contribute to a Marxist analysis? Put otherwise, What can a Marxist analysis gain by adopting aspects of Innis's work? Fundamentally, this means abstracting from Innis those concepts and observations that contribute to an understanding of the forces of production and developing their implications for the relations of production.

Why bother with such an exercise? Quite simply, Innis has made a major contribution to Canadian political economy and his work is too valuable a resource to ignore. More than any single scholar, Innis has traced the progression of a series of resources at the core of the Canadian economy and provided valuable insights into its movements and 'biases.' He provides a foundation of empirical observations and insights that can be integrated into a Marxist framework, even though he clearly was not himself a Marxist.[1]

For Innis, labour and capital are analysed as part of the forces of production, not in terms of their relations with each other. They both tend to enter his analysis as extensions of technology. In *Settlement and the Mining Frontier*, Innis views labour from the perspective of capital; that is, simply as a cost of production that is highly variable, subject to movements of supply and demand. Contrary to Innis, the analysis to be suggested here views staples as raw materials which capitalists wish to transform into capital. Staples do not, of course, do this themselves. It is done by labour. Initially, staples are treated as commodities, gathered or produced by someone else, and exchanged by merchant capitalists, an example being gold acquired through placer mining. With the introduction of capital directly into the production process, as characteristic of industrial capitalism, labour is then performed by wage labour. This then becomes the dominant relation in the economic system. There is a dynamic in Innis's work but the dynamic is primarily external; that is, the relationship between Canadian staples and external markets. The missing dynamic, and one which complements the external one, is internal class relations. Internal class relations should not be abstracted from external relations for either capital or labour. The capitalist

---

[1] A similar conclusion has been arrived at by Stanley Ryerson. He comments on Innis's "creative work" and "massive pioneering operation in exhaustively examining some of the main areas of economic activity on which the economy of Canada has been founded" (1963:57-58). Ryerson also criticized Innis for failing to examine the class and socio-political relations involved in resource activities (62-63).

class in Canada is clearly related to international capitalism through both capital and markets. Similarly, the working class in Canada has been built on immigration and organized, especially in the resource industries, by U.S.-based unions. Thus, one needs to integrate the external and internal dynamics — the struggle between classes in Canada and the struggle of Canada within the world system. The forces of production — capital, markets and technology — are related by Innis to the relationship between Canadian resources and the demands for these resources, but it is equally important to analyse how these factors condition relations of production in the movement from petty commodity production to capitalist production and, within capitalist production, from entrepreneurial to corporate capitalism.

The staples thesis places paramount importance on the technology necessary to extract raw materials from nature and move them to markets. It is equally important, however, to recognize that the resulting "technical division of labour" is infused with relations resulting from the "social division of labour."[2] There results conflict, as Marx argued, "between the material development of production and its social form" (1967:884).

Equipment or machinery is not necessarily capitalist; it becomes so only under certain social relations. For example, a sluice box is as easily the equipment of petty commodity producers as the capital of a capitalist. It is reasonable to assume, however, that once the equipment or machinery reaches a certain scale, requiring more than a handful of men to operate and large sums to purchase, such as a mechanical dredge, then it can no longer be utilized under petty commodity class relations. It must either become the common property of all those using it as in cooperative ownership, an unusual development under capitalist-dominated social relations, or, more likely, it will become the property of capitalists, who in turn employ the labour power of others to operate it. The experience of capitalism has been that petty commodity relations are unable to sustain the competition of capitalist relations and are absorbed, with most of the actors becoming proletarian. This means offering only their labour power for sale, rather than the commodities they produce. There also tend to be tangential developments. For example, the more costly instruments of production (equipment or machinery) are themselves products of labour by other than those directly engaged in mining and thus create a capitalist manufacturing system to supply capitalist mining, albeit not necessarily in the country where they will be utilized.

---

[2]Wright argues that "the technical division of labour represents structural positions derived from the particular technologies used in production (or forces of production), whereas the social division of labour is derived from the social organization of production (or relations of production)" (1978:37).

Under petty commodity production (as in all modes of production), it is necessary to obtain subsistence, such as food and shelter. In agrarian petty commodity production, this class tends to produce much of its own food and construct its own shelter. In mining, petty commodity producers are likely to construct their own shelter but usually rely on others for supplies. These supplies are by and large sold by shopkeepers, other members of the petite bourgeoisie. Under capitalist production, all of these activities tend to be drawn into capitalist relations.

In Canada the historical moment of petty commodity production in mining was quite short. Part of the reason for the speed of its demise was the prior existence elsewhere of capitalist mining, which rapidly penetrated this new activity in Canada, sometimes directly through branch plants and sometimes mediated by indigenous capitalists expanding their activities. At first, simple commodity producers worked alone or in pairs, using handicraft methods to obtain precious metals. They first met capitalists in a trading relationship, exchanging precious metals for cash. Cash was then used in consumption, with those selling supplies also turning cash into capital. Early miners relied on savings (or deferred consumption) as a means of becoming capitalists themselves. Many failed, but some succeeded. Most often it was outside (either central Canadian or foreign) capitalists who took advantage of the transition.

Central to the transition from petty commodity to capitalist production is the relationship between capital and technology, since the transformation typically involves increased use of technology (or 'stored-up' labour) to replace 'living' labour. It is important to establish the nature of this relationship. It requires large amounts of capital to develop and, more importantly, implement sophisticated technology in large-scale capitalist production. Since only the largest capitalists have access to such large capital pools, either internally generated or from outside financial sources, they tend to monopolize the benefits of technological advance. This undercuts the relative productivity of small firms and inhibits the emergence of others.

As already suggested, it is necessary for capitalists to dominate petty commodity producers for two reasons: first, for access to their valued resources, such as land, mineral rights, or markets; and, second, for access to their labour power. Thus, the capitalist class continually dominates, displaces and integrates petty commodity producers, either as labourers (wage labour) or as managers of their enterprises (salary labour) to perform some of the tasks of capital in overseeing the process of production. The petty commodity producer can be dominated in several ways, such as in the capital market, the commodity market, the capital goods market (cost of machinery), access or rights to land (the state), or by transportation charges. In Canada the state has had a particularly active role in facilitating this domination and the rapid creation of highly concentrated corporations in command of mining. Innis underplays the centrality of the state in this transformation and fails to analyse the state as an institution reflecting the class struggles of society.[3]

Various processes and transformations of the forces and relations of production have been discussed theoretically. It is now appropriate to make concrete application of this to transformations of mining in Canada, relying largely on the work of Innis.

The Unfolding of Canadian Mining

In *Settlement and the Mining Frontier,* Innis's approach was to take a "sample" of "regions with widely divergent characteristics," including the Yukon (placer mining of gold), the Kootenays (lode mining of gold, copper, lead and zinc) and northern Ontario (lode mining of gold, silver and copper), and deal with each during its formative stages (1936:171). The major omission from this sample is coal mining. Innis has some comments on coal mining in the West as it affects developments in the Kootenays, but very little on the actual nature of production. His failure to discuss the many dramatic class conflicts in coal mining is a major omission. It would be beyond the scope of this paper to comment extensively on these operations and struggles, but there is some value in briefly reviewing aspects of the relationship between capital and labour in the coal industry.[4]

East and West: Coal Mining

Coal miners have been among the most militant workers in Canada and among the first to unionize. The coal miners of Nova Scotia formed the Provincial Workmen's Association in 1879 and led important strikes in 1904 and 1907. The struggles of Alberta coal miners in 1906 precipitated implementation of the Industrial Disputes Investigation Act of 1907, and the Western Federation of Miners, active since 1895, were avid supporters of

---

[3]In a detailed analysis of Canadian state actions facilitating capital accumulation in the resource sector, Melissa Clark has demonstrated its active role in patent legislation, facilitating foreign markets, tariff concessions and encouragement of foreign capital. This intervention by the state has most often benefited dominant capitalists over smaller ones and both over the working class (1980). Innis does, however, make an important observation on federal-provincial conflicts in the mining industry when he says "the political and economic structure of the federation of Canada with its emphasis on coal and iron, rigid debts and protectionism has tended to conflict with the political and economic structure of the provinces with their emphasis on the new industrialism of hydro-electric power, oil and minerals. The results have been evident in the financial and labour problems of the iron and steel, coal mining and railroad industries, of federal debts and of interprovincial and international constitutional stalemates" (1941:xiv).

[4]Also see David Frank, 1976, and S.D. Hanson, 1975. Bill Moore has done a review of pre-Klondike mining in Canada, as well as an analysis of three modes of production in mining from an international perspective: feudal, petty commodity and capitalist (1978). The most notable event in the mining industry after Innis wrote occurred in Asbestos, Quebec, 1949; see Trudeau, 1974.

the Industrial Workers of the World after its formation in 1906. Dramatic evidence of their militancy is evident in the fact that coal miners in Canada, representing under 2 per cent of all non-agricultural workers, accounted for 42 per cent of the time lost due to strikes between 1900 and 1913 and 53 per cent of the time lost between 1921 and 1929.[5]

Part of the Royal Commission on Relations of Labour and Capital of 1889 concentrated on Maritime coal miners, and the commission's report provides a good source of information on the social relations of production in that industry. One mine, Springhill Mines, Nova Scotia, employed about 1,500 people at the time, including about 150 boys. The boys, who drove horses pulling boxes of coal, loaded and unloaded boxes, and opened traps in the mine, were paid from 45¢ to 80¢ for a ten-hour day. The men, however, worked on a different system. Coal cutters worked in pairs, removing the coal from the face of a drift and were paid by the box. While the company furnished the tools they worked with, the cutters had to pay for their own powder and hire a loader to put the coal into boxes. Besides the loader, who was paid from the cutters' income, the miners also collectively employed a checkweighman to oversee the company's weigher and report any irregularities back to them, since they were regularly docked for too much rock or underweight boxes. This system involved time as well as contract work. The company required the miners to work complete shifts and not stop when they felt they had done enough work for that day (see Royal Commission on the Relations of Labour and Capital 1889, 1973:404-42). This form of work is obviously a transition between petty commodity production and wage labour, involving elements of each type, but is clearly dominated by capitalist relations. The contract system common in early mining took two forms. One was 'tut-work,' where miners were paid by the amount of ground they cut, and the other 'tribute-work,' where miners were paid by the value of dressed ore. A substantially revised form of contract work remains prevalent in mining today but now takes the form of a bonus system above an hourly wage.

In his review of Vancouver Island coal mines, Bill Moore comments that

> like the coal mines of Nova Scotia, the mines on Vancouver Island were worked under a system of contract similar to the tribute and tutwork systems since the miners were paid by the ton or yard while having to pay for the powder which they used. In the late 1870s, wages were $1.20 per ton, then were slashed to $1.00 per ton, resulting in a strike by the miners; however, this was not the first, and certainly would be followed by numerous more strikes. This system of contract continued in use into the twentieth century, since it was a central issue in the coal miners' strikes in 1913 and 1917, along with the issue of union recognition. The miners had

---

[5]See Jamieson, 1968:95, 197; there is an account of some of these strikes in Innis and Ratz, 1940:359.

managed, however, to win by this time a minimum day rate of $3.00 per day, regardless of the tonnage produced or yardage mined. [1978:200-201]

As is evident, the method of payment in the early mines was quite complex and had not yet evolved into primarily wage labour. Moreover, these early mines were for the most part quite small, averaging between twenty-five and forty men using hand drills and little equipment besides steam-powered drainage pumps and hoists (see Moore, 1978:205).

Saskatchewan miners in the Souris coalfields, numbering over six hundred in 1931 working in a dozen deep-seam mines, were employed under conditions similar to those prevailing in Nova Scotia and Vancouver Island. Their pay consisted of a daily wage plus payment for timbering and the weight of coal mined, but the cost of blasting powder was deducted from their income. The nature of the coal industry in Saskatchewan did, however, create important differences with other regions. The work was seasonal with the mines operating only during the late fall and winter months because the major market was for domestic use, thus providing little demand outside the cold months. During the long layoffs, the miners often worked on farms. In the early 1930s, this situation was upset by the Depression, which undercut demand for coal and availability of off-season work for the miners. Adding to their difficulties was the introduction of mechanized strip-mining techniques in the Truax-Traer mines, which required much less labour. Together these developments led to implementation of wage cuts by mine owners. The ensuing struggle, led by the Mine Workers' Union of Canada, resulted in a bloody clash between the miners and the Royal Canadian Mounted Police on 'Black Tuesday' in September 1931. The miners were crushed and their union broken so thoroughly that they remained unorganized until 1945. This clash between capital and labour in Saskatchewan coalfields demonstrated the bias of the state in containing labour through coercion and the courts while serving the interests of capital (see Hanson, 1975:33-35, 66, 70; more generally, see Jamieson, 1968:96).

Mining practices varied in different regions and for different types of minerals. Struggles between capital and labour were particularly acute in coal mining, as even this limited overview has shown, and were of great importance in sustaining the militancy of Canada's resource proletariat. Coal was the first mining industry in Canada to experience capitalist relations, led in part by its direct relationship to railway and manufacturing companies. Its omission from Innis's sample thus biases his conclusions. Generally, however, the cases selected by Innis provide a good overview of the formative stages of mining in Canada and illustrate the most notable systems of labour.

The Klondike: Placer Gold
Placer gold was first discovered in British North America in 1857 in the gravel of the Fraser River. The golden year of the Cariboo was 1863 when

thousands of miners flocked to the region. Many of these miners had experience in the earlier California gold rushes and were quickly mobilized. The land was common property, open for anyone to stake a claim, and little equipment was needed, since it was basically a handicraft activity, essentially requiring hand-picking of the gold, using pans. There were few barriers to entry. It was possible to pan a ton of gravel a day, although it was difficult work. The miner had simply to shake a pan and gradually wash the sand and gravel away, leaving the heavier particles of gold mixed with black sand. For fine dust, the residue was placed in a tub of water with mercury, where the two stuck together. The mercury was then squeezed out in a porous sack, and the remainder roasted to leave the gold.

Rudimentary technology was soon adapted to cope with problems of frost and underground gravel, which was frozen throughout the year in the Klondike. After locating a pay-streak by panning, the miners, usually working in pairs, would build a log fire to melt a hole in the ground, then remove the gravel and repeat this until the shaft ran to the pay-streak. They would then begin to drift a hole (running parallel) to the surface, using the same log-firing method. A windlass hoist was erected over the shaft, and the ore drawn to the surface and washed. Once a drift went far enough, a wooden track was laid and a car loaded with ore was pushed by hand to the hoist (see Haskell, 1898). This drift was then taken across the creek bed. Normally two men could hoist a hundred buckets a day, each containing seven or eight pans of gravel, for four to five months a year (see Innis, 1936:199-203). This ore was stored in a dump until spring, when water trapped in a dam above the claim could run over the ore, which was placed in a sluice box to wash out the gold. The sluice was a wooden trough about twelve inches wide and nine inches deep with a trap at the bottom. Access to large volumes of water was crucial to this method, and this problem offered the first area for capitalist penetration of the petty commodity mode of production. As Moore has shown, "Petty producers were at the mercy of the flume owners for water . . . . capitalists became the dominant feature of sluicing and flume operations, integrating the operations" (1978:203).

While the Pacific Coast had been hit by a series of "cyclones," as Innis would say, the most turbulent rush came in Dawson in 1896-98. Dawson, in January 1898, had some five thousand inhabitants; by mid-summer there were over twenty-one thousand. The lateness of its discovery is attributable to the difficulty of access. The law required that each miner have one year's supplies (about fifteen hundred pounds), which he had to transport over the three-thousand-foot Chilkoot Pass and down the six-hundred-mile Dawson River. This resulted in many men losing their lives in the attempt, and over five thousand horses were lost on the Skagway Trail from Alaska. Speed was central to success for the individual miner, since the main stakes were made in 1896-97. There soon developed a speculative market in stakes, resulting in what Innis calls "pool-room prospecting." Once a mining exchange was established, auctions for the claims were held, and, as Innis notes, this "purchase and sale of claims laid the basis for concentration and, in turn with higher labour costs, for the development of the 'lay' system" (1936:198, 207).

The lay system was, like the contract system, a transition between petty commodity and capitalist modes of production. For industrial capitalism to work, there must be available a labour supply willing to work for 'reasonable' wages. Given the ease of movement into petty commodity production and the scarcity of labour in the Klondike during this period, this condition was not met. The lay system was the capitalists' compromise. With it, the alluvial claim is "let out by its owner to two or more miners on condition that the miners pay all expenses connected with the mining and washing of the gold, the owner receiving half the gross output but paying all the royalty" (A.N.C. Threadgold, quoted in Innis, 1936:207n). As the capitalists saw it, this was "a mere temporary expedient designed to meet the owner's want of capital and mining knowledge, an expedient too, of use in retaining labourers when labour was scarce." This was the most common means of working claims in the Klondike, accounting in 1897-98 for three-quarters of the claims (see Innis, 1936:207).

Concomitant with the mining activity were developments among those supplying miners. The demand for labour in constructing "roads, railways, buildings and saw-mills raised wages to the [then] high figure of $10 a day" (Innis, 1936:259). It also encouraged the development of other trades, such as tinsmiths and blacksmiths. In Innis's imagery, each rush "acted as a gigantic pump, unpredictable as to time and strength of stroke, which drew enormous supplies of labour and capital to the field concerned" (1936:176). Capitalist companies soon became established, particularly in the areas of transportation, supplies and commerce, including two banks, which established branches in 1899.

With the penetration of capitalism, the petty commodity system was undermined. The leading edge was the transportation system in the form of the railway, since it made possible the delivery of heavy mining equipment, a point central to Innis's argument. This capitalization reduced by one-half the cost of moving a cubic yard of gravel between 1899 and 1903, and most of the reduction was in labour. This meant the end of the lay system and an end to the premium on the cost of labour. The population of the Yukon fell from twenty-seven thousand in 1901 to eighty-five hundred in 1911 to four thousand in 1921, but not without a fight over the rights of access to the land essential to the capitalists monopolizing production.

During the initial rush, the claims were limited to 100 square feet, and the allocation of lands "was carried out along principles established at miners' meetings" (Innis, 1936:197). As mining companies began to acquire entire creek claims, pressure began to mount on the state, but its interest was in maximizing production and royalties, best accomplished by capitalists. Hydraulic-mining regulations were set in 1898, with long-term leases and areas covering one to five miles along waterways. Rental was set at $150 per year for each mile and a condition that at least $5,000 capitalization be invested annually (see Innis, 1936:226-27). State policy thus undercut the position of the petty producers and supported capitalist production. The miners, of course, protested the new lease arrangements, arguing they would "hand the country over bodily to a gigantic monopoly whose interest it will be to carry out their operations with Chinese or Japanese labour" (quoted in Innis, 1936:228). A royal commission was appointed in 1903 to examine the hydraulic concessions and in particular the Threadgold concession. While the commissioners rejected Threadgold, "he was able shortly to acquire by other methods the claims necessary for large-scale operations," and the overall trend toward large concessions was firmly established (Innis, 1936:268). By 1906 a Placer Mining Act was in place, but this only served to stabilize the field for capitalist firms and encourage individual prospecting, not mining. Since capitalist firms had already gained rights of control over the claims, they were free to exploit them. The transformation from petty commodity to capitalist relations in mining was accompanied by increased state activity in this industry, thus reinforcing the strength of capitalist production and in particular large-scale capitalists capable of taking advantage of expensive technology.

The mechanics of capitalization of alluvial mining began most dramatically in 1900 with the introduction of dredges, which destroyed the lay system and reduced the demand for labour. "Three men running the dredge handled 700 cubic yards of gravel in 20 hours, representing 'the labour of 156 men working with a shovel and pick'— a material saving with the decline of wages to $5 per day and board" (Innis, 1936:223-24). One such dredge cost $300,000 in 1905, thus limiting entry to only well-capitalized firms. Further savings resulted for the capitalists from the development of hydroelectric power, which reduced the cost from 30¢ per cubic yard using gas as fuel to 10¢. The Yukon Gold Company had eight electric dredges by 1913, and only a few large companies controlled the entire output (see Innis, 1936:238-39). The transition was rapid. Aided by state policies and capital equipment developed in other countries, the domination by capitalist firms was complete. Labour became wage labour, and the dominant means of extraction became capital intensive.

The Kootenays: Lode Gold, Copper and Zinc
In contrast to the Klondike where capitalist relations dominated petty commodity production, in the Kootenays petty commodity production in the form of placer gold mining had been exhausted in the mid-1870s, well before capitalist relations were introduced. There was, however, a link, as pointed out by Innis, between the earlier placer mining and the development of transportation systems in the region. These transportation systems in turn facilitated the rapid introduction of capital-intensive methods of mining,

providing the opportunity for lode mining (in solid rock). In 1887 a crushing mill was built by the Selkirk Mining and Smelting Company, and ore from that mill was exported to San Francisco for smelting. Mining in Trail, British Columbia, began in the 1880s with a smelter-railway complex being constructed by F. Augustus Heinze from U.S. Mining. This began operation in 1896. In 1898 it was sold to the Canadian Pacific Railway (CPR), which desired the railway rights. Railways became interested in stimulating mining in the area "as a means of encouraging traffic in relatively non-remunerative, high cost of construction, operation and maintenance territory, and of contributing important long-haul westbound continental traffic in the form of machinery and passengers from the industrial east" (Innis, 1936:313). The railway also allowed the cheap transport of coal from the Crowsnest area to fuel the smelters.

From a very early point the conditions necessary for the rapid development of large-scale capitalist operations were met, facilitated, of course, by generous state subsidies to the CPR. Eastern financial interests were quick to take advantage. For example, the Gooderham family of Toronto purchased the War Eagle Mine in 1897. The CPR began to expand rapidly, buying mine options in 1905 to complement its smelter and forming them into Consolidated Mining and Smelting Company (Cominco). It bought out the Centre Star and War Eagle mines and leased the Snowshoe Mine. These developments were looked upon favourably by the state. The *Annual Report* of the minister of mines commented in 1903: "This viewing of mining from a more strictly business standpoint is gradually tending to the elimination of enterprises which were not based upon substantial mines and which therefore could not succeed but by their very existence cast a shadow of doubt upon legitimate enterprises" (quoted in Innis, 1936:294-95). As Innis notes, it was necessary for Cominco "to protect itself" against the vagaries of small mining operations by assuming their control to ensure stability (1936:314). Other factors also took their toll; while the First World War drove the price for metals up, as did the lowering of the U.S. tariff on zinc concentrates in 1913, the price decline in 1919-20 meant "only the large mines were able to operate" (1936:229). The booms and busts of mining eliminated those unable to weather such storms.

Unlike in the Klondike, labour was never in serious shortage in the Kootenay region. The completion of the CPR, plus the end of petty commodity production in the Klondike, created a major labour pool. Two other factors were significant. The production facilities from the outset were capital intensive, thus requiring little labour, and the CPR was expert in importing the necessary labour through immigration. Innis notes that

> the overwhelming importance of capital equipment and technical management tended to weaken the position of labour from the standpoint of unionism and to accentuate mobility, particularly with the marked increase

in immigration to the adjacent plains area. Settlers worked in the mines for a small stake and moved on to their homesteads. Mining like railway construction was a source of cash to large numbers of immigrants. [1936:316]

Innis does not note that immigration was used in other much more conscious ways by capital to control labour. As Stanley Scott notes in his analysis of this subject, there was a systematic gathering of immigrant Italian labourers to work the smelters. He quotes Edmund S. Kirby, manager of the War Eagle Mine:

> In all the lower grades of labour, especially in smelter labour, it is necessary to have a mixture of races which includes a number of illiterates who are first class workmen. They are the strength of an employer and the weakness of the Union. How to head off a strike of muckers or labourers for higher wages without the aid of Italian labour I do not know. [1977:58]

Based on their experience building the railway, the CPR's owners encouraged the employment of Italians in their mining operations; they accounted for 60 per cent of mill workers and 40 per cent of the residents of Trail (see Scott, 1977:59). The mining companies fought the organization of labour by firing the leaders and striking fear in immigrant workers.

The initial mode of payment in the mines was a contract system, paid on the basis of the number of feet drilled. This later gave way to wage labour plus a bonus system. While organization was difficult, the International Mine, Mill and Smelter Workers were able to form Local 15 in the Cominco plant at Trail in 1916. Their first contract represented a 15 per cent increase, but this "hardly dented the inflationary rate of almost forty-seven per cent since the previous raise in 1911" (Scott, 1977:64). With labour in abundance and a relatively low demand for labour in the operations, the company was successful in breaking the union in 1917 when five hundred men were not called back to work after an unsuccessful strike. Workers in this plant remained unorganized until 1938. The Kootenay region of British Columbia proved to be an important battleground for capital and labour, and signalled the turbulent struggles that became characteristic of labour relations in Canadian mining. It also provided an important illustration of the transformation that had taken place within capitalism itself.

During the first stages of capitalist penetration of mining, there was a great deal of competition. The competitors came from two sources: *internally*, from those successful in accumulating savings from independent commodity production who transformed this money into capital; and, *externally*, through the penetration of financial capital (as in the case of Inco Limited, to be examined shortly), by backward integration by industrial capital (such as smelter operators), or by extension of corporate capitalism (as with Cominco and the CPR). Each development represented different forms of accumulation as capitalists restructured themselves through combination and merger to minimize the destructive effects of competition. This restructuring left the industry dominated by large companies better able to embark on capital-intensive operations and resist struggles by labour.

In an attempt to explain different patterns of ownership in the mining industry, Innis offers an interesting account of the important position Canadian companies occupied in the British Columbia mining industry compared with the U.S. control in Ontario:

> The dominance of Canadian control in British Columbia through the Consolidated Mining and Smelting Company contrasted sharply with American control in eastern Canada through International Nickel. American control over International Nickel was established in the construction stage of the Canadian Pacific Railway and Canadian control over Consolidated Mining and Smelting in the developmental stage. [1956a:314]

Northern Ontario: Silver Mines
Like Innis, the Ontario Department of Mines noted in its *Annual Report* of 1892 that outsiders dominated the province's mining industry:

> Ontario has been disappointingly slow in developing its mines, and what has been done has been the work not of Ontario men, but of Americans or Europeans, and has frequently been carried on in ways unsuited to our conditions. . . . No mining region can reach the highest prosperity merely by shipping its ores to other countries, and it is safe to say that until Ontario ceases to sell its ores and low grade mattes and begins to smelt and refine its own iron, steel, nickel and copper, no great advance is likely to be made. [205]

There was no boom in placer gold mining as had occurred in the Yukon and British Columbia to set the stage for Ontario's mining. The closest was the discovery of silver in Cobalt in 1903, a boom that collapsed in the early 1920s. In 1904 there were only fifty-seven miners in Cobalt, but by 1912 this had increased to thirty-five hundred. Initially, there was fear by capitalists that the silver finds were confined to the surface, but after 1907 it became evident that the veins ran deeper and older pit mines were transformed into shaft mines. Shaft-mining required large amounts of capital, skilled miners and advanced technology. Most of the skilled miners were recruited from Nova Scotian coal mines, while "back-breaking labour was performed by unskilled immigrants from continental Europe — Poles, Italians, Austrians, Hungarians and Finns" (Baldwin, 1977:82). A long, bitter strike over wages in 1907 caused many of the skilled Nova Scotian miners to leave. "In the spring of 1908 unskilled workers were reported as plentiful and skilled workers as scarce. The end of the strike was an indication of the declining importance of labour and of the increasing importance of capital," according to Innis (1936:326). While this may have been the case for the number of labourers required, it was not correct for the skill levels required of the workers.

With a desire to control labour, the mine owners formed the Mines Free Employment Bureau in 1907

> to coordinate the hiring policies of the operating mines. . . . Its stated purpose was to advance the mining industry in the Temiskaming District, to consider changes in mining legislation, to maintain a hospital in the area, and to promote a spirit of cooperation amongst the various mines in the camp. In reality, however, it was a union of the leading mine managers designed to regulate hours, wages and working conditions. By controlling both the labour supply and the type of employees that were hired, the Employment Bureau allowed the mine owners to discipline the work force effectively. [Baldwin, 1977:85-86]

The bureau proved advantageous to capital, and by 1910 virtually all mines in Cobalt were involved. This was an important indicator of the need for corporations to rationalize their supply of labour, both in terms of availability and quality. It became evident to the mine owners that a supply of skilled miners needed to carry out lode mining was critical to their operations. It was no longer sufficient to continually recruit the unemployed. It also represented a stage in the battle between capital and labour over wages and work conditions; capitalists had been hurt by the 1907 strike and sought to contain such uprisings.

The First World War once again shook the silver-mining industry. First the markets for silver were cut off and mines had to be closed, but then the price rapidly rose and the mines reopened. "The gains were not passed on to the workers whose real wages declined due to an inexorable rise in the cost of living. These conditions provided fertile ground for union organizers" (Baldwin, 1977:87). The Western Federation of Miners attempted to organize the workers in 1916, and membership rose from four hundred to fifteen hundred. The mine owners countered through their association with wage increases, but this only postponed the strike until 1919. This strike marked the end of the silver mines of the area. The best ore had been extracted and the price of silver again fell. The boom was over, and for Cobalt the future was a bust, as it fell victim to the inevitable outcome of mining communities — the exhaustion of ore and the end to jobs.

The Cobalt silver industry did have a longer impact than this suggests. As Innis points out, "Companies transferred their activities from Cobalt to Porcupine and began the development of such gigantic properties as Dome, McIntyre and Hollinger" (1956c:229). Many of the miners followed suit. In these new operations much more attention was paid to labour relations, since the value of skilled labour had become evident through the silver experience and the owners knew profitability required the mines to stay open. For example, Hollinger Mines introduced a 'loyal service' system to reduce labour turnover, rewarding workers with an hourly bonus above wages for each year as an employee. More attention was paid to living conditions, and in 1922 the company imported a hundred Cornish miners to shore up the quality of their work force (see Innis, 1936:360-62). Under corporate capitalism much of the cost of production shifts from labour to capital, but the quality of the labour required for capital-intensive operations also increases. Important distinctions within the working class between different skill levels begin to emerge, and skilled workers are able to command much better conditions and pay levels from companies. It is in the skilled trades that labour union activity has its greatest momentum, but it is a momentum whose first interest involves only a fraction of the working class. Capital-intensive industries consequently promote divisions within the working class; capitalists in these industries are in the position to pay much higher wages than are capitalists in labour-intensive industries.

Northern Ontario: Nickel Mines
Sudbury, Ontario, has been the centre of Canada's, and indeed the world's, nickel industry since it was first surveyed by the CPR in 1887 on its way west. From the outset the industry was dominated by large foreign-controlled companies. As Innis points out, "The international character of capital and technique in the mining industry was illustrated in the development of nickel mining and smelting in Sudbury. The mature development of refining in the United States facilitated competition in the refining industry of Great Britain, and International Nickel became an important rival of the Mond Nickel Company" (1956f:168).[6] While Innis has very little to say about nickel mining, it is valuable to review its highlights because it represents an important example of the early movement into highly concentrated corporate control and volatile demands for labour.

The mining and processing of nickel required large amounts of capital and access to technology, even more than required in the mountainous Kootenay region, because of the nature of the ore bodies. Quickly the companies rationalized production and the work force, consolidating their operations. Sudbury itself was not initially a mining town; rather it acted as a service centre for the small communities at the mine and smelter sites. It grew from a thousand residents at its incorporation in 1893 to eighteen thousand in 1931. "Most of the early settlements at the mines disappeared after 1900 as the mining companies centralized their smelting operations and built the permanent company towns of Copper Cliff, Creighton, Coniston and Levack" (Stelter, 1974:6). Not until 1920 did Sudbury itself become the home of nickel miners; about 25 per cent of its 1931 labour force and 50 per cent of its 1941 labour force were engaged in mining (Stelter, 1974:7).

The first smelter was established at Copper Cliff in 1888, and the first mine opened at Murray Mine in 1890. The Orford Copper Company was

---

[6]Since it was published in 1936, *Settlement and the Mining Frontier* covers only the formative stages in Sudbury, and Innis had little to add in his later works.

established in the Eastern Townships of Quebec in 1877 and began to smelt copper and sulphur but had problems smelting nickel. The sulphur fumes destroyed the neighbouring farms, and the company had to move to New Jersey, where it produced sulphuric acid for sale to the Standard Oil Company. About the same time, the Canadian Copper Company was formed to mine the copper outcroppings discovered near Sudbury. Canadian Copper used the Orford Copper Company to refine its copper matte, but found that it was contaminated by nickel. In 1889 nickel-steel was discovered as valuable for armour plate, and it suddenly became a semi-precious metal. After experimentation, the 'Orford process' to extract nickel was developed, and in 1902 the Orford Copper Company and the Canadian Copper Company merged to form the International Nickel Company of Canada (Inco) in New Jersey. Since Canadian Copper owned the best ore bodies, it dominated extraction in Sudbury, accounting for 71 per cent of the nearly two million tons mined between 1887 and 1902.

The early mines originally had a contract with the miners based on production, supplemented by a minimum daily rate. Not until 1917 was a wage system in place, supplemented by production 'incentives.' During this formative period and down through the years, the company had been plagued by labour shortages during boom times and practised massive layoffs during bust periods.

In the summer of 1903, after only a year as International Nickel, there was a scarcity of labour and the mines had to be briefly closed, since the available labour was utilized in construction. Construction finally got under way for a smelter that could convert the ore to a Bessemer matte containing 80 per cent nickel-copper. Additional refining was inhibited, however, by a U.S. tariff, and attempts to force refining in Canada met with threats to develop the newly purchased New Caledonian ore bodies. Inco continued to do its refining in New Jersey, in the company's old Orford Copper plant, refusing to build a Canadian refinery until the Ontario government, under the pressure of war, established a commission to investigate the possibility of nickel refining in Canada. The Ontario commission and the Munitions Resources Commission resulted in Ottawa telling Inco it must construct a refinery because of the salience of its product for the good of the 'empire.' Under threat of nationalization, Port Colborne was born as the location for a Canadian nickel refinery, close to the U.S. market and supplies of hydroelectric power. Construction of the Port Colborne refinery began in 1916 and was completed in July 1918, just as the war ended. The nickel industry, which had enjoyed strong wartime markets, immediately began to feel the price of peace. It closed the Port Colborne refinery in the autumn of 1921 and laid off the workers, not to reopen until the spring of 1922. In 1928, it was determined, under pressure of antitrust action in the United States, that the International Nickel Company of Canada should become the parent company, and shares were exchanged with the International Nickel Company

(New Jersey), which became a subsidiary for the United States market and sold the mill products from its Huntington, West Virginia, rolling mill. Although Canada gained a refining capacity for the nickel industry, the actual manufacturing of nickel products still took place outside Canada, thus leaving important manufacturing jobs to Inco's foreign operations.

The Mond Nickel Company had been founded in 1900, and in Sudbury it was engaged in mining the same ore body as International Nickel, the Frood Mine; through an issuing of stock to Mond, the two companies were merged in 1929 under the International Nickel name. This brought into the organization another set of operations: most importantly, a nickel refinery in Clydach, Wales; a rolling mill in Birmingham, England; and a smelter in Coniston, near Sudbury. Inco also expanded its market considerably within Europe. The company emerged with a 90 per cent share of the world's nickel market, retaining some 80 per cent until the outset of the Second World War. Born under the International Nickel monopoly, Falconbridge Nickel was formed in 1928 and enjoyed the high prices Inco was able to command. Falconbridge developed under the tutelage of Thayer Lindsley, an engineering and financial wizard. After a period when control passed between continental financial circles, it finally came to rest with Howard B. Keck, owner of Superior Oil in Texas (with the gracious assistance of the Canadian Imperial Bank of Commerce, which held the crucial balance of shares). International Nickel was until the early 1970s controlled by U.S. financial interests associated with J.P. Morgan. Today, control is in the hands of some of the world's leading financial organizations.

The next major development associated with International Nickel occurred in the mid-1950s with the discovery of nickel in northern Manitoba and the opening of Thompson in 1961. Thompson is the child of corporate capitalism at its most advanced stage, including generous state subsidies in the form of road construction and hydroelectric facilities. It was constructed full-scale out of the wilderness and from the outset was equipped with the most advanced mining technology. The third largest town in Manitoba is totally dependent upon Inco for its existence. The labour force in Thompson continues to be plagued by turnover rates of 125 per cent per year, thus creating a very mobile working class. Recruitment during recessions in the Canadian economy is not difficult, but during other periods there is a constant labour shortage. Since Thompson, there has been an important international expansion by Inco into Indonesia and Guatemala and diversification into other activities.

Today there exist several giant Canadian-based companies specializing in mining but operating throughout the world, including Inco, Noranda, Falconbridge and Cominco. From the entrepreneurial stage Innis discussed, there have emerged dominant integrated companies capable of shifting production from country to country. This, of course, weakens the position of Canadian labour, since companies are capable of supplying parts of their markets from non-unionized facilities in the event of strikes in Canada. The Canadian labour force continues to bear the brunt of the booms and busts of this resource-based industry and frequently experiences, massive layoffs, particularly prior to contract negotiations.

While the nickel industry has been riddled with periods of labour shortage and layoffs, it has not been as cyclical as the newest mining industry, uranium. Elliot Lake, the heart of Canada's uranium mines, had twelve mines open between 1954 and 1958, with an additional four in nearby Bancroft. Employment in Elliot Lake rose from five hundred in 1954 to ten thousand in 1958. By 1962 this had fallen to three thousand, and in 1973 only two uranium mines remained open, employing a mere sixteen hundred. Recently, the industry and town have experienced another boom. The 'cyclonics' of mining are still with us, and the ones blown about the most are the wage labourers employed — or unemployed — by the industry.

Conclusion

A wage labourer sells his power to work, not the product of his labour. This is the essence of the working class. Petty commodity producers sell their products and thus enter into market relations. Wage labourers enter the paid labour force where they sell their own labour power and compete with other workers for jobs. A capitalist buys the labour power of workers and puts it to work with the aid of means of production to produce or provide goods and services. The traditional miner was a petty commodity producer; often he worked as a prospector or a lumberjack or farmer or fisherman besides mining, but he worked for himself. Petty commodity production in mining was characterized by a low level of technology, little equipment, low capitalization and easy access to markets. The technology required was often not much more than sluice boxes, flumes and ditches, and the organization of work usually involved only partnerships and small groups; the labour was basically manual labour. This was true for alluvial ore bodies and placer gold where small claims could be staked. Petty commodity production in mining gave way to capitalist production around the turn of the century. A number of factors entered into this transition. The technology and capitalization needed to work underground rather than 'grubbing' was extensive; the state introduced larger claims in order to increase its royalty revenues from mining (particularly as it became an industrial staple); and the relationship between miners or those producing the ore and smelter owners became important, particularly as they extended their operations back into extraction. Basic, however, was the creation of a labour force separated from its own means of production with only its labour power to sell.

In the early stages of capitalist production, the owners extracted ore by means of tribute or a tut-work system whereby work was contracted out by auctioning it to groups of miners who in turn were charged for their materials and paid for the amount of ore produced. Gradually this gave way to wage labour, but a bonus system was retained for the volume, weight or amount of work done. The tut-work system combined elements from both petty commodity and capitalist modes of production but was clearly moving toward the latter. The capitalist owned the mine and its products; the workers worked 'for themselves,' yet they did not own the means of production (a central component of petty commodity production). Today there remains an important remnant from this past mode of payment; it is the bonus or incentive system. Besides this is the 'loose' supervision traditional in mining, where a miner likely sees his shift boss only once or twice a shift for a few minutes. The independence of the miner, the control he has over the pace of his work, and how he organizes his work are important characteristics but ones that are now giving way with advances in mechanized-mining and bulk-mining techniques.[7]

Capital's relationship with labour is ambiguous. On the one hand, living labour is the source of its surplus and thus crucial to the realization of profits; on the other hand, capital strives to minimize the amount of living labour it requires by introducing stored-up labour in capital-intensive technology. The reasons are twofold: it reduces the cost of production and hence improves profitability, and it minimizes the amount of direct control the capitalist must exercise over labour. Both reasons are central to understanding the dynamics of capitalism. Capitalists are required to accumulate or die. They must expand their operations through profit realization or be absorbed by other capitalists. At the same time, capitalists wage a continuing struggle with labour. Labour must continually strive to gain sufficient wages to sustain itself, and particularly in Canada, it must continually struggle to find a place where it can sell its labour power. These two processes are the central dynamic of capitalism. Only by placing them at the centre of analysis is it possible to understand, explain and change the course of Canadian history. Reading Harold Innis will help provide the raw material, but only once a thorough understanding of class dynamics is mastered will the motor forces be uncovered.

---

[7]This is the subject of the following paper, chapter 8.

Chapter 8
The Subordination of Labour in Canadian Mining

Following from the previous paper, this one traces class transformations within Canadian mining by using the International Nickel Company as a case study. After first summarizing the major conclusions regarding the transition from simple commodity production to capitalist relations, this paper explores the movement from the formal to real subordination of labour. Both the technical and social aspects of this subordination are examined. As with many skilled workers, miners have enjoyed a high degree of autonomy in their work. The mechanisms whereby capital erodes this autonomy are central to understanding the specifics of class struggle. The processes explored here are by no means unique to mining. Similar developments are occurring within other resource sectors, such as forest products, having occurred at an earlier period in manufacturing sectors, such as the automobile industry, and, it appears, will soon be followed with the advent of automated offices in clerical institutions, such as in finance or the state. In each case the purpose is to decrease the autonomy workers have over their own labour power and transmit control to management. Not only is the number of jobs being reduced, but the content of the remaining jobs is also undergoing dramatic changes. To understand changes in the class structure and the experiences of workers, it is necessary to locate detailed transformations under way in specific labour processes.

The past century has witnessed two fundamental changes in Canadian mining's class relations. Around the turn of the century there was the transformation from petty commodity to capitalist relations of production representing the formal subordination of labour. More recently there has been the real subordination of labour accomplished by transformations within the capitalist mode of production. Both resulted in radical reorganizations of the social relations of production and were carried out with the infusion of large amounts of capital and technology. The first change, from owner-operated mining to capitalist control, was accomplished by capitalist ownership of mining sites. The second change is characterized by mechanization of underground operations and automation of surface plants, reducing the amount of direct labour required and the autonomy of the remaining mine workers, thus increasing the direct control of capital over the labour process.

This paper will analyse the impact of technology on the nature of work in mining, focusing on the implications for the number of workers required and their skill levels. In the analysis of the first change from petty commodity to capitalist production, mining will be examined historically; for the second change, concentration will be on recent transformations in the underground and surface operations of the International Nickel Company (Inco), Canada's largest mining company.[1]

Introduction

Property relations involve a series of rights that determine control over various aspects of production.[2] Independent commodity producers control, for example, access to the means of production, their own labour power, the products of their labour, and the way they organize the labour process. With the subordination of petty commodity production by capitalist relations, these rights are eroded. A transformation results under capitalist relations, as Guglielmo Carchedi has argued, from the formal subordination of labour to real subordination. Formal subordination of labour means that only the products of labour are appropriated by capital, while the prior technological conditions of production remain intact; that is to say, "at first, capital subordinates labour on the basis of technical conditions in which it historically finds it" (Marx, 1967:310). Real subordination means that the labourer is not only stripped of control over the products of his labour but also of control over the way his labour power is utilized in the social organization of work. Workers are transformed into "collective labourers" and subjected to a detailed division of labour (Carchedi, 1975:14-16, 1977:53-55). This process is accomplished, Marx argued, by the "decomposition of handicrafts, by specialization of the instruments of labour, by the formation of detail labourers, and by grouping and combining the latter into a single mechanism" (1967:364). Thus, workers are stripped of the rights to property associated with petty

---

[1]This paper draws upon a thread of argument within my larger study, *Hardrock Mining: Industrial Relations and Technological Change at Inco* (1980), which documents changes in the technology of mining and the labour process only touched upon here. The purpose of this paper is not to provide a history of mining, or even a survey of the labour process in that industry. Rather, it is to make a specific argument about changes in the labour requirements within the industry as it progresses through various relations of production.

[2]For a discussion of this point, see the following paper, chapter 9.

commodity production, only partially eroded with the formal subordination of labour, and are left with only detailed labour to perform. Capital appropriates all the rights of property and uses technology to subject the labour process to minute units devoid of previously acquired skills.

In Canadian mining, the formal subordination of labour occurred very rapidly, cutting short the independent commodity producer's premier place within the industry. Formal subordination was accomplished primarily by capitalists gaining control over access to mining property by having the state transform mining areas from common property available to anyone to private property that the capitalists could appropriate.[3] The real subordination of labour in mining has, however, been a longer process. Control over the labour process within the mines has been accomplished primarily by the introduction of capital-intensive technology and training methods that dramatically reduce workers' autonomy and bring them directly under the control and supervision of capital. While mechanization has been the principal expression of capitalization underground, in surface operations the change has been toward greater automation; that is, interdependent control systems that involve both electronic machines directing other machines to perform predetermined tasks, thus minimizing workers' intervention, and the centralization of reporting control information. Mechanization and automation have altered the skill levels of mining workers and made possible their loss of control over the production process. In both settings capitalization has decreased the amount of 'bull-work' (heavy labour) performed, but it has also decreased the requirement for craftsmen and tradesmen within the mining industry. The mechanization of mines and automation of surface plants have been an important dimension of management's strategy to contain labour in what has always been a militant fraction of the working class. Additional strategies not to be discussed in detail here have included internationalization of mine production centres and diversification of profit centres.

In response to the militancy of Canadian labour, cyclical shortages of labour, and threats to its control over the international nickel market, Inco embarked on a multi-pronged strategy to enhance its profitability in the late 1960s. Its program of internationalization meant the development of laterite ores in Indonesia (at a cost of $850 million) and Guatemala ($235 million). Its diversification program included purchases of ESB Limited, the world's largest battery manufacturer ($241 million), as well as investments in a rubber company, a machinery company, an energy company and an investment company, all designed to reduce its dependence on the metal mines industry (hence on the workers in that industry).

The thrust of this paper, however, is to explore the implications of

---

[3]See Harold A. Innis's documentation of the development of mining exchanges and state regulations providing long-term leases on large mining areas requiring heavy capitalization in the Yukon at the turn of the century in *Settlement and the Mining Frontier* (1936:226-27).

capitalization for workers within the mining industry as they are expressed in new types of technology and the reorganization of work. The forces of production are related to the relations of production in such a way that capital dominates labour and uses technology and the organization of work to reinforce its control to facilitate capital accumulation. Production is both a technical and social process in which the social dominates the technical. Decisions governing the introduction of technology are determined by profitability (a social imperative for capitalists) and require that workers can be induced to accept them. It will be argued that the relation between the social and technical aspects of production presented here explains the development of class relations within Canadian mining.

Petty Commodity Production to Capitalist Relations[4]

In Canada the historical moment of petty commodity production in mining was relatively brief. Part of the reason for its rapid demise was the existence elsewhere of capitalist mining, which rapidly penetrated this activity in Canada, sometimes directly through branch plants and sometimes mediated by indigenous capitalists expanding their activities. The relationship between capital and technology is at the heart of the transition from petty commodity production, and the realization of capital's success was made possible by favourable state policies. It is important to establish the relationship between capital and technology. Large amounts of capital are required to develop and, more importantly, to implement sophisticated technology in large-scale capitalist production. Since only the largest capitalists had access to such large capital pools, either internally generated or from outside financial sources, large capital tended to monopolize the benefits of technological advance. This advance tended at the same time to undercut the relative productivity of earlier forms of production. Further prerequisites to capitalism are control over the factors of production (in this case, mine sites) and the availability of labour unable to seek out its own means of production. Both of these conditions were met by the destruction of petty commodity mining and aided by state policies.

The gold rushes on the West Coast between 1863 and 1898 were the heyday of petty commodity production in Canadian mining. Land for mining was readily available and only rudimentary technology was required for production. The major toe-hold of capitalist penetration occurred through the development of a speculative market in mine stakes and the emergence of a mining exchange to auction claims. This market made it possible for capitalists to concentrate many claims under their own ownership. The high cost and scarcity of labour in the area, however, prevented widespread use of

---

[4]See the previous paper, chapter 7, which explores in more detail the trends identified in this section.

wage labour. Instead a 'lay system' was created. It was a transitional form of production between petty commodity relations and capitalist relations of production. Formal subordination occurred in the sense that capitalists owned the claims but let them out to miners who worked the claims using the same techniques as before. The miners covered all the costs of production, while the owners paid the royalties and received half the gross output of the mines, the other half going to the miners. During the height of the gold boom of 1897-98 in the Klondike region, the lay system accounted for three-quarters of all claims (Innis, 1936: 207).

After the construction of railways into the region, heavy equipment was introduced in the form of mechanical dredges. These dredges allowed capital to eliminate the lay system; the premium on labour was reduced. Mechanical dredges meant three men could perform the labour of 156 men using hand methods, making possible the monopolization of production by a few large firms (Innis, 1936:223-24).

The removal of ore from alluvial soils along creek beds by placer mining encouraged petty commodity production, but such primitive techniques could not withstand competition with capital-intensive ones. Lode mining, in which ore is removed from hard-rock underground, encouraged capitalist relations from the outset because of the high capital costs involved. Initially lode mines did not use wage labour. Throughout the mining industry — in coal, copper, nickel, zinc and silver mines — a contract system of employment developed. Miners were paid either by the amount of ore removed (tribute-work) or ground cut (tut-work). In a sense, they sold the products of the mines to the mine owners. Miners worked in pairs or small groups and organized their own production. Coal cutters, for example, were paid by the box of coal and hired their own loaders and checkweighmen. The mine owners furnished the tools, but the miners had to pay for their own blasting powder (Royal Commission on the Relations of Labour and Capital 1889, 1973:404-42). Although the contract system common throughout mining gradually gave way to wage labour, supplemented by bonus payments for output above a minimum amount of production, the miners continued to retain a good deal of autonomy in their organization of work underground.

These systems combined elements of both petty commodity and capitalist production, but the direction of the relations of production was clear. The capitalists owned the mines and their products; the workers worked 'for themselves,' yet did not own the means of production. Today many remnants of these earlier systems persist in mining. There is still a bonus system distinct from hourly wages, as well as a 'loose' supervisory system, and miners still control the organization and pace of their work. Recent developments, to be discussed shortly, are beginning to strip away these remnants and complete the real subordination of labour in mining.

Social labour is created when workers are drawn together to produce as a unit, whereas individual labour occurs primarily in craft settings. Technology has the potential to socialize labour, but control over that technology by capital distorts this potential by directing it towards particular ends—capital expansion through profitability — and not necessarily towards the benefit of workers or of society. Advanced capitalism socializes the means of production but not the relations of production. The means of production are organized for the purpose of capital expansion.

Transformations within Capitalist Relations

There has always been a formal subordination of labour in Canada's nickel mines, but the real subordination of labour has involved a fairly lengthy process. This section will examine the way capital has penetrated the organization of work in nickel mines and undercut the relative autonomy of miners. These are processes still under way; by analysing mines and surface operations at different stages of capitalization, it is possible to understand the direction of the forces at work.

Until the late 1960s, there were few changes in the labour process or the level of technology in Inco's mines. Miners worked in small crews performing an entire cycle of work: drilling, blasting, removing the ore, timbering and so on. There was a minimal amount of supervision: most miners saw a shift boss (or supervisor) only once a shift for a few minutes. Prior to large-scale mechanization, the only significant technological innovations were the development of pneumatic drills to replace hand hammering, or screw-drills and slushers to replace shovellers to move ore within the workplace. Slushers reduced the amount of bull-work and were simple, mechanical blade-like devices, operated by a member of the mining team, which scraped ore along the stope (production work area) into an ore pass. Neither the pneumatic drills nor slushers seriously reorganized the social relations of production.

Since 1976, Inco has introduced over five hundred pieces of trackless diesel equipment into its Canadian mines.[5] There are now four basic types of mines: traditional hand mines, captured-equipment mines, ramp mines and open-pit mines. Traditional hand mines continue with essentially the same level of technology and organization of work that has been in place since the turn of the century. Captured-equipment mines have introduced scooptrams (diesel-powered, front-end loaders) into traditional stopes. The effect has been to enlarge these work areas somewhat, but the basic organization of production is retained. In captured stopes, the scooptrams are disassembled on the surface and taken into the work areas where they are reassembled and maintained. They replace slushers in traditional mines and increase the

---

[5]All information in this section on Inco's operations comes from the management of its surface operations and mines, union officials, mining workers or trade journals. For a thorough overview, see Clement, 1980. The research for this study was completed in 1979. Since then, further layoffs and closures have occurred with production not expected to resume in Sudbury until early 1983.

miners' capacity to move ore. They are integrated into the traditional mining cycle, and a scooptram operator (in captured-equipment stopes) is also responsible for other phases of mining, together with the driller and stope leader. Ramp mines have revolutionized the organization of work underground. In them, there is a ramp built from the surface so that heavy diesel equipment can be driven throughout the mine. Ramp mines are of two types: either blast-hole mines (like Creighton No. 3), where huge slices of ore are blasted at one time after months of long-hole drilling; or enlarged stope mines (like Levack West), where different phases of the mining cycle are performed by specialized crews rotating through the giant stopes. In both types, the number of work areas in a mine is dramatically reduced and the scale of the workplace enlarged. Rather than being responsible for an entire cycle of work, each miner is essentially a machine operator and continuously performs one aspect of the work process (drilling, blasting, removing ore, bolting and screening, or sand-fill). The final type of mine, and the one that has induced much of the mechanization underground, is the open-pit mine. Here, heavy diesel equipment is used in a surface mine and each person has a specialized task involving the operation of a particular piece of equipment. The major limitation of open-pit mining is the depth below surface it can practically go before true underground procedures must be used (only about 11 per cent of ore removed from nickel mines in Canada is from open pits).

A sense of the difference between types of mines is provided by a comparison of two mines standing side by side near Sudbury. Levack Mine was opened in 1900 and continues to use traditional mining methods. Employing 1,000 workers, the mine's capacity is five thousand tons of ore a day. Levack West, a ramp mine, has been operating since 1974, and the 185 workers are able to produce thirty-eight hundred tons per day. It has forty-seven pieces of diesel equipment for only 50 men per shift working underground, and 32 maintenance workers. Repairs are made to the diesel equipment in a huge maintenance bay built into the rock underground. Each worker at Levack produces an average of five tons of ore per day; at Levack West the average is twenty-one tons per day.

In Inco's Sudbury mines, the cost of labour as a proportion of the overall production cost varies from less than 40 per cent in the most mechanized mines to over 70 per cent in the least mechanized. Increasing mechanization is being introduced into the mines, requiring less labour and less-skilled miners to operate the equipment. The output of ore in the metal mining industry as a whole increased by 114 per cent between 1964 and 1973 and its value increased by 158 per cent, while the labour force grew by only 15 per cent. Obviously fewer workers using more equipment can produce more ore than they could using traditional methods.

The major types of trackless mining equipment introduced include diesel ore-moving machines such as scooptrams and load-haul-dumps (or ore carriers). A scooptram can move fifteen times the amount of ore per man-shift as a slusher. Multi-boom jumbo drills, in which a driller stands on a platform and uses levers to control three drills, are more common, together with another new form of drill, adopted from the petroleum industry, the in-the-hole drill, which drills 6½-inch holes two hundred feet in preparation for large-scale blast-hole mining (such as the Creighton No. 3 ramp mine). Compared to conventional drilling, in-the-hole drills reduce the drilling cost per ton from 55¢ to 24¢. Raise borers have also been introduced. These machines make eight-foot diameter raises between levels underground; these raises are used for service passages, ore passes and ventilation. Traditionally this task has been performed by the most-skilled miners, driving openings between the two-hundred-foot levels. Raise borers drill 6½-inch holes from one level until they break out through below and then draw up huge bits eight feet in diameter to carve out an opening. In 1968 there were only 10 raise borers in the world; by 1975 there were 200 (but only 25 in North America). In 1977 Inco had 14 of these machines and they had drilled thirty-seven *miles* of raises in the Sudbury area alone. Each of the tasks now performed by these types of equipment was once done by skilled miners. Indeed, drilling, slushing and driving raises were the three most-skilled tasks underground. These same activities are now performed by machine operators, who can be trained in a few weeks to perform tasks skilled miners took years to perfect.

The more equipment used underground, the more likely a miner will perform only one aspect of the mining cycle, the quicker he can be trained to perform his appointed task, and the greater the scale of the work area. From management's perspective, more mechanization means less reliance on the skills or individual initiative of the miner. Traditionally miners have trained one another in a *de facto* apprenticeship system. As a new miner was introduced into a mining crew, he acquired the knowledge of the necessary skills from those he worked alongside. After a period of about two years as a driller working with a stope leader, the miner would move into another work area as a stope leader and train another driller. Both of these miners would be responsible for the entire cycle of work as outlined earlier. With the introduction of mechanized mining, management has appropriated the training process and designed it around each piece of equipment. This training will be discussed shortly.

Supervision in the mines is ambiguous in a number of respects. On the one hand, it has traditionally been very tough. Supervisors have exercised arbitrary and at times ruthless power over workers in the past. On the other hand, miners have enjoyed a great deal of autonomy and have seldom seen their supervisors. They organized and paced their own work. In addition to this basic ambiguity, the nature of supervision has been changing in response to mechanization and to larger work areas. The transformation of the mines from many small production stopes, numbering upwards of one hundred in traditional mines, into a few large areas means that supervisors can keep a closer watch over workers and that workers themselves have less discretion in organizing or pacing their own work, since they are confined to the operation of one machine and one task.

Supervisors (or shift bosses as they are called by the miners) are themselves in an ambiguous position in the hierarchy of the mines. They are directly on the firing line between workers and management. In all of the shaft mines, they are expected to cover a very large area with many distinct workplaces — all on foot. In ramp mines supervisors have access to vehicles that can move quickly from one area to another, and the workers themselves are concentrated into a few work sites. In the shaft mines the supervisor is pressured by management to ensure production but cannot directly oversee the men's work. Moreover, a greater differentiation takes place among the miners themselves as a result of centralized production. Not only do they become specialized in one task, but the stope leader who used to work alongside his driller in a partnership now becomes stope boss, giving direction to several machine operators rather than performing the tasks himself.

In place of close supervision, mines have traditionally used a system of production 'incentives' or a bonus system. During the formative period and through the years, the bonus became an institution integral to mining. It came to be called an 'invisible supervisor' by the workers, which induced miners to maximize production. This bonus is outside the wage structure negotiated by the union and is controlled by management. In theory the bonus is a simple incentive or inducement, to reward miners for producing more ore or doing more development work quickly. In practice it is much more complex. It is a source of pride for many miners, since it sets them apart from most workers in other industries and among miners it is a measure of skill and dedication to their trade; it is also a justification for taking the risk of working underground. To the unions, it is a source of danger, luring miners to work unsafely and to take jobs away from other miners. To the companies, it is a means of social control, the carrot that reduces the amount of supervision needed. In the minds of many, it is 'what makes the miners go.'

About one half of all those working underground are on bonus. Underground, the miner still commands a great deal of control and the company relies on his ability, not just his hard work. Tradition in the mines has had it that anyone who can affect the rate of production is on bonus. This system is still evident in all underground operations of Inco, but there are important variations as a result of mechanization. The most notable is Levack West, mentioned earlier as a ramp mine, where the entire mine is on a single contract rather than a bonus geared to a crew of miners in a single work area. Other mines have had the bonus system adjusted with mechanization as the rates of production needed to attain bonus have been revised upwards, mainly because the machine operator has less control over the rate of production and is deemed not to require as much inducement simply to keep his machine functioning. When the machine sets the pace and supervision is direct, the bonus loses its original 'invisible' control purpose.

Given the great distance between work crews and management, the bonus system has been used to fill the gap. As tasks are subdivided and the coordination role of management takes on greater importance as a result of mechanization, there is a trend away from this system. Supervisors have greater mobility and workers less control over their rate of production, leading some managers to conclude that the bonus is no longer necessary. The relationship between the bonus and the skill of the traditional miner has been very close. There is not simply a correspondence between hard work and more money; technique has a lot to do with whether or not the miner will end up the month with no bonus or five hundred dollars. This has at least been true in traditional mining. What is currently in dispute within Inco is whether or not the bonus is anachronistic in mechanized mines; that is, now that the real subordination of labour has been accomplished. Levack West may well be indicating the direction for the future; the open-pit mines, the most mechanized form of mining, have already abandoned the bonus.

The way technology has been introduced and the interests it serves have been controlled by capital, not by labour. Work has been reorganized *for* the miners, not by them. To be sure, it has reduced the amount of bull-work within the mines, but at the expense of miners' jobs, not to create better ones. With the increase in mechanization, it has been possible for management to penetrate — to a greater extent than in the past — the miner's control over the pace of his work and the skills he brings to bear. Management's strategy in introducing technology has been to decrease its reliance on the skills of the miners and to minimize the number and quality of workers needed, thus increasing its control over the work process and maximizing its profits from the benefits of technology. The miners have lost in many ways — in their ability to demand a bonus as a result of their control over the pace of work, in their knowledge of mining practices, in their numbers and, all too often, in their health and safety.[6] Technology is not neutral in the struggle between capital and labour because it has been employed from the outset to meet the needs of capital, not those of labour. It has been used to accomplish the real subordination of labour and to embellish the command of capital. Technological development does, however, offer the potential to humanize the labour process but only if it is adapted in a way most beneficial to those most directly affected — the miners.

Dramatic changes in the organization of work underground are matched by those on the surface in the mills, smelters and refineries. Surface mining operations have traditionally combined bull-work and craft production. They have been labour intensive even though highly mechanized, since workers perform a great deal of detail labour, much of it directly determining the quality of production. Workers usually control the machinery they work

---

[6]For an analysis of the relationship between health and safety and mechanization, see Clement, 1980:chap. 7.

with rather than being controlled by it. With automation, the bull-work is eliminated, but so is craft production. It is replaced by dial watching and patrol duty. The tasks are no longer those of controlling machinery; instead, workers monitor equipment and make repairs when necessary.

Automation has been introduced into the milling and refinery operations of Inco on a large scale, but only certain aspects of the smelting operations have experienced automation.[7] The Copper Cliff Mill, built in 1930, has only one-half the capacity of the Clarabelle Mill, built in 1971 for $80 million, but employs 322 people compared to 235 for the new mill. Mills have always been quite capital intensive, with the older mill having an operator to maintenance ratio of 1.3 to 1. The newer automated mill, however, actually has more maintenance workers than operators, with a ratio of 0.8 to 1.

Developments in refining are even more significant than in the mills. The Port Colborne Nickel Refinery (PCNR), built in 1918 and using a labour-intensive electrolytic process, produced an average of 60,000 pounds of nickel a year per employee, while the Copper Cliff Nickel Refinery (CCNR), built in 1973 for $140 million and using an automated high-pressure carbonyl process, produces six times as much per employee, or 360,000 pounds per year. With one-quarter the number of employees, the CCNR produces 50 per cent more nickel than the PCNR. The more labour-intensive refinery has an operator to maintenance ratio of 1.8 to 1 compared to the automated plant where the ratio is 0.9 to 1. It should come as no surprise that in 1978 the PCNR was mothballed, aside from a few specialty items, and the CCNR has assumed virtually all the nickel refinery duties for the Ontario division.

Because it experienced mechanization much earlier than underground, surface supervision has always been much more direct. Workers are located in centralized operations. After automation, however, the nature of supervision changes again. With fewer workers, spread over a broader area, there is again a different form of supervision. Management does not need workers to perform constant operations; instead they need people to service equipment, to watch for problems and to be available for maintenance. Contact is ensured by instrumentation to monitor the equipment and through radio

---

[7]In the Sudbury operations of Inco, the milling operations on one side of the Copper Cliff Smelter and the refining operations on the other have been automated. Between these automated operations stands the labour-intensive smelter with 1,650 hourly workers and 200 staff. It is without doubt destined for automation, likely requiring the construction of an entirely new building. It is interesting to note that this smelter is the base for the 1,250-foot 'super-stack' which daily disperses 3,600 tons of sulphur dioxide into the atmosphere. A great public outcry over this pollution has occurred, and the Ontario government has rescinded its order to cut emissions, effectively licensing the company to continue polluting at its present level until 1982. One must wonder whether Inco is fostering the outcry to strengthen its case with the state for subsidies to build a new plant, legitimized by sulphur dioxide reductions but having the effect of reducing its demand for labour.

contact with individual workers. Workers no longer have a direct hand in production and have virtually no control over the rate of production. The real subordination of labour reaches its ultimate form: capital can directly control production by controlling instrumentation.

Mechanization underground and automation of surface operations have dramatically reduced Inco's labour requirements. From 1972 to 1979 the size of union locals at Inco shrank from 2,800 to 750 at Local 6200 at Port Colborne; from 18,500 to 11,100 at Local 6500 in Sudbury; and from 2,910 to 2,250 at Local 6616 in Thompson.[8] There was an overall decline of hourly paid workers by 42 per cent. Not only has there been a drastic reduction in the number of workers required, there has also been a decline in the quality of labour required by new labour processes. As the full implications of capitalization work themselves through the entire Canadian operations of Inco, it can be anticipated that even fewer and lower-skilled workers will be required.

Implications of Mechanization and Automation for Skills and Training
Changes in the use of equipment in mining have been accompanied by another form of technology — 'people technology' as Inco managers refer to it — a form of training intended to meet the changed skill requirements brought about by greater capitalization and designed to give management even greater control over the labour process. The first major application of the MTS program (modular training) was at the highly automated Copper Cliff Nickel Refinery in 1972. As a result of operators being required to do maintenance work (at operators' rates), there were over a thousand grievances filed in the first year. Arbitration ruled for an expansion of operators' tasks without an increase in pay. Modular training gives management the tools for pushing operators into more maintenance work, and for designating an expansion of tasks contained in each job. The tasks themselves are simplified and regularized with the minute division of labour and standardization inherent in modular training. Since March 1977, Inco has pursued a policy of extending modular training across its entire Ontario division, both underground and on the surface.

Modular training means that each operation is broken down into its parts; these parts become interchangeable and can be arranged in a variety of ways. At the same time, performance rates and standards allow management to precisely control the performance of workers. Every process and piece of equipment is documented in a systematic way and inventoried. Production is rationalized and each task subdivided into minute parts, whether it is an operating or maintenance task. A training manual is produced for each piece

---

[8]Inco has announced a further cut as of January 1983 to 8,900 hourly workers in Sudbury and 1,850 in Thompson. The cutoff point for layoffs in Sudbury will be eight years seniority. Over the past decade Inco has reduced its Canadian hourly labour force by about 13,000 workers. Given the use of labour-saving technology, even full market recovery will not result in recovered jobs.

of equipment and is administered largely by self-learning.

The system is not yet entirely in place, but according to the MTS report outlining the program for Inco, "Many operators will learn (or be asked to learn) to do things that do not fall within their present duties" (Management Training System, 1976:10). Maintenance workers will have more manuals than production workers, but production workers will be trained on more than one manual. The unit is the equipment, not the person. In a trade there is a common core of skills. Principles and techniques are learned, and these are then adapted to the situation. The training is broad. In modular training, however, the situation is determined by specific equipment; training is more immediate and 'practical' (from the company's, not the worker's perspective). The result for the workers is a limit of the marketability of their skills, hence reducing their mobility between companies and industries, unlike the wide applicability of skills learned by tradesmen.

MTS is an extension of technology and is only applicable to highly mechanized and automated tasks. It gives management leverage in utilizing and policing the time it takes workers to perform predetermined and measured tasks. A person can be trained for a number of tasks, and these tasks then become codes attached to the worker. Inco is moving ahead rapidly in the area of people technology, just as it has in other forms of technology.

While management has been attempting to narrow the jobs its employees perform in the mining industry, workers have been attempting to broaden their skills. This is expressed in a program known as 'miner-as-a-trade.' The intent is to certify miners as in trades such as plumbing and mechanics that require 'tickets' to practice. Miners have been certified in several European countries since 1951, but the first program in North America began in January 1975 in Manitoba. The apprenticeship is over a three-year period and requires eight weeks of school a year, with the rest of the time spent working in specified areas. The mining companies were reluctant to become involved, but the program was implemented by the New Democratic government because of union pressure. 'Grandfather' tickets were issued to about three hundred experienced miners with four or more years of mining in 1975, but the program was not made compulsory, denying the essential exclusive quality of traditional apprenticeship practices. Miners in Ontario have not yet been successful in having the program implemented.

Miner-as-a-trade in its present form is not going to revolutionize the industry. As present it is a mere drop in the bucket. In 1977 the first graduates completed the course; there were only six of them. There are only about twenty people currently enrolled in the apprenticeship program at Inco's Thompson operation. As long as it is not a prerequisite to being a miner, there is little possibility that miner-as-a-trade will counteract the tendencies of fragmented labour inherent in mechanization and MTS as Inco is implementing them.

Contrary to the popular opinion that increased technology leads to greater skill requirements, the overall effects of automation and mechanization in combination with modular training have been the opposite. In part this is attributable to workers having less control over the functioning of machinery, but it is also the result of simultaneous changes in the organization of work and the way workers are trained. In a classic study, James Bright of the Harvard School of Business identified this trend in 1958, arguing that "we tend to confuse the maintenance and design problems or exceptional operator jobs with the most common situation: namely that *growing automaticity tends to simplify operator duties*" (1958:183, emphasis in original). Capitalization clearly results in deskilling within mining if, following Bright, we define skill as a "blending of several things — manual dexterity, knowledge of the art, knowledge of the theory, and comprehension and decision-making ability based upon experience" (187). While there has not been an increase in skill for production work, there has been in designing equipment and, in some cases, maintenance. In Canadian mining, most of the equipment design takes place outside the country, thus reducing many of the potential benefits for the skilled component of the Canadian labour force in manufacturing (Britton and Gilmour, 1978:94).

Moreover, maintenance work is itself being subjected to modular training practices that threaten the traditional tradesmen who have performed these activities. Elaborate educational systems and apprenticeships have traditionally been developed to transmit their skills, giving these workers considerable power, a power reflected not only in their higher wages but in their leadership position within the working class. Much of the tradesmen's leverage came from their freedom to change employers because of general skill shortages. Recent developments such as MTS, however, threaten to eliminate the company's need for their skills and hence undercut their power. Individuals no longer have traditional training and become tied instead to specific equipment and specific companies. Tradesmen become more expendable as companies develop means to rapidly transmit aspects of their trades to unskilled workers. Increased capitalization will certainly demand a great deal of maintenance work, but these tasks are being performed by workers trained to maintain specific equipment rather than by tradesmen. This will probably lead to a fall in the value of the labour power of maintenance workers and a diminishing of apprenticeships.

For the most part, management has been successful in implementing changes in the techniques of production and training. They serve the twin goals of increasing the ability of capital to accumulate and of management to control the workers. These strategies have been costly; tremendous amounts of money have been invested in capital equipment and training programs. But in the long term, management thinks these investments will increase their power at the expense of workers. There is every reason to believe they are right, particularly since unions, at least at Inco, have been unsuccessful in resisting these developments.

Conclusion

Two aspects of class transformation have briefly been explored in the case of Canadian mining. The first was the transformation from petty commodity to capitalist production. It was argued that the autonomous organization of work, craft skills and bonus system meant that all the characteristics of this form were not completely destroyed with the formal subordination of labour. These remnants are, however, disappearing with the real subordination of labour. The most obvious change in the property relations of mining occurred with the destruction of the petty commodity form, but there have also been significant changes within capitalism itself. As a result of mechanization, the autonomous organization of work and the bonus system are threatened.

The quality of labour required to operate and maintain a traditional electrolytic refinery differs from that required for an automated carbonyl process refinery. There is not a mere mechanical relationship. On the one side, capitalists seek to minimize their variable costs in the form of labour and maximize their fixed costs in capital, thus reducing the amount of labour required. On the other side, labour struggles against its own elimination and against changes in the demands made by capitalists. The forces and relations of production are dynamically related, each having implications for the other. The fundamental relation is, however, a social one: capital controls labour in order to maximize profitability and uses the technical division of labour as a means to accomplish this end.

As a consequence of capitalization, management strategies toward workers have changed. Underground, there has been a strong tendency to move away from the traditional 'responsible autonomy' of mining crews towards greater direct control. On the surface, direct control has always been more prevalent, but with automation, new strategies have been devised. Automated plants like the Clarabelle Mill and the Copper Cliff Nickel Refinery have different labour requirements than do labour-intensive operations. Workers are required more for patrol and maintenance than for detailed labour. As a result, there is at least the appearance and ideology of a responsible-autonomy strategy on the part of management. In fact, workers and first-line supervisors find that what they are responsible for is accountability, not decision making. They have virtually no control over the actual work process, this having been programmed into the equipment.

The effect of capitalization is to decrease dramatically the need for both skilled and unskilled labour. They are replaced by semiskilled labour. Both heavy manual labour and craft skill give way to machine tenders and those patrolling equipment programmed to perform pre-designed tasks. This is not an automatic process — labour resists management strategies because many jobs are lost and the strongest fraction of the working class, the tradesmen, are directly threatened. The consequence of the overall trend is towards a homogenization of the working class in mining. The net effect may well be a stronger, more unified class in a political and ideological sense, since the impact of these processes tends to decrease traditional divisions within the working class between operations and maintenance, labourers and craft workers, and even surface and underground workers.

Class struggle focuses on control over the production process and the distribution of the expanding surplus that technology makes possible. Having broken the power of the craftsmen and eliminated most labourers, capital can afford to increase the wages of the remaining workers and still appropriate the lion's share of the surplus. Struggles for control rather than those for wages are much more threatening to capital. The forces outlined may well open the possibility for broad-based action by workers to appropriate the means of production.

It is not the introduction of technology per se or the technical division of labour that has caused the negative effects of technology, rather it has been the social relations of production and the way technology is used as a strategy by management to minimize control by workers. As Marx observed for the initial industrial revolution, "It took both time and experience before the workpeople learned to distinguish between machinery and its employment by capital, and to direct their attacks, not against the material instruments of production, but against the mode in which they are used" (1967:429). It is no longer possible (or even desirable) to return to petty commodity production in mining. The forces of production have become 'socialized' by giant multinational corporations. The only progressive direction would be to socialize the relations of production; that is, to create a system of property relations whereby the means of production become the common property of those working them and to provide rights and claims to the consumers of the products. It may first be necessary to nationalize the mines and processing facilities by turning them into state property, but this would have little bearing on the relations of production. If there are to be equitable and just relations of production and a guarantee of the safest working conditions, it will be necessary for those most directly affected to control the conditions and organization of their work.

Chapter 9

Class and Property Relations: An Exploration of the Rights of Property and the Obligations of Labour

The following paper is the most abstract in this collection. It is also the most tentative and exploratory. As an attempt to build a dynamic analysis of class, the paper explores the theoretical basis of that concept's components. Class is understood as a relational concept derived from property, which itself is fundamentally understood as specifying relationships between people in relation to things. I am seeking to use the concepts developed here in two related projects. One, as in the previous paper on mining and the paper following this one on simple commodity production, serves as a guide to an understanding of the labour processes in a series of workplaces. The other is a way to organize the data from a national survey entitled The Canadian Class Structure. *Both projects — the case studies and the national survey — are ways of gathering evidence that allow the development of a theory of class. This paper presents, in rudimentary form, the fundamentals of such a theory. Clearly, it will evolve and be fleshed out over time, but as a blueprint it provides the premises upon which my current research is based. Important to note, as the conclusion indicates, is that class includes not only economic relations but political and cultural/ideological ones as well. Control over property rights, it is argued, is central to an understanding of the dynamics of class struggle.*

Property is one of the most basic, yet least-developed, concepts for the understanding of class. It incorporates a series of relationships characterizing different relations of production. The various *forms* of property (such as personal, communal, cooperative and corporate property or common, state and private property) each designate specific relations between people and objects. They also designate, more importantly, relations between people and understandings about the rights of individuals to the use or benefit of things. To appreciate the concept of property, it is necessary to subdivide it into its various rights and specify the relations involved.

Property is a set of rights that determine *relationships* among and between people and things. The specification of relationships to the means of production as they affect relations between people is the essence of class analysis. The core relationship in a society dominated by the capitalist mode of production is that between capital and labour such that capital appropriates the right to the products of the labour power of workers. This relationship is not, however, the sole one. Other relationships, which it is argued are specified by the various rights of property, condition this core relationship. The most obvious example is the traditional petite bourgeoisie, which combines many of the rights of capital and obligations of labour in itself through independent commodity production whereby this class owns its own property and uses its own labour power. Aside from this core relationship, however, there are other property relations into which the petite bourgeoisie enters, such as market and capital relations with the capitalist class, or intermittently into wage relations with capital, or employer relations with labour. Each must be disaggregated from the total bundle of relationships associated with various forms of property.

Crucial to understanding how the rights of property are reproduced and transformed is the existence of a state to mediate each process. Property rights always have some limitations on their exercise. As the embodiment of social relations, there must be limits, since various rights invariably interact and, as such, require means to establish bounds. The state is often regarded as the 'umpire' of these various claims. In some senses it is primarily arbitrating competing claims among capitalists (hence the Supreme Court's primary activity) and conditioning capital's right to exploit other classes. This is, however, too narrow a view of the state. The state in capitalist society has as its principal task the legitimation and enforcement of the rights of property, including the supply and containment of labour (the economic *and* social reproduction of the working class), ensuring that labour meets its obligation to provide capital with labour power. This task imposes severe limits on the state's infringement on the rights of capital. While it appears that the state creates property rights for capital, it is actually capital that created the capitalist state to enforce the rights capital has appropriated. The state, moreover, exercises the rights of state property, and an increasing part of labour enters its employ.

To perform an analysis of property rights, that is, their dissection, as complex as it might be, is not as difficult as a synthesis, for when these various rights are drawn back together in their myriad of interactions and conditioning, the clinical clarity of analysis becomes swept along by history. How can the various rights be weighed in terms of their historical significance? How do they become transformed in their reproduction? How have they been influenced by labour's resistance? How do they become simplified or made more complex? Or how can they be made transparent? These are critical questions.

The Meaning of Property
Property is a social creation (*jure humano*) that orders and maintains specific relations between people. It is not, as it is used in an everyday sense, *what* is owned (or an object) but the rights attached to ownership; specifically, it is the right to control the use or benefit to which ownership is put. In the words of Morris Cohen, an American jurist, "'Property' denotes not material things but certain rights." He elaborated the specifically social content of the concept by saying, "A property right is a relation not between an owner and a thing, but between the owner and other individuals in reference to things" (1978:158-59). It is also a social relationship in another respect. Not only is it a right but "an enforceable claim to some use or benefit of something," in the words of C.B. Macpherson. As he goes on to say, "What distinguishes property from mere momentary possession is that property is a claim that will be enforced by society or the state, by custom or convention or law" (1978:3). We are obviously referring to property as much more than personal possessions (or chattels); it is the right to the use or benefit of things, tangible or not, enforceable by law.

Historically, property has been expressed in various forms of ownership. A brief summary of the pre-capitalist property forms has been provided by Marx and Engels (1970:34-36):

(1) [*Tribal ownership*]: It corresponds to the undeveloped stage of production, at which a people lives by hunting and fishing, by the rearing of beasts or, in the highest stage, agriculture. . . . The division of labour is at this stage still very elementary.

(2) [*Ancient communal and state ownership*]: Which proceeds especially from the union of several tribes into a *city* by agreement or by conquest, and which is still accompanied by slavery. Beside communal ownership we already find movable, and later also immovable, private property development, but as an abnormal form subordinate to communal ownership.

(3) [*Feudal or estate ownership*]: Like tribal and communal ownership, it is based again on a community; but the directly producing class standing over against it is not, as in the case of the ancient community, the slaves, but the enserfed small peasantry. . . . This feudal system of land ownership had its counterpart in the *towns* in the shape of corporative property, the feudal organisation of trades. Here property consisted chiefly of the labour of each individual person. . . . Thus the chief form of property during the feudal epoch consisted on the one hand of landed property with serf labour chained to it, and on the other of the labour of the individual with small capital commanding the labour of the journeyman.

Out of feudalism grew capitalist ownership, which itself underwent changes in its property relations corresponding to an increasing division of labour. It is change in the content of capitalist property relations and its destruction of other forms that concerns us here.

Capitalism requires the subsumption of earlier property forms by "the complete separation of the labourers from all property in the means by which they can realise their own labour," as Marx argued, for two reasons. One is the requirement to transform "the social means of subsistence and of production into capital" and the other to transform "the immediate producers into wage-labourers" (1967, I:714). This destruction turns individual property into social property by concentrating, in Marx's words, "the pigmy property of the many into the huge property of the few" (762). By divorcing labour from ownership of its means of production, it is transformed into wage labour capable of reproducing itself only by selling its labour power to capitalists, who own the means of production. Corresponding changes occur for both landed and manufacturing property. Both begin to correspond to the capitalist mode of production.

All forms of property under the capitalist mode of production are not capitalist, although all are shaped by capitalism as the dominant mode of production. As a first approximation of basic types of property relations under capitalism, we can begin with the three distinctions offered by C.B. Macpherson. *Private property* is "the right of an individual (or a corporate entity) to exclude others from some use or benefit of something." *State property* is "a right of a corporate entity — the state or the government or one of its agencies — to exclude others, not [as *common property* is . . .] an individual right not to be excluded" (1973:123). In analysing private property, it is important to recall, as Marx argued, there are "two very different kinds of private property, of which one rests on the producers' own labour [and] the other on the employment of the . . . labour of others . . . the latter not only is the direct antithesis of the former, but absolutely grows on its tomb only" (1967, I:765). This distinction within private property is, as will be argued later, the essential criterion separating the traditional petite bourgeoisie and the capitalist class (at the economic level).

State property arises, according to Macpherson, because the capitalist market fails to meet the necessary conditions of allocation. He points, for example, to transportation and communications "facilities necessary for, but not profitable to, private enterprise" (1973:134), and we could readily add a range of social welfare activities such as hospitals and schools.[1] The state as an employer has adopted the *form* of capitalist relations and, as controller of state property, sets up similar relationships with labour to those used by capital.

It is crucial to correctly locate the state in our understanding of property,

---

[1]State property is used in two distinguishable ways: to gain revenues and to meet *politically defined* needs. The latter may be the social welfare needs of its citizens or the need to subsidize private capital. In either case, the administration of state property, as with private property, is designed to maximize the labour power of its workers and does not endow them with the rights of property (with the exception, of course, of the new petite bourgeoisie).

particularly to distinguish state from common property and specify the relationship between the state and private property. Macpherson convincingly argues that "the state indeed creates and enforces the right which each individual has in the things the state declares to be for common use [i.e., common property]. But so does the state create and enforce the exclusive rights which are private property. . . . The state *creates* the rights, individuals *have* the rights." And he quickly adds, corporate property (which is the recognized rights of a group) is an extension of individual property.[2] The key, as far as state property is concerned, is that it "consists of rights which the state has not only created but has kept for itself" (178:4-5). There is no essential contradiction between state and private property. Both are hierarchically organized such that those claiming the property rights have what will later be referred to as economic ownership and possession, while those excluded have the obligation to labour. The only contradiction appears between these two types of property and common property; that is, the right not to be excluded, which undermines an essential quality of state and private property, since everyone can claim the use and benefit of this form of property.

A thorough discussion of state property and the class relations established as its result would take us too far afield for present purposes, although the conclusion would be that at the socio-economic level classes in the state correspond to those under capitalist property relations (see Carchedi, 1977). It is important, however, to further discuss the relationship between the state and private property.

It is the dictum of Montesquieu that "by political laws we acquire liberty and by civil law property" (quoted in Cohen, 1978:155). The contradictions between liberty and private property, however, have been posed by many theorists, namely that the freedom of the few to accumulate private property necessarily excludes the many from its benefits, hence weakening formal political equality. While the state appears to be the source of private property and is justifiably seen as its guardian, it would be more accurate to see the state in capitalism as arising to sanction private property and protect it from the antagonisms of civil society. Nonetheless, the state does have a crucial role in adjudicating and regulating the claims of property. The state can and often does regulate the profitability of particular activities; that is, it makes more or less valuable, various property rights. For example, the striking of tariff duties determines whether certain industries will likely survive or be

---

[2]Macpherson argues that "common property is always a right of the natural individual person, whereas the other two kinds of property are not always so: private property may be a right of either a natural or an artificial person, and state property is always a right of an artificial person" (1978:6). The significance for our purposes, as will be illustrated shortly, is that the rights of an artificial person (corporation) can be subdivided or delegated, hence the authority of management in exercising the rights of capital in a joint-stock company or senior civil servants exercising state property rights in the state.

destroyed by imported goods. In fishing, it determines the jurisdictions; that is, makes into private property certain territories for the exclusive benefit of those it deems to use it. It also has the power of taxation, which is the right to take part of property (or revenue derived thereof) as its own. For the most part, however, it ensures what R.H. Tawney has referred to as "private taxation which the law allows certain persons to levy on the industry of others" (1978:143).

In order to understand property relations within, for instance, the farming and fishing industries, including the positions of independent commodity producers and capitalists, it is valuable to examine the relations between the state and property. It can be asked: Is the sea private property? As far as rights of access to fish, the sea has been transformed from common to private property for the most part. The state excludes some from the use or benefit of the products of the sea, not simply regulating its use (as can be the case with common property). The licences themselves, which are 'tickets' to the amount of fish which may be gathered, the species, time and location, take on a value of their own. They become private property — the state grants the rights, individuals (or corporations) have the rights, and in the case of some fishing rights, these can be sold as private property. An important illustration of the state creating private property out of common property occurred in the initial stages of colonization in North America when the bulk of the land was alienated from the native people and turned into private property, often given over to corporations, such as the Hudson's Bay Company or the Canadian Pacific Railway (having passed through the various stages of common and state property).

The state is constantly engaged in creating or adjudicating private property rights for capitalists. Two cases that surfaced during the drafting of this paper illustrate this role. In both, the state creates the conditions whereby capital can realize itself by overcoming the barriers imposed by alternative systems of production. The first was a ruling concerning the lands of the Inuit of the Baker Lake area:

> A Federal Court judge ruled yesterday that the Inuit have aboriginal title to about 130,000 square kilometres of the Northwest Territories. In his 65-page judgment, [Judge Patrick Mahoney] said the Inuit have no surface rights. He added that on Dec. 17 he will lift the order which has restricted exploration in the Baker Lake area since 1977. . . . [Federal Government lawyer Luther Chambers is quoted as saying] "All they got was that they have the right to hunt and fish. The way I see it, the Government is free to deal with the land as it sees fit . . . to issue mining permits after Dec. 17." [*Globe and Mail*, 16 November 1979:4]

A second case concerns the lack of rights of farmers not only to the resources under their lands but to control access to these resources:

> Contrary to popular belief, a farmer or rancher cannot prevent an industry operator from entering his property to drill, build storage and processing

facilities or to drive pipelines through his fields and meadows. He has to yield the right of entry to a company that bought provincial mineral leases to explore and, if successful, develop crude oil, natural gas or coal reserves beneath the surface.

That is, unless the farmer owns the mineral rights himself. Only descendants of a few early homesteaders in what was then part of the Northwest Territories, before Alberta became a province in 1905, and beneficiaries of land grants, such as the Canadian Pacific Railway, control both surface and mineral rights. . . .

On average, a well site would earn the farmer $3,000 to $5,000 in a once-only lump sum payment. If found productive the completed well — fenced off and with a service road — would be worth up to $2,500 in annual rental payments. [*Globe and Mail*, 19 November 1979:B6]

In both illustrations, capitalist mining and energy companies are ensured access to 'their' property rights (as created by the state) in the form of mineral claims. In both cases, these are claims created by the state and turned into private property, overriding the claims to the lands by those outside the capitalist class. Thus, in an analysis of class and property it is crucial to understand how the rights of property are subdivided, reproduced and transformed. The state is often the mediary and acts to enforce the claims of capital.

The dominant ideology concerning the state and property is that the state is simply acting to ensure that those who own things are able to enjoy the benefits; that is, protecting the 'natural' rights of the owners. Morris Cohen's observation that "the essence of private property is always the right to exclude others" and hence that "domination over things is also *imperium* over our fellow human beings" places this dominant ideology in a different light. As Cohen illustrates, the state's protection of property does not simply protect that property from others but "determines what men shall acquire. Thus, protecting the property rights of a landlord means giving him the right to collect rent, protecting the property of a railroad or a public service corporation means giving it the right to make certain charges," all of which ensures that the distribution of the benefits of these activities accrue to the property owner and exclude others (1978:159-60).

Property relations under feudalism involved mutual sets of rights and obligations and were limited to specific uses of land. The most important limitation was that the land was not disposable, particularly because different groups had various claims to the same land. Under capitalism these rights tended to become consolidated (that is, absolute). Contrasting modern private property with feudal rights, Macpherson says it "may be called an absolute right in two senses: it is a right to dispose of, or alienate, as well as to use; and it is a right which is not conditional on the owner's performance of any social function" (1978:7-10). Hence, the restrictions on property under capitalism are less than under feudalism, with many of the obligations characteristic of property ownership under feudalism now falling to the state to perform. The rights of property under capitalism are, nonetheless, qualified in several respects, principally that the exercise of one person's rights does not impede another's use or benefit of his property.[3] These qualifications are mainly to protect property holders from their fellows and not to ensure that the benefits of property enhance all. Property itself, however, has undergone some significant transformations with the development of capitalism.

Forms of Ownership
An important distinction that Marxists have come to accept for advanced capitalist societies is that between legal (or judicial) and real (or active) ownership. With the advent of the joint-stock company, a disjuncture became possible between what has often been called the ownership and control of corporations. It is clear that not all stockholders control corporations in which they have holdings. Indeed, for most the only claim their ownership ensures is that of revenue derived from dividends. Nonetheless, for a smaller number of concentrated owners, their claims do extend to control. This distinction is necessary to avoid the position that all legal owners are capitalists, when in fact only a fraction of owners are able to realize the *actual* property rights of corporations. The rest are *rentiers*, who retain only the right to income from their property, not the right to direct labour or the products of labour. These rights are transferred to capitalists in return for investment income. Most stock and bond holders are in a *rentier* position. Not all loan capital embodies this passive relationship. Banks, for instance, typically set conditions on their temporary 'investments' and retain the rights of possession upon default or even a voice in direction of the company (economic ownership). When sufficient capital is invested to command a say in management, then at least some additional rights of property are retained. The distinction, then, is basically between active and passive ownership, with capitalists as active and *rentiers* as passive.

Within active ownership it is possible to make a distinction between economic ownership and possession. The need for this distinction arises with the increased division of labour that occurs with the development of corporate capitalism and its expanded hierarchy of control. Since the rights of capital are no longer activated by a single capitalist or even a handful of top managers, they become collectively performed by what Guglielmo Carchedi refers to as "a complex hierarchically organised ensemble of people" (1977:70).

---

[3]This obviously has limited application when it comes to common property. Private-property owners have notoriously infringed on common property — the air and water — with their industrial wastes. The same infringement on private property of other capitalists would not be tolerated. For private capital, pollution is a way of socializing costs.

Nicos Poulantzas has defined the two forms of active ownership as follows: *economic ownership* is "real economic control of the means of production, i.e., the power to assign the means of production to given uses and so to dispose of the products obtained," while *possession* is "the capacity to put the means of production into operation" (1975:18-19). The two forms of control are directed at different levels within the firm: economic ownership refers to the activities of accumulation and investment, while possession refers to direction of the labour process. The capitalist class has both forms of ownership, while the working class is excluded from both; that is, the products of its labour and the control of the labour process. What is critical in this distinction is the recognition that possession is subject to a division of labour such that possession can be distinguished from economic ownership and thus assigned to a large number of positions within the labour process. For Poulantzas, economic ownership "is determinant in defining the places of social classes, that is to say, the place of the dominant and exploiting class" (1975:19). Possession is nevertheless crucial for determining the place of the intermediate class. The development of capitalism has meant the alienation of control over the labour process (possession) from the working class and subjected it to scientific control. The right to control one's own labouring practices, as has been the case for independent commodity producers and the early stages of capitalist relations characterized by the formal subordination of labour, has passed to the capitalist with the real subordination of labour. The real subordination of labour has been accomplished by a detailed division of labour (see Braverman, 1974). To the extent that control over the labour process has been retained by labour, it is only for that fraction of the working class still able to enforce the claims of tradesmen and craftsmen. This, of course, is a rapidly dwindling portion of the working class. The rest of the working class performs only the obligations of labour[4] and not the rights of capital. The significance of the distinction between economic ownership and possession as two active aspects of property will become evident as we begin to apply them to class relations.

Class Relations

Class may be defined at the economic level in terms of relationships to property and control over labour. What, then, is the capitalist class? Those who control property rights[5] and command the labour power of others. And the working class? Those who are excluded from control over property rights

---

[4]An important question, beyond the scope of this paper, is the extent to which labour has been able to establish its own rights both as labourers and citizens. Such rights might include minimum wage legislation, the right to form unions, or the right to refuse unsafe work.

[5]The property referred to here is *both* state and private, each of which excludes others, and not common property.

and are obliged to sell their labour power. Estrangement from their *means* of labour and the rights of property are the key criteria for determining the working class. This distinguishes the working class from the traditional petite bourgeoisie, who control their own property (that is, their ability to labour). The modern petite bourgeoisie (or new middle class) performs both the tasks of capital (including surveillance and control, coordination and unity) and the tasks of labour, thus exercising both the rights of property and the obligations of labour, even though, like the working class, it has only its labour power to sell. The working class thus includes those excluded from the rights and benefits of property who also perform the obligations of labour. Its labour power is a living commodity sold to capitalists. In so doing, labour gives over to capital control of its labour power and is subject during specified periods to the command of capital. Labour is thus obliged to obey the rule of capital or face penalties. By virtue of their control over property and over employment of the labour power of others, capitalists control the means by which capital is accumulated, the products of labour, the use of labour, and the direction of the labour process. As a first approximation, this defines the basic classes of capitalism.[6]

With the formal subordination of labour, capital strips labour of its rights to the products of its labour, but with the real subordination of labour, capital also strips labour of control over the labour process (that is, the right to conceive, design and direct its own labour). In both cases capital appropriates the rights as its own. In the first case this right is retained as *economic ownership* and in the second subjects workers to a detailed division of labour as *possession*, thus leaving workers with only their obligation to labour under the direction of capital and without claims on the products of their labour.

The purpose of the remainder of this paper is not to explore property relations through an examination of capitalist and working classes but to examine the class which combines elements of each, namely the petite bourgeoisie. It will be argued that what Carchedi calls the "functions of capital" and the "functions of labour" can be identified as the rights of capital and the obligations of labour within property relationships and that these can be exposed through an examination of the petite bourgeoisie, which contains elements of both sets of rights and obligations.

---

[6]The traditional petite bourgeoisie entered into relations of *unequal exchange* with capitalists ('buy cheap, sell dear'), whereas the relationship between the working class and capitalists is predicated on *surplus value* (the difference between the value produced by the worker and the wages paid for a worker's labour power). The relationship between the new petite bourgeoisie and capitalists does not fit precisely into either of these relations and remains an important point of debate, the most convincing argument being that capital (private or state) appropriates *surplus labour* from the new petite bourgeoisie

The first distinction that must be offered is one which identifies fractions of this class found inside and outside capitalist relations. The classic petite bourgeoisie are those who own their own property and are thus 'independent' of the capitalist class in the sense that they 'work for themselves.' This can be designated as the *old middle class* to distinguish it from the *new middle class*, which is located within bureaucratic settings and performs both the "functions of capital and labour" (Carchedi, 1977:43-91).[7] The key element of this analysis for the relationship between capital and labour will be to provide insight into the process known as proletarianization, whereby both the old and new middle classes are increasingly being drawn into a relationship with capital that destroys their rights of property — either their independent ownership in the case of the old middle class or their performance of the rights of capital in the case of the new middle class — and requires them to increasingly perform the obligations of labour.[8] The analysis will proceed primarily on the economic level, but the political and ideological implications will partially be addressed. In terms of my immediate empirical interests, I intend to document the economic processes of proletarianization identified and correlate them with their political and ideological implications. I have chosen first to examine two elements of the old middle class, farmers and fishermen,[9] who have been the traditional independent commodity producers in Canada. In the future I intend to turn my empirical investigations to the urban elements of the old middle class (shopkeepers and independent professionals such as doctors and lawyers) and eventually to the new middle class, including the bureaucratized elements of the old middle class and those performing the mixed rights and obligations of capital and labour within capitalist firms and the state. This entire empirical undertaking should allow an answer to the process of proletarianization and uncover its implications for the class struggle between capital and labour.

The existence of the middle classes has modified and to some extent cushioned the political and ideological struggle between capital and labour. The degree of proletarianization will, it is argued, facilitate the development of direct confrontation between capital and labour. Although Marx had little to say about the classes outside capital and labour under capitalism, he did observe "the continual increase in numbers of the middle classes . . . situated midway between the workers on the one side and capitalists and landowners

---

[7]Key to the distinction is that the organization of work is *individual* for the old middle class but *collective* for the new middle class; i.e., the old middle class is based upon fragmented property and individual labour, while the new middle class is located in the nexus of social property and collective labour.

[8]Proletarianization is a process; to become proletarian is a condition. Proletarianization means to become more like the proletariat in that control over one's own means of realizing one's labour is being lost.

[9]See the following paper, chapter 10.

on the other. These middle classes rest with all their weight upon the working class and at the same time increase the social security and power of the upper classes" (1956:190-91). This suggests that the proletarianization of the middle class would serve to polarize the two great classes of capitalism, thus laying bare the contradiction between them. This prospect runs counter, of course, to most analyses, which identify the expansion of the middle class with the development of capitalism. The present formulation recognizes that the old middle class shrinks with the development of capitalism but that the new middle class expands. The point in question is whether the new middle class will continue to expand or eventually begin to experience proletarianization as the labour process becomes further socialized. It is here suggested that the latter may be occurring, although it has not been demonstrated.

The traditional petite bourgeoisie, which was particularly characteristic of the early stages of capitalism, prior to its absorption into or destruction by the concentration and accumulation of capital on a large scale, includes two fractions. Those engaged in production are independent commodity producers, most notably artisans, farmers and fishermen; those engaged in service, who may be called the urban petite bourgeoisie for lack of a better term, are small businessmen such as restauranteurs, shopkeepers and independent professionals (like accountants, doctors and lawyers). The traditional petite bourgeoisie own their own property and use their own labour power with limited additional labour (usually family members or marginal workers). The ideal-type traditional petite bourgeoisie (who seldom existed) was one who owned his own means of production, controlled his supplies and directly sold his commodities or services to consumers. In practice, there has been a constant erosion of control over these dimensions, in addition to the overall displacement of the traditional petite bourgeoisie as a class. At the level of property, the petite bourgeoisie represent an identity between legal ownership, economic ownership and possession, as well as a non-exploitive relationship with labour; that is, property controlled by the labourer is the means for realizing labour. Even though it no longer accurately reflects property relations (if it ever did), this continues to be a dominant *image* of property even in advanced capitalism. It is proposed here that an appropriate understanding of the process of proletarianization for the traditional petite bourgeoisie requires a specific analysis of the *various* property rights they have held.

Questions of economic ownership and possession of property relations are critical for the traditional petite bourgeoisie, but so too are those relations concerned with markets for the commodities of independent producers (particularly since they are engaged in exchange). Also of importance is the relationship to sources of finance, since petty commodity producers in Canada have traditionally been restricted in their effectiveness as primitive accumulators of capital and hence have relied on external financial sources; also included are sources of essential supplies, which are elements of the means of production. The traditional petite bourgeoisie are subordinate to capital insofar as they relate to capitalists in the capital, supply and sales markets. Concentrated financial capital in the money markets (e.g., mortgages), industrial capital as the suppliers of instruments of production (e.g., equipment) or as buyers of their products (e.g., fish or food processors) are all illustrations of areas of possible subordination to capital. To the extent they are subordinated, they are no longer independent; that is, they lose some of the rights of property and experience proletarianization. Whether they actually become proletarian is determined by whether they lose all the rights of capital.

The persistence of the traditional petite bourgeoisie retards the development of capitalism and the forces inherent in the capitalist mode of production. The property of petty producers is, in the words of Marx, "the antithesis of social, collective property." As he goes on to argue:

> This mode of production presupposes parcelling of the soil, and the scattering of the other means of production. As it excludes the concentration of these means of production, so also it excludes cooperation, division of labour within each separate process of production, the control over, and the productive application of the forces of Nature by society, and the free development of the social productive powers. [1967, I:761-62]

The centralization of capital, which destroys petty production, transforms the labourers into a proletariat and their means of production into capital, Marx argues, and further socializes the labour process itself. The struggle by the petite bourgeoisie against their proletarianization is necessarily conservative, Marx and Engels contend:

> The lower middle class, the small manufacturer, the shopkeeper, the artisan, the peasant, all these fight against the bourgeoisie, to save from extinction their existence as fractions of the middle class. They are therefore not revolutionary, but conservative. Nay more, they are reactionary, for they try to roll back the wheel of history. [1969:57]

The key ideological characteristic of the traditional petite bourgeoisie is independence. This is the independence of working for oneself, of 'being your own boss,' and thus distinct from both big labour and big capital. The crucial economic relationship of the petite bourgeoisie in Canada, however, has been its dependence, its failure to remain autonomous from capital.

As for the new middle class, it experiences proletarianization differently but (one suspects) with similar ideological reactions. Its independence, or, more accurately, autonomy within the labour process, comes from its intermediary position between capital and labour such that it simultaneously has some of the rights of property and obligations of labour. Carchedi has argued that the process of proletarianization for the new middle class involves the "progressive decreasing of the time dedicated to the global function of capital and thus with a progressive increase of the time during which the function of collective work is performed" (1977:9). Stated in the terms used here, this means the new middle class progressively loses its rights of property, and its obligations as labourers increase. To determine precisely how this occurs is beyond the scope of this paper, but it is clearly an important political question for determining the relations of class with the further socialization of the means of production under capitalism.

Conclusion

Property relations, including both state and private property, are the axis upon which classes are drawn in capitalism. It is not a simple dichotomous structure but a complex dichotomy whereby the major criterion is the relationship of control over property. There are, however, other property relations to be considered. The principle task, therefore, is to locate the rights of ownership and hence the relationships involved in property. Only then is it possible to locate agents within these relationships. Some relationships may be 'pure' in the sense of absolute rights or total absence of rights, while others may be mixed. In the latter it will be crucial to establish the determinant rights as they affect the economic, political and ideological location of agents. Agents may 'feel' independent and act politically on this belief while at the same time be economically dependent. In such cases, it will be valuable to determine how this inconsistency is handled by agents; that is, by acceptance of a dominant ideology inconsistent with their subordinate location.

Individuals, particularly those within the middle classes, can stand in different relationships to various rights of property and can be expected to simultaneously experience a number of relationships through their position. For example, franchise dealers running corner stores, gasoline service stations, and so forth, may own their own 'property' but enter into contracts with capital to market specific products under specific conditions, thus restricting their control over their property. These types of restrictions are particularly evident in agriculture, where outlets for products, generally under the control of monopoly capital, determine for the farmer both what is to be produced and how it is to be produced; that is, both the economic ownership and possession dimensions of their property relations are restricted.

The study of property, because it focuses the study of classes on their relationships and, hence, struggles between them, must incorporate the political and ideological confrontations over the rights of property that result. Since control over the rights and forms of property is at the core of class struggle, it brings to the fore the question of class alliances. Speaking of the traditional petite bourgeoisie, Marx commented:

> Against the coalesced bourgeoisie, a coalition between petty bourgeois and workers had been formed, the so-called *social-democratic* party. . . . The peculiar character of the Social-Democracy is epitomized in the fact that

democratic-republican institutions are demanded as a means, not of doing away with the two extremes, capital and wage labour, but of weakening their antagonism and transforming it into harmony. However different the means proposed for the attainment of this end may be, however much it may be trimmed with more or less revolutionary notions, the content remains the same. This content is the transformation within the bounds of the petty bourgeoisie. [1963:49-50]

One may suspect, at first glance, that a focus on property might be in danger of economism. However, it is not property as a thing but its relationships that are being investigated, and these relationships inherently contain political and ideological dimensions. The struggles over the benefits or uses of property rights constitute the political dimensions; the justification of interests by those controlling or excluded from property rights constitutes the ideological dimension. There need not be a direct mechanical correspondence between the economic, political and ideological. To begin to determine the specific nature of the relationship is an empirical problem.

It is argued that the justifying theory of property, as used to unmask the political and ideological content of property in advanced capitalism, is one developed to correspond to petty commodity producers, or at best small capitalists, in terms of competition, free markets, the ingenuity of the owners, the hard work, the risk of innovators, etcetera. Modern capitalism continues to rely on this justifying theory (which is particularly useful for alliances with the petite bourgeoisie), but the economic structure it describes has been transcended. Nonetheless, the power of the ideology persists. It remains an important task to determine the resilience of this ideology under pressure from the proletarianization of the middle classes.

Chapter 10

Property and Proletarianization:
Transformation of Simple Commodity Producers
in Canadian Farming and Fishing

Based on the theoretical formulations of the previous paper, this one builds a more detailed analysis of the position of simple commodity producers in the class structure of Canadian society. It attempts to enrich our understanding of the dynamics of class by specifying the processes under way within simple commodity production. Traditional Marxist theories of proletarianization are placed in a different light by examining how simple commodity producers can be subordinated without joining the proletariat. My current research investigates how the process of proletarianization affects the organizational forms fishermen create to resist domination by capital. These include unions, cooperatives and associations, each of which corresponds to differing degrees or types of subordination to capital. When this research is completed, I intend to examine forms of resistance by farmers and later to study the flourishing of franchises as a way capital uses contracts to expand its control. Each of these case studies is moving towards a comprehensive analysis of class in Canada and is building upon the theoretical formulations of the last two papers in this collection.

Penetration of simple commodity production by capitalist relations can be understood as a process of proletarianization whereby former independent producers become wage labourers, thereby joining the ranks of the proletariat. There are, however, intermediate locations. To understand these, it is valuable to distinguish the variety of relationships involved in simple commodity production and to examine their erosion with the penetration of capitalism. Using illustrations from Canadian farming and fishing, it will be argued that capitalism does not necessarily fully proletarianize labour, which instead maintains certain characteristics of so-called independent commodity production.

It has been assumed within much of the Marxist literature that the logical extension of capitalism is the subordination of the petite bourgeoisie (who own their own means of production and work 'for themselves') to capital by being transformed into wage labourers. This assumption is largely correct, yet some activities (particularly farming and fishing) persist in the *appearance* of petty bourgeois relations of production. In these activities, capital sustains simple commodity production (albeit in a distorted form) and does not turn all producers into wage labourers. By maintaining a distorted form of petty production, capital is able to shift much of the capital risk and supervision of labour onto the producers themselves. Through contractual obligations and market domination, capital exercises sufficient control over production while minimizing its own capital investment and expenditure on supervision.

The limits of individual/family production are clear and have been reached in virtually all economic activities in Canada outside farming and fishing.[1] Simple or 'independent' commodity production is based on individual/family units, hence precluding extensive *cooperation* in the labour process, restricting the division of labour in society, and limiting the introduction of machinery (even though machinery has allowed simple commodity producers to expand and intensify their operations in some ways without the need to purchase labour power). These factors — so prevalent in industrial production — also have their effects on farming and fishing but are not usually expressed as wage labour.

The Dynamics of Capitalism

Marx argued that "the continual tendency and law of development of the capitalist mode of production is more and more to divorce the means of production from labour, and more and more to concentrate the scattered means of production into larger groups, thereby transforming labour into wage-labour and the means of production into capital" (1967, III:885). Why? Because capitalism requires continuous expansion in its drive for surplus value. It must continue to seek out surplus value or die. Extraction of absolute surplus value by lengthening its employees' working day has obvious limitations. These limitations are overcome by the extraction of relative surplus value, which intensifies labour's productivity through mechanization (or

---

[1]Many areas of retail trade, another traditional sector of the petite bourgeoisie, have also experienced capitalist domination, but here it is through the instrument of *franchises* such as grocery stores, fast food outlets, service stations, etc., which are a type of contract between individual owners and capitalist firms having consequences similar to the ones to be outlined here for simple commodity producers.

development of the technical relations of production). This means overcoming the barriers posed by pre-capitalist relations of production. As Marx argued, "The technical and social conditions of the labour process, and consequently the very mode of production must be revolutionized, before the productiveness of labour can be increased. By that means alone can the value of labour-power be made to sink" (1967, I:315). A necessary condition for the flowering of relative surplus value is the emergence of social labour, also known as cooperation. Alongside the introduction of machinery, it is possible to introduce labour that is both collective and simplified (a detailed division of labour). Thus the labour process must become a social process to maximize the exploitation of labour's productiveness.

As argued in the previous paper, capitalism requires the subsumption of earlier property forms by separating labourers from the means of realizing their labour for two reasons: the requirement to transform "the social means of subsistence and of production into capital"; and the need to transform "the immediate producers into wage-labourers" (Marx, 1967, I:714). There is an antagonism between individual and social property. As Marx specified, there are "two very different kinds of property, of which one rests on the producers' own labour [and] the other on the employment of the . . . labour of others . . . the latter not only is the direct antithesis of the former, but absolutely grows on its tomb only" (1967, I:765).

Much debate surrounds the emergence of capitalism from pre-capitalist relations of production and capitalism's domination of pre-capitalist relations. For present purposes, only a limited aspect of these debates is relevant.

Whether there has ever been a truly independent petite bourgeoisie is questionable. Simple commodity producers and shopkeepers alike have been subject to the designs of merchant capital from the outset, and later to the requirements of financial capital, transportation capital, wholesale capital and industrial capital. Even the earliest free peasants and artisans often entered the market with their commodities dominated by merchant capital.

There are, however, degrees of independence experienced by the petite bourgeoisie; the most fundamental aspect of this independence is freedom from wage labour through ownership of their own means of realizing their labour. Aside from this minimal requirement, however, the independence of the petite bourgeoisie has been subject to varying degrees of domination by capitalism. Even the minimum requirement has been eroded to the extent that the petite bourgeoisie are compelled to enter into wage labour for part of the year, as is the case for many farmers and fishermen, to sustain or subsidize their simple commodity production.

Under some circumstances (for example, in regard to native people and the fur trade), it was necessary for capital to create simple commodity production (thus changing the original relations of production, in this case from subsistence hunting and gathering). This development represented the *commodification of products* and established a 'trading' relationship. In other circumstances (as in early carriage makers, who were artisans), it was necessary to develop capitalist relations if the machinery of the industrial age was to be fully utilized (as in the ensuing automobile industry, where labour becomes proletariat). This means the *commodification of labour*. The carriage makers were formally subordinated to capitalism by being brought together under a single roof but with their prior techniques of production still used. Later, with the introduction of machines, they were really subordinated and subjected to a detailed division of labour. In advanced capitalist societies like Canada, the problem is not to explain the real subordination of labour, as in the industrial example. Rather, the problem is to explain the apparent persistence of independent commodity producers. It will be argued that much of what remains takes the *form* of independent commodity production but that the *content* has been shaped by the capitalist mode of production. Independent commodity producers retain *formal ownership* and *possession* of their means of production but capital captures *economic ownership* or control.

Not-So-Independent Commodity Production
The essential question for a materialist understanding of class is: How are immediate producers linked to the means of realizing their labour? To address this question, as the previous paper argued, requires an understanding of the way property rights are organized. *Formal ownership* is the legal or nominal claim some individual or abstract individual (corporation) has with respect to something. It can be distinguished from *real or active ownership*. Real or active ownership can be divided into two aspects corresponding to two levels of production. Nicos Poulantzas defines *economic ownership* as "real economic control of the means of production, i.e., the power to assign the means of the production to given uses and so to dispose of the products obtained" and *possession* as "the capacity to put the means of production into operation" (1975:18-19).

The argument to be advanced here is that the proletarianization of independent commodity producers means they retain possession of the means of realizing their labour (and formal ownership of the means of production) but lose real economic control in terms of the use of the means of production and the marketing of their products. Proletarianization is a process whereby capital progressively appropriates the property rights of independent commodity producers, thereby increasingly reducing them to performing exclusively the obligations of labour. Proletarianization is a *process*, hence it can be understood as a variable, as the previous paper argued.

Under conditions of the full development of capitalism, capitalists control the following as a result of their property rights: (1) the means by which capital is accumulated; (2) disposal of the products of labour; (3) the technical development of the labour process; and (4) the supervision of labour. A proletarianized independent commodity producer retains only the final aspect of property rights, that is, the direction of his own labour power (possession), while the other three aspects (economic ownership) are dominated by capital.

Returning to the central question (How are the immediate producers linked to the means of realizing their labour?), three distinct types of commodity production can be identified:[2]

(1) *Independent commodity production*: links the producer with capital through the mechanism of a market. There is a unity between the direct producer and his means of realizing his labour. Production is based on individual/family labour.

(2) *Capitalist commodity production*: separates the direct producer from the means of realizing his labour and forces him into wage labour. Capital directly organizes production, which is based on social labour.

(3) *Dependent commodity production*: wherein market relations are bypassed and the direct producer is compelled into a contract or monopoly relation with capital. Capital directly penetrates the relations of production by dominating economic ownership, while the direct producer retains formal ownership and possession. It is also based on individual/family labour, but only in terms of labour control and surveillance; in terms of coordination and unity, it becomes social labour organized by capital.

Capitalist production includes, because of the necessity to extract surplus value from the labour power it has purchased, control and surveillance of the social relations of production. It also involves, in terms of the technical relations of production, coordination and unity of the production process. Dependent commodity producers retain control and surveillance (supervise their own labour process), while coordination and unity are imposed by capital, thus making this form of production simultaneously individual and social.

Another way of expressing these distinctions is with the ideas of conception and execution. In independent commodity production these are unified

---

[2]Other ways of organizing commodity production exist, such as communal ownership as practised by Hutterites, which involves common property and social labour, but these remain to be theorized. It may be that in a society where capitalist relations dominate, communal ownership involves common property relations internally but private property relations externally. Cooperatives may be considered in similar terms, whereby individual ownership prevails internally while corporate ownership characterizes external relations and relations to the employees of cooperatives.

within the direct producer, and in advanced capitalist production (character-ized by the real subordination of labour) the direct producer is divorced from conception and simply executes. Dependent commodity production retains the unity of conception and execution with respect to possession (operating the means of production) but separates them in terms of economic ownership (uses given to the means of production and disposal of products).

The 'ideal' independent commodity producer represents an identity of formal ownership, economic ownership and possession, as well as a non-exploitive relationship with labour; that is, property controlled by the labourer is his means for realizing his labour. This ideal has seldom been achieved, and the clear pattern has been the disappearance of independent commodity producers. Not only have they failed to claim surplus value (thus acting as an effective means of primitive accumulation), but they have even failed to meet their cost of reproduction. If independent commodity produc-ers are unable to cover the cost of reproducing the labour power of their family, then they are forced to: (1) sell part of their means of production —land, stock, equipment—thus further eroding their position; and/or (2) enter part-time wage labour to subsidize their independent commodity pro-duction; and/or (3) 'rationalize' production, which means subjecting them-selves to control by capital (typically by specialization and entering into contractual obligations for their products); or (4) cease to be independent commodity producers and sell their means of production; depending upon the ease of entry-exit and value of their means of production, they will either retire on this income or enter full-time wage labour. Only with this final option do the commodity producers become proletarian. Otherwise they are experiencing proletarianization.

Capital's tendency to appropriate the economic ownership of independ-ent commodity producers by controlling the way production is organized and products are distributed means an emasculation of their independence. This is not, however, the same as being proletarian. Simple commodity producers can struggle against capital's domination by forming financial cooperatives (credit unions), producer cooperatives or consumer coopera-tives to sell products, to purchase equipment or place political pressure on the state concerning such matters as transportation tariffs or marketing boards. They can form associations to act as political lobbying agencies, or they can form unions to negotiate prices for their products (unlike traditional labour unions, which negotiate the price of labour power).

Simple commodity producers (whether independent or dependent) should not be confused with the proletariat proper. Possession of the means of realizing their labour is an important condition that can be expected to cause distinct political and ideological interests. The more they become proletarian-ized, the more they may be expected to tend toward proletarian interests; but they should not be expected to develop identical interests unless they fall fully into the proletarian condition.

The basis for a peculiarly petty bourgeois ideology has been explored by Jairus Banaji, who argues that

> the historical roots of all varied forms of simple commodity production lie in the patriarchal-subsistence mode of production based on small scale parcellised property and the exploitation of family labour. This connection is important because when simple commodity production arises, the economic logic of the more archaic patriarchal enterprise *continues to dominate this form of production.* The chief expression of this fact is that products are sold without regard to price of production. [1977:32]

He goes on to quote Marx to the effect that the sale of products by a simple commodity producer "appears to him as profit" because "he looks upon it as something that cost him nothing" so long as the product's price covers "his actual costs" and "a physical minimum" for subsistence. Banaji's argument is that the "devalorization of labour-time" serves to transfer value to capital. Resistance to extinction by simple commodity producers aids this transfer, since it takes the form of overwork and underconsumption. This line of argument is challenged by Jacques Chevalier, who argues that simple commodity producers do calculate the value of their labour and this value is "commodified" if not "monetized": "As for the labour power of this not-so-independent producer, it is indeed 'purchased' by capital insofar as it is a 'calculable' ingredient which enters into the products that are purchased by capital" (1980:17-18). This assumes a capitalist rationality rather than the pre-capitalist rationality argued by Banaji. It may well be that these two world views of commodity producers correspond respectively to the dependent and independent commodity producers identified earlier. While independent commodity producers may border on a form of subsistence ideology and may incorporate into their production some subsistence practices, such as growing their own food, dependent commodity producers are compelled to confront capitalist assumptions of 'rationality,' which include not only the adoption of technology to increase productivity, as will be argued shortly, but also the market value of labour power. Because they are compelled to specialize, dependent commodity producers become detached from subsistence production. Rather than resistance taking the form of overwork and underconsumption, it would be expressed as exits from dependent commodity production and entry into wage labour. The ease with which this can occur depends, of course, upon the available market for wage labour. Resistance to adversity does, however, suggest two different strategies: retrenchment to subsistence production for independent commodity producers; or movement into wage labour for dependent commodity producers. This would suggest a greater prospect for the alliance of the proletariat with dependent commodity producers than with independent commodity producers.

Commodity Production in Canada

As capitalist relations of production developed in Canada, as elsewhere, they came up against pre-capitalist ways of organizing production. In Canada these were initially exemplified by subsistence producers (the indigenous peoples), who were often transformed into independent commodity producers, and by non-native independent commodity producers who had immigrated from Europe to take advantage of the abundance of the land and rich resources of the sea. Most independent commodity producers were engaged in agricultural production, while others were in mining, forestry, furs, fishing and artisan trades. In most of these activities it was necessary for capitalism to destroy the earlier forms. Destruction was made necessary for two principal reasons: in order to capture the land, resources or markets controlled by the independent commodity producers; *and* in order to separate these producers from their means of labouring so as to turn them into wage labourers. This pattern has clearly been the dominant trend. There has been a dramatic numerical and proportionate decrease in Canadians 'working-for-themselves' and an expansion in those 'working-for-others.' Whereas in most of these activities wage labour has become the dominant relationship, in some — particularly farming and fishing — the trend is less clear.

Unlike earlier periods when most people laboured in the activities of farming and fishing, today relatively few work in these occupations. At the turn of the century nearly one-half of the labour force was occupied in these activities; today only about one-twentieth. Those who remain, moreover, have relations of production that differ substantially from those of their ancestors. Only agriculture (49 per cent self-employment) and fishing (56 per cent) remain as preserves of self-employment; in retail trade (10 per cent), construction (11 per cent) and forestry (3 per cent), the destruction is nearly complete — and *is* complete in manufacturing and mining (less than 1 per cent each). Why has this occurred in farming and fishing? What changes have taken place *within* these activities? What relationships exist between so-called independent commodity producers and capital? These are the questions the rest of this paper will seek to address.

With only minor exceptions, the market for agricultural and fishing producers is capitalist. Thus, simple commodity producers within these activities must articulate (that is, link) with capitalist firms, and they do so on terms where they are subordinate. They become, in a sense, extensions of capitalist firms, locked into 'captured' markets. Rather than being separated from the means of realizing their labour, they remain owners of their means of production. Depending upon their degree of subordination, however, they lose control over their labour process and ability to make decisions about the nature of production (conception) while at the same time being reduced to carrying out the directives of capital (execution). Ownership of their own means of production becomes an empty shell (Marx once called it "sham property"), the content of which is determined by capital; the façade of independence remains but not the content.

With the subordination of simple commodity producers, capital is able to ensure its source of produce yet is absolved from (1) the natural risks of weather, disease or stock/soil depletion; (2) the need to invest capital in the first stages of production; and (3), likely most important, the need to supervise labour. The final point is significant in several respects: in terms of the cost of supervision, of the need to recruit a labour force, of the skills and experience of farmers/fishermen, and of the willingness of simple commodity producers to exploit themselves and their families by working long hours and engaging in intensified labour. While capitalist and simple commodity production are articulated, they are simultaneously contradictory. Capital seeks to maximize production and minimize costs, yet at a certain level it needs to have the persistence of production (at least so long as other sources are not available for less cost). It squeezes but does not choke, at least once simple commodity production has been sufficiently reorganized (that is, consolidated) to accommodate the currently available levels of technology. Given this reorganization, capital has further captured 'its' producers. These factors explain why capitalist agriculture/fishing has not simply destroyed simple commodity production altogether. It has done so in areas where social labour is necessary to secure maximum production, as in the case of offshore or trawler fishing; it has not done so where individual labour can organize production, as in inshore fishing. Ironically, mechanization actually *expands* the number of activities where individual labour can operate, although it decreases the number of people (farmers and fishermen) who can participate. A dual process operates such that capital requires producers to reorganize and intensify production while producers compete against one another by expanding their operations and reducing their overall numbers.

Farming and fishing refer to specific activities and the products of these activities derived, respectively, from the land and the sea. The way these activities are organized — the social and technical relations of production — can vary from subsistence production for the use-value of the product to independent or dependent commodity production for the exchange-value of the product; it can also vary from collective production for use (self-sustaining communities) to collective production for exchange. Collective production for exchange can be organized in a variety of ways, including communal, cooperative or capitalist. Individual producers (who own their own means of production) can engage in exchange (1) by selling/exchanging their products directly to the consumer, (2) by marketing their products cooperatively through membership in a producers' cooperative, or (3) by selling their products to capitalists. The nature of exchange (the market) influences the way individual producers organize production (social relations) and the equipment or techniques they use (technical relations). It is important to keep in mind, however, that the market itself is an expression of the social relations of production. If capital dominates the market, then it captures the direct producers and does not allow them to freely engage in exchange.

Some Illustrations from Farming

Capitalist agriculture exists in Canada, although it is not the primary form. Examples include a variety of situations. Those most resembling factory production include some large-scale greenhouse operations producing year-round supplies of vegetables or flowers, some mushroom operations, and some ranching, dairy, poultry and pork operations. Each has the characteristic of the regularized use of wage labour and a separation between management and labour. Other large-scale agriculture also uses wage labour but does so only seasonally, thus calling upon the reserve army during the peak harvest periods for fruit, tobacco or vegetables. This labour may be hired directly by the farmer or mediated through labour contractors — either private or state. Harvest involves a brief period in the farmer's season, and often the labour power of the farm family is all that is used for the remainder of the year. So long as the use of wage labour is not regularized and the farm family directly uses its labour power in production, these farmers can be considered simple commodity producers. When the farmer assumes a primarily management role and relies upon wage labour to perform the obligations of labouring, then capitalist agriculture can be said to exist. When the farm family is responsible for both management and labouring, then simple commodity production prevails. The intermittent hiring of temporary labour cannot be a criterion for capitalist agriculture. The labourers themselves are not part of the regular labour force; typically, they are students or other temporary workers who cannot rely on agricultural labour as a regularized way of reproducing themselves (unlike migrant labourers in the southern United States who can follow harvests throughout the year). This is not to say that all intermittent agricultural labourers work for simple commodity producers; capitalist agriculture also relies on temporary labour pools, but this is to supplement permanent wage workers.

A key question to be asked of the simple commodity mode of production is: Who survives? The keynote of survival within commodity production has become specialization. With specialization, dependence on capitalist firms increases as does the reliance on capital-intensive machinery. Specialization is a process of competition among petty commodity producers themselves. As soon as some adopt the most advanced techniques of production, others must follow or fail. In sour cherry production, for example, it was possible for many small producers to participate as long as the major method of harvesting was by hand. As soon as mechanical harvesting was introduced, the cost of picking was reduced and those using hand techniques could not compete. Mechanical harvesters range in cost from $30,000 for a light "Friday" machine to $77,000 for a "FMC" harvester. With the introduction of mechanical harvesters, processors changed their methods of receiving cherries from baskets (as with hand-picking) to water tanks.[3] The use of tanks requires hydro-coolers (costing about $10,000), tanks themselves (about twenty-five at $150 each), tow-motors or front-end loaders to handle the tanks (minimum $3,000, if attached to an existing tractor) and larger trucks than previously required ($18,000). Consequently, the handling of the product changes with the method of production and effectively excludes those not specializing. The cost of converting from hand- to machine-harvesting varies from $65,000 to $100,000 in capital investment.[4] To invest such large sums requires specialization in cherry production and expansion of the land holdings planted in cherry trees.

Under conditions of mixed production, farmers were able to spread their labour over an extended season by dealing with a variety of crops; with specialization labour becomes concentrated in specific seasons but can be dramatically reduced by the use of specialized machinery. The extensive use of machinery, however, breeds debt and another form of domination by capital. According to the Canadian Imperial Bank of Commerce's *Commercial Letter*, "In Canada's agricultural industry farm machinery expenses are now the largest single component of farm operating outlays, accounting for about 30 per cent of the value of farm inputs over the past couple of decades" (1977:5). In addition to machinery, there has been a steady growth of commercial fertilizers and chemicals, inputs requiring purchase from capitalist firms and required by processors buying the commodities. The value yielded to the commodity by machinery or other inputs purchased by the farmer is not 'new value.' It simply transfers value added to their original production through the farm products. Thus, contained within the price of products grown under these conditions is value created by workers in capitalist manufacturing, reducing the actual value added by simple commodity producers themselves.

Even the land itself can be a means by which capital can extract surplus from agricultural producers. This is most evident in cases where capital leases land to farmers[5] who in turn acquire the right to its use for a specific period

---

[3]Only a few major processors of cherries exist in the Niagara fruit belt (Canada's main sour-cherry-growing area). Three processors do cherries on a large scale (2,000 tons), and there are several smaller processors (150-200 tons). The market for processed cherries, in turn, is also concentrated, since the main outlets are bakeries dominated by companies like Weston Bakeries or canning factories controlled by the processors themselves, such as E.D. Smith, thus limiting entry.

[4]Using mechanical harvesters, as few as three people can pick and deliver over one hundred tons of cherries in less than two weeks (the period when cherries are ready to be harvested and when processors receive them). Hand-picking would require about one hundred workers.

[5]Farmers are now often required to lease land in addition to that directly owned because the specialized investment in capital-intensive machinery, such as tomato, soya bean or grain harvesters, requires large volumes. Land is made available by the exit of farmers no long able to survive.

(hence having access to their means of realizing their labour). Even with what is normally thought of as landownership, the farmer often has a mortgage relationship to the land with a financial institution, which extracts part of the surplus in the form of interest. The financial institution has a claim on the land should the farmer be unable to meet his contractual obligations, and the same could also be said of the instruments of production for both farmers and fishermen.

Independent commodity producers thrived as long as there were local or regional markets for agricultural products. This was particularly true for Ontario. Small fruit-processors grew up alongside fresh fruit and vegetable farmers; market gardeners sold their produce through local or regional outlets; dairy farmers sold to many local dairies and cheese factories. There was a symbiotic relationship between the producer and small-scale processor or retailer (themselves typically organized by petty bourgeois relations of production). A classic example was the relationship between grain farmers and grist-mill owners who in turn sold to local bakeries or local merchants. Each was dependent upon the other and was predicated on a scattering of the means of production. This situation prevailed only as long as the markets were local or regional and controlled by petty bourgeois relations of production; once capitalist relations entered and began to concentrate the means of production, the market situation changed. The fact, for example, that the twelve hundred small cheese-producers in Ontario at the turn of the century have been reduced to fewer than thirty capitalist firms today altered the market situation for dairy farmers.

In Canada the market for agricultural products became national and international once there was the entry of large, integrated multinational companies into the processing and distribution of farm products.[6] There was a rationalization of production and specialization. Farmers became captive to their demands. Operations became capital intensive. Only the largest could survive and then only by purchasing their neighbour's land and investing in costly equipment. As a result, there was a dramatic increase in the number of farmers. Until 1941 agriculture was the largest sector of the Canadian labour force, taken over by manufacturing in 1951; as late as 1926, 57 per cent of Canadian immigrants went to the farms, but by 1952 this had fallen to 10 per cent and to less than 2 per cent by 1975. Alongside the decline in numbers was a reorganization of production.

The mixed-vegetable farmer, who grew corn, radishes, lettuce, carrots, onions, potatoes, etcetera, had more independence relative to one now concentrating singularly on potatoes, soya beans or tobacco. The mixed-fruit farmer, who grew sweet cherries, sour cherries, peaches, plums, pears, apples

---

[6]On the effects in the peach industry of the consolidation around Canadian Canners and its eventual sale to the U.S.-based multinational Del Monte, see Wallace Clement and Anna Janzen, "Just Peachy: The Demise of Tender Fruit Farmers," *This Magazine* 12:2 (1978).

and so on, was freer from market control than one who now only grows a specialized crop. Once 'all their eggs are in one basket,' they are captured. They are compelled, however, by the demands of capital and the requirement to intensify production (usually through mechanization) to concentrate in this manner. This method of production requires greater capitalization, hence greater debt. To secure financing, they need contracts with processors; it becomes a spiral of dependence, often ending in the only available exit — wage labour.

Contracts have become the major way capital can control simple commodity producers. Poultry, egg and pork producers are vulnerable to feed companies like Ralston Purina or Master Feed who provide the stock and feed while farmers provide the land and labour. The companies set conditions on how production is to take place, including the number of hours of light, temperature, amount of water, grade, additives to feed, amount of feed, and growing time. Companies like Heinz in the Leamington, Ontario, area dominate tomato processing, and farmers wishing to sell to them must meet their conditions in terms of the type of plants, fertilizers, chemicals, method and timing of harvest, and so on.

Potatoes provide a classic illustration of dependent commodity producers. McCains controls potato production in the upper St. John River Valley. Farmers contract their potatoes to McCains, since it gives them a guaranteed outlet and a pre-season contract is a prerequisite to securing financing. McCains also owns fertilizer and equipment companies. Built into the farmer's contract is a guaranteed repayment of any outstanding debt to any of the McCain Group of Companies before the farmer sees any money. Two-thirds of New Brunswick's potato crop is handled by McCains, and less than a quarter of the potatoes are destined for the less concentrated fresh market. Production is highly mechanized, indeed the most efficient in the world in terms of output per man-hour, but the farmers are held in a price squeeze by the company. They bear the capital investment in land and machinery, are in a monopoly situation with respect to fertilizer and chemical inputs, and are unable to effectively negotiate the price for their potatoes. McCains has some of its own production (between five and eight thousand acres), yet prefers to buy most of its potatoes from dependent commodity producers. It uses its own production as leverage against the local farmers and, when this is not sufficient, imports potatoes from the United States (93 million pounds in 1977) to keep the local price depressed. The potato farmers have formal ownership and possession of their means of production, but real economic ownership is appropriated by McCains.

As a result of domination by capital, many Canadian farmers are compelled to give up their own means of realizing their labour and enter wage labour. There is, however, another pattern whereby simple commodity producers enter wage labour to supplement their incomes. This is the pattern of part-time work. Between 1941 and 1971, 28 to 36 per cent of Canadian farmers reported off-farm incomes, with the proportion standing at 34 per cent in 1976. The most impressive statistic, however, is that the ratio of family farm income from off-farm work has quadrupled from 0.18 in 1941 to 0.74 in 1971. By 1971, "37.8 per cent of total dairy products, 55.3 per cent of total chickens and 62.4 per cent of the soybeans were produced by operators with some off-farm work" (Bollman, 1980:11-12). By 1976 non-farm sources accounted for 67 per cent of total farm income in Canada; thus, non-farm income in wages or salaries, social security payments and/or investments are used to supplement farm income. Unable to reproduce themselves through farming, many simple commodity producers must offer their labour power for sale. This is another expression of proletarianization, an expression characteristic of dependent commodity producers who already find themselves proletarianized within their own means of production by capital appropriating real economic control over their labour process.

Some Illustrations from Canadian Fishing

The process of proletarianization has been uneven within Canadian fishing. East Coast fishermen illustrate this rather emphatically: offshore fishing (which has been transformed into factory-like conditions with great capital investment, such as factory freezer trawlers costing $15-20 million, the application of science and an extensive division of labour) has become organized by a combined share and wage system controlled directly by capitalist firms; inshore fishing, however, remains craft-like (with low capitalization, little technology and a low division of labour) and is organized by simple commodity producers. Capital has captured the fish-packing industry, the simple commodity producer's main market. The inshore fishermen take cod and hake by hook and line, herring and mackerel using drift nets, fish traps or weirs, and lobster by traps (see Dickie, 1980). Production is organized by individual producers and spread along the coastline, "often revolving economically around a local merchant trader who had a virtual monopoly on transfers to market. In many cases he also supplies all merchandise required by the fisherman and his family" (Dickie, 1980:17). The major change occurring for inshore fishermen is a change in their market. Rather than a local merchant, large industrial processors have taken control. Giant companes like National Sea Products and Unilever absorbed local processors and centralized production. Rather than relying exclusively on the inshore fishery, these companies began to use their own offshore draggers. Traditionally deep-sea fishing had been done by schooners from France, Portugal, Spain, Newfoundland and the Maritimes. In the early 1960s, with the support of federal and provincial governments, a Canadian fleet of otter-trawlers was built. These are operated on the principles of capitalist relations of production.

Corresponding to these changes has been a weakening of simple commodity producers. The most dramatic illustration is the Newfoundland

Resettlement Program with relocated traditional outport fishermen who were replaced by offshore draggers. In spite of these changes, simple commodity producers remain central to East Coast fishing. Inshore fishing accounts for 95 per cent of the Atlantic fishing vessels (28,000), 75 per cent of the fishermen (40,000), and 50 per cent of the value of fish caught. Richard Williams has classified these inshore fishermen into three groups:

(1) Some 10 to 15% of the total are highly capitalized full-time fishermen who conform to the image of primary producer as small businessmen. They may have hundreds of thousands of dollar invested in well-equipped all-weather long liners or inshore draggers, and inshore facilities. They regularly employ other fishermen as wage workers. While the overall numbers of such fishermen has remained fairly constant over the past decade, their share of the catch has increased substantially.

(2) Approximately 50% of the inshore fishermen are full-time or part-time fishermen who are not able to accumulate enough capital to make it into the small businessmen's club. Because of their numbers, this group produces collectively the largest share of the inshore catch, but still they are individually mired in a cost-price squeeze that prevents them from developing their productivity. These fishermen are not necessarily impoverished (although a large proportion are among the working poor), but they are subsidizing the industry overall since they do not earn close to a just return for their labour inputs.

(3) The third level are the part-time and occasional fishermen who are just hanging on. They may be people who merely fish lobster or other particular species in season (Gaspereau, smelts, Irish moss) for a few dollars cash income. These producers are among the hard core of the multiple-income multiple-vocation rural poor in the Maritimes. [1977:4]

Atlantic fishermen are in a dependent relationship with the fish companies. The companies employ many of them as wage workers on their offshore dragger and seiner fleets, thus clearly placing them among the proletariat. Simple commodity producers, however, are dependent in other ways. The first group mentioned by Williams is able to survive by entering into contracts with the processors, much like the contracts discussed earlier for farmers. The financing is necessary to pay for the expensive capital equipment these fishermen must buy as a prerequisite to the type of fishing the companies require. For the type of fishing they do, they have the most productive technology in areas where the huge factory ships are not practical. The second group Williams identifies serves as a marginal source for the companies, which are able to take advantage of their marginality by paying low prices for their catches, if and when it suits them. The final group are basically subsistence producers who enter some form of fishing for short periods as a source of cash income. The first group are small capitalist commodity producers; the second group are independent commodity producers, clearly dominated in the market; the final group vacillates between subsistence and independent commodity production.

How is it possible for fishermen to reproduce themselves under these conditions? The well-capitalized fishermen are able to survive by conforming to the requirements of capitalism; the others can survive only through government support. R.D.S. Macdonald has explored this situation in some detail for Prince Edward Island. He found that the average net fishing income in 1978 was $5,862 for a skipper/owner and $1,034 for a helper. Unemployment insurance made up about 40 per cent of non-fishing income for skippers in 1978 ($2,443). Besides these subsidies for the reproduction of these commodity producers, the state provides many other forms of support. The level of state support is so high that "it cost more than $41 million [in state expenditures] to produce $28 million worth of fishery products in P.E.I. in 1978. However, if a more kindly view of the P.E.I. fisheries performance is taken (i.e., assuming the opportunity costs of labour to be zero), then it cost as low as $25 million to produce $28 million" (1980:27-29). State subsidies have permitted the persistence of simple commodity producers in fishing; by paying part of their cost of reproduction, the state is indirectly subsidizing the low price the processing companies can pay for fish (not to mention the direct subsidies they already receive). Many of these fishermen would have entered wage labour long ago had jobs been open, but since such jobs are not available in the Atlantic provinces, they continue as marginal simple commodity producers.

The situation is obviously complex. Some Atlantic fishermen have become members of the proletariat, working for wages or shares on large company-owned ships. Most continue to own their own means of production in the form of small boats and nets. Those who own their own boats, however, clearly divide into two types: (1) those who have conformed to the most developed technology for fishing by entering into contracts with the processors, thus retaining formal ownership and possession while losing real economic control; and (2) those kept on the margin by the processors and lacking real economic control because the processors maintain market control. These latter are able to reproduce themselves only because of state subsidies. Were such subsidies removed, only the first type would survive and a situation resembling the decline in marginal agricultural producers would follow. Exits by these marginal fishermen would also occur if there were wage-labour alternatives, but in the context of a depressed economy, no such options exist. Thus, fishing becomes a distorted form of subsistence for many, a livelihood made possible only through state subsidies but one which in turn subsidizes fish processors, who pay fishermen less than the value of production for their catch.

Pacific fishing tends to be somewhat more homogenous than on the Atlantic coast. Seine boats, ranging from fifty to eighty-five feet, and smaller gill-netters and trollers are the mainstays of the industry. The industry itself is highly concentrated, with B.C. Packers holding the predominant position; processing has become increasingly concentrated with the closing of smaller processing plants along the coast and consolidation of the larger companies. This has compelled the use of larger, faster boats to move rapidly from the fishing grounds to port. The expense of the boats has also created a form of hidden proletarianization. Fewer and fewer 'captains' on the giant seiners own their own boats; increasingly they operate boats owned or financed by the processor. Moreover, the only way for those owning their own boats to have a secure, large-scale market for their catch is to contract with the processor for a minimum price.

Payment for fish is built around a complex share-system that divides the revenue from the sale of a catch (minus the cost of provisions). On a typical seine boat the shares would be divided among the captain, the crew, the owner of the net, and the boat owner. The captain may own the boat and/or the net, or these can be owned by the processor. The right to catch fish is determined by a licensing system, tied to the boat; the licence itself takes on a value.

Licensing is a result of state policy for the regulation of what is called a 'common property resource' and is designed to limit access to the fish. The term is a misnomer. As far as rights of access to fish, the sea has been transformed from common to private property by the state, first establishing its claims (state property), then granting individuals/corporations licences to take fish (private property). The current state policy began in 1967 with restrictions on new lobster licences, and was extended in 1968 to cover Pacific salmon and Atlantic herring, and further reinforced by the declaration of a 200-mile limit in 1977.

The experience of fishermen illustrates some of the complexity of class struggles for simple commodity producers. Williams has pointed out that inshore fishermen "may have fished for a co-operative, or on contract to a company, or within the traditional truck system" or even intermittently as wage labourers. These various relationships have led to distinct political and ideological responses to the condition of fishermen. Three major responses can be distinguished: associations, cooperatives and unions.

> The ideological pitch of inshore fishermen's associations, most of them government-sponsored, has been to the fisherman as independent producer. Free and competitive markets [are held out and] collective bargaining . . . posed as a threat to the independence of the individual producer. . . .

> Co-operatives have similarly addressed the petite-bourgeois and independent-producer interests of the fishermen. They have held out the promise of control over markets and processing as an alternative to monopoly structure. . . .

> . . . unionization, the fishermen obviously do not approach this alternative with a straightforwardly proletarian consciousness. [1979:173]

Unionization is evident among fishermen on both coasts. On the East Coast, Newfoundland is the most organized, with both inshore and offshore fishermen represented by the Newfoundland Fishermen, Food and Allied Workers Union. In the Maritimes much of the offshore fleet is represented by the Canadian Brotherhood of Railway, Transport and General Workers, but the inshore fishermen remain unorganized, aside from the Maritime Fishermen's Union, which has been struggling to gain recognition for the right of inshore fishermen to bargain collectively. In the early 1970s the United Fishermen and Allied Workers Union (UFAWU) from British Columbia attempted to organize Maritime fishermen but were repelled by capital and the state (see Cameron, 1977). In British Columbia the UFAWU is a strong union but does not have the right to negotiate wages for fishermen, only the price of fish (although it does negotiate wages for shore workers and tendermen). Cooperatives are also significant fishermen's organizations, ranging from the giant Prince Rupert Fishermen's Cooperative to the smaller United Maritime Fishermen or the Central Native Fishermen's Cooperative. Finally, fishermen's associations, based either on species, gear type or area, have proliferated on both coasts. An exploration of the conditions under which either unions, cooperatives or associations are formed is the subject of my current research. It will be argued that each is a response to the degree of proletarianization experienced by fishermen.

Conclusion

Property is a social creation that orders and maintains specific relations between people. It is not, as it is used in an everyday sense, what is owned (or an object), but the rights attached to ownership; specifically, it is the right to control the use or benefit to which ownership is put. Simple commodity producers have traditionally been distinguished by the ownership of their own means of production. It has been argued here, however, that the nature of their ownership has been undergoing a process of proletarianization. Major portions of simple commodity producers retain formal ownership of their means of production and possession, but capital has managed to gain real economic control. This has been accomplished by the erosion of part of the rights of property. Property is an enforceable claim, and capitalists who have contracts with simple commodity producers are able to determine the way production is organized and how the products are to be distributed. A simple commodity producer who enters into a contract with McCains, Heinz, National Sea Products or B.C. Packers is no longer independent. He has become a dependent commodity producer. It is not a matter of the will of the producer; he is compelled by the forces of centralization and concentration to specialize his production and take advantage of the most productive technologies. Formal ownership remains individual but real economic control is social; in other words, the dependent commodity producer becomes an extension of capitalism.

To lament the demise of the independent commodity producer is to dream about an earlier era, an era that was difficult and not very productive.

There is an appeal to the unity of conception and execution that the independent commodity producer possessed but not when understood in terms of the dominating relationship that is inevitable in its articulation with capitalism. A society built on independent commodity production without capitalism is impossible to conceive. It is possible, however, to conceive another alternative offered by Marx in an optimistic moment:

> Capitalist production begets, with the inexorability of a law of Nature, its own negation. It is the negation of a negation. This does not re-establish private property for the producer, but gives him individual property based on the acquisitions of the capitalist era: i.e., on co-operation and the possession in common of the land and of the means of production. [1967, I:763]

References

Abella, Irving
1973 *Nationalism, Communism and Canadian Labour: The CIO, the Communist Party, and the Canadian Congress of Labour, 1935-1956.* Toronto: University of Toronto Press.
1975 *The Canadian Labour Movement, 1902-1960.* The Canadian Historical Association Booklets, no. 28. Ottawa.
Abella, Irving, ed.
1975 *On Strike: Six Key Labour Struggles in Canada 1919-1949.* Toronto: James Lorimer & Co.
Abella, Irving, and Millar, David, eds.
1978 *The Canadian Worker in the Twentieth Century.* Toronto: Oxford University Press.
Acheson, T.W.
1972a "The Social Origins of the Canadian Industrial Elite, 1880-1885." In *Canadian Business History, Selected Studies, 1497-1971,* ed. D.S. Macmillan. Toronto: McClelland & Stewart.
1972b "The National Policy and the Industrialization of the Maritimes, 1880-1910." *Acadiensis I.*
1973 "Changing Social Origins of the Canadian Industrial Elite, 1880-1910." *Business History Review* 47:2 (Summer).
1977 "The Maritimes and 'Empire Canada.'" In *Canada and the Burden of Unity,* ed. David Jay Bercuson. Toronto: Macmillan.
Acton, Janice et al., eds.
1974 *Women at Work: Ontario 1850-1930.* Toronto: Canadian Women's Educational Press.
Aitken, Hugh G.J.
1952 "A Note on the Capital Resources of Upper Canada." *Canadian Journal of Economics and Political Science* 18:4 (November).
1965 "Government and Business in Canada: An Interpretation." In *The Canadian Economy,* eds. J. Deutsch et al. Revised ed. Toronto: Macmillan.

Allaire, Yvan; Miller, Roger-Emile; and Dell'Aniello, Paul
1977   *The Newspaper Firm and Freedom of Information*. Royal Commission on Corporate Concentration, Study no. 23. Ottawa.
Armstrong, Hugh
1977   "The Labour Force and State Workers in Canada." In *The Canadian State: Political Economy and Political Power*, ed. Leo Panitch. Toronto: University of Toronto Press.

Babcock, Robert
1974   *Gompers in Canada: A Study in American Continentalism before the First World War*. Toronto: University of Toronto Press.
Baker, John
1977   "The Underdevelopment of Atlantic Canada, 1867-1920." Master's thesis, McMaster University, Hamilton.
Baldwin, Doug
1977   "A Study in Social Control: The Life of the Silver Miner in Northern Ontario." *Labour/Le Travailleur* 2.
Banaji, Jairus
1977   "Modes of Production in a Materialist Conception of History." *Capital and Class* 3 (Autumn).
Berger Commission
1977   *Northern Frontier, Northern Homeland: The Report of the Mackenzie Valley Pipeline Inquiry*. Vol. 1. Ottawa: Supply and Services Canada.
Bernier, Bernard
1976   "The Penetration of Capitalism in Quebec Agriculture." *Canadian Review of Sociology and Anthropology* 13:4 (November).
Bollman, Ray
1980   "The Phenomenon of Part-time Farming." *Agrologist* 9:3 (Summer).
Bourgault, Pierre
1972   *Innovation and the Structure of Canadian Industry*. Ottawa: Science Council of Canada.
Bourque, Gilles
1979   "Class, Nation and the Parti Québécois." *Studies in Political Economy* 2 (Autumn).
Bourque, Gilles, and Laurin-Frenette, Nicole
1972   "Social Classes and National Ideologies in Quebec, 1760-1970." In *Capitalism and the National Question in Canada*, ed. Gary Teeple. Toronto: University of Toronto Press.
Braverman, Harry
1974   *Labor and Monopoly Capital: The Degradation of Work in the Twentieth Century*. New York: Monthly Review Press.

Bright, James
1958 *Automation and Management.* Cambridge, Mass.: Harvard University Press.
Britton, John N.H., and Gilmour, James M.
1978 *The Weakest Link: A Technological Perspective on Canadian Industrial Underdevelopment.* Science Council of Canada, Background Study no. 43. Ottawa.
Brownstone, Myer
1961 "Agriculture." In *A Social Purpose for Canada*, ed. Michael Oliver. Toronto: University of Toronto Press.
Brunst, A.S.
1978 "Farm Debt in Canada." *Canadian Farm Economics* 13:1 (February).
Bryce Commission,
1978 *Report of the Royal Commission on Corporate Concentration.* Ottawa: Supply and Services Canada.

Cameron, Silver Donald
1977 *The Education of Everett Richardson: The Nova Scotia Fishermen's Strike 1970-71.* Toronto: McClelland & Stewart.
Canadian Imperial Bank of Commerce
1977 "Canada's Food Land Resource." *Commercial Letter*, no. 3. Toronto.
Caplan, Gerald L., and Laxer, James
1970 "Perspectives on Un-American Traditions in Canada." In *Close the 49th Parallel etc.: The Americanization of Canada*, ed. Ian Lumsden. Toronto: University of Toronto Press.
Carchedi, Guglielmo
1975 "Reproduction of Social Classes at the Level of Production Relations." *Economy and Society* 4.
1977 *On the Economic Identification of Social Classes.* London: Routledge and Kegan Paul.
Chevalier, Jacques
1980 "On the Complexity of Simple Commodity Production." Departmental Working Paper 80-11. Sociology and Anthropology, Carleton University (December), Ottawa.
Chodos, Robert
1977 *The Caribbean Connection.* Toronto: James Lorimer & Co.
Clark, Melissa
1980 "The Canadian State and Staples: An Ear to Washington." Ph.D. thesis, McMaster University, Hamilton.
Clement, Wallace
1974 "The Changing Structure of the Canadian Economy." *Canadian Review of Sociology and Anthropology: Aspects of Canadian Society*, pp. 3-27.

1975 *The Canadian Corporate Elite: An Analysis of Economic Power.* Toronto: McClelland & Stewart.

1977 *Continental Corporate Power: Economic Elite Linkages between Canada and the United States.* Toronto: McClelland & Stewart.

1978 "A Political Economy of Regionalism in Canada." In *Modernization and the Canadian State,* eds. D. Glenday, H. Guindon and A. Turowetz. Toronto: Macmillan.

1980a *Hardrock Mining: Industrial Relations and Technological Change at Inco.* Toronto: McClelland & Stewart.

1980b "Searching for Equality: The Sociology of John Porter." *Canadian Journal of Political and Social Theory* 4:2 (Spring-Summer).

Clement, Wallace, and Drache, Daniel
1978 *A Practical Guide to Canadian Political Economy.* Toronto: James Lorimer & Co.

Clement, Wallace, and Janzen, Anna
1978 "Just Peachy: The Demise of Tender Fruit Farmers." *This Magazine* 12:2.

Clement, Wallace, and Olsen, Dennis
1974 "Official Ideology and Ethnic Power: Canadian Elites 1953-1973." Presented at the American Sociological Association meetings, Montreal (29 August).

Cohen, Morris
1978 "Property and Sovereignty." In *Property: Mainstream and Critical Positions,* ed. C.B. Macpherson. Toronto: University of Toronto Press.

Conway, John
1978 "Populism and the United States, Russia and Canada: Explaining the Roots of Canada's Third Parties." *Canadian Journal of Political Science* 11:1 (March).

Craven, Paul, and Traves, Tom
1979 "The Class Politics of the National Policy, 1872-1933." *Journal of Canadian Studies* 14:3 (Fall).

Cross, Michael, ed.
1974 *The Workingman in the Nineteenth Century.* Toronto: Oxford University Press.

Cuneo, Carl J.
1978 "A Class Perspective on Regionalism." In *Modernization and the Canadian State,* eds. D. Glenday et al. Toronto: Macmillan.

Deaton, Rick
1972 "The Fiscal Crisis of the State." *Our Generation* 8:4.

Development Education Centre
1977 "Corporate Power, the Canadian State and Imperialism." In *Imperialism, Nationalism and Canada*, eds. John Saul and C. Heron. Toronto: New Hogtown Press.
Dickie, L.M.
1980 "The Gulf of St. Lawrence: Requirements for Fishery Management." *Canadian Issues* 3:1 (Spring).
Dosman, Edgar
1975 *The National Interest: The Politics of Northern Development 1968-1975*. Toronto: McClelland & Stewart.

Ferns, Henry S., and Ostry, Bernard
1976 *The Age of Mackenzie King: The Rise of a Leader*. Toronto: James Lorimer & Co. (original 1955).
Forsey, Eugene
1974 *The Canadian Labour Movement, 1812-1902*. The Canadian Historical Association Booklets, no. 27. Ottawa.
Fournier, Pierre
1976 *The Quebec Establishment*. Montreal: Black Rose Books.
1980 "The New Parameters of the Quebec Bourgeoisie." *Studies in Political Economy* 3 (Spring).
Fowke, V.C.
1946 *Canadian Agricultural Policy: The Historical Pattern*. Toronto: University of Toronto Press.
Frank, David
1976 "Class Conflict in the Coal Industry: Cape Breton 1922." In *Essays in Canadian Working Class History*, eds. Gregory S. Kealey and Peter Warrian. Toronto: McClelland & Stewart.

Goldthorpe, John
1966 "Social Stratification in Industrial Society." In *Class, Status and Power*, eds. R. Bendix and S.M. Lipset. 2nd ed. New York: Free Press.
Griezic, Foster J.K.
1975 "Introduction to the University of Toronto Edition" of *A History of Farmers' Movements in Canada: The Origins and Development of Agrarian Protest 1872-1924* by Louis Aubry Wood. Toronto: McClelland & Stewart (original 1924).
Guindon, Hubert
1968 "Two Cultures: An Essay on Nationalism, Class and Ethnic Tension." In *Contemporary Canada*, ed. R.H. Leach. Toronto: University of Toronto Press.

Hanson, S.D.
1975 "Estevan 1931." In *On Strike: Six Key Labour Struggles in Canada 1919-1949*, ed. Irving Abella. Toronto: James Lorimer & Co.

Haskell, William B.
1898 "Two Years in the Klondike and Alaska Goldfields." In *Let Us Be Honest and Modest: Technology and Society in Canadian History*, eds. R. Sinclair, N.R. Ball and J.O. Petersen. Toronto: Oxford University Press (original Hartford, 1898), 1974.

Haythorne, G.
1941 *Land and Labour*. Toronto: University of Toronto Press.

Hedley, M.J.
1976 "Independent Commodity Production and the Dynamics of Tradition." *Canadian Review of Sociology and Anthropology* 13:4 (November).

Heidrick and Struggles Inc.
1973 "Profile of a Canadian President." Chicago.

Heron, Craig, and Palmer, Bryan
1977 "Through the Prism of the Strike: Industrial Conflict in Southern Ontario, 1901-14." *Canadian Historical Review* 58:4 (December).

Hill, Christina Maria
1973 "Women in the Canadian Economy." In *(Canada) Ltd.: The Political Economy of Dependency*, ed. Robert Laxer. Toronto: McClelland & Stewart.

Howard, Roger, and Scott, Jack
1972 "International Unions and the Ideology of Class Collaboration." In *Capitalism and the National Question in Canada*, ed. Gary Teeple. Toronto: University of Toronto Press.

Information Canada
1972 *Foreign Direct Investment in Canada*. Ottawa.

Innis, Harold A.
1930 Review of *Gold Fields of Nova Scotia* by W. Malcolm. *Canadian Historical Review* 11.

1936 "Settlement and the Mining Frontier." In *Canadian Frontiers of Settlement* (a series in nine volumes), eds. W.A. Mackintosh and W.L.G. Soerg. Toronto: Macmillan.

1937 Introduction to *Labour in Canadian-American Relations*, ed. H.A. Innis. Toronto: University of Toronto Press.

1939 Review of *International Control in the Non-ferrous Metals* by William Yandell Elliot et al. *Canadian Journal of Economics and Political Science* 5.

1941 Editor's foreword to *American Influence in Canadian Mining* by E.S. Moore. Toronto: University of Toronto Press.

1945 Review of *The Romance in Mining* by T.A. Rickard. *Canadian Historical Review* 26.

1956 *Essays in Canadian Economic History*. Toronto: University of Toronto Press.

1956a "The Canadian Mining Industry." In *Essays* (original 1941).

1956b *The Fur Trade in Canada*. Toronto: University of Toronto Press (original 1930).

1956c "The Canadian Economy and the Depression." In *Essays* (original 1934).

1956d "Government Ownership and the Canadian Scene." In *Essays* (original 1933).

1956e "Recent Development in the Canadian Economy." In *Essays* (original 1937).

1956f "An Introduction to Canadian Economic Studies." In *Essays* (original 1937).

Innis, H.A., and Ratz, B.

1940 "Labour." In *Encyclopedia of Canada*. Vol. 3, ed. W.S. Wallace. Toronto: University of Toronto Press.

Irvine, William

1976 *The Farmer in Politics*. Toronto: McClelland & Stewart (original 1920).

Jamieson, Stuart

1968 *Times of Trouble: Labour Unrest and Industrial Conflict in Canada, 1900-66*. Task Force on Labour Relations, Study no. 22, Ottawa.

Johnson, J.K.

1976 "John A. Macdonald and the Kingston Business Community." In *To Preserve and Defend*, ed. Gerald Tulchinsky. Montreal: McGill University Press.

Johnson, Leo A.

1972 "The Development of Class in Canada in the Twentieth Century." In *Capitalism and the National Question in Canada*, ed. Gary Teeple. Toronto: University of Toronto Press.

1973 "Incomes, Disparity and Impoverishment in Canada Since World War II." Toronto: New Hogtown Press.

Kalbach, W.E., and McVey, W.W.,

1971 *The Demographic Base of Canadian Society*. Toronto: McGraw-Hill.

Kealey, Greg

1974 *Hogtown: Working Class Toronto at the Turn of the Century*. Toronto: New Hogtown Press.

1976 "'The Honest Workingman' and Workers' Control: The Experience of Toronto Skilled Building Trades Workers, 1896-1914." *Labour/Le Travailleur* 1.

1980 *Toronto Workers Respond to Industrial Capitalism 1867-1892.* Toronto: University of Toronto Press.
1981 "Labour and Working-Class History in Canada: Prospects for the 1980s." *Labour/Le Travailleur 7.*
Kilbourn, William
1960 *The Elements Combined: A History of the Steel Company of Canada.* Toronto: Clarke, Irwin.
Knox, F.A.
1936 "Settlement and the Mining Frontier." *Canadian Journal of Economics and Political Science 2.*
Kunz, F.A.
1967 *The Modern Senate of Canada, 1925-1963.* Toronto: University of Toronto Press.

Langdon, Stephen
1972 "The Political Economy of Capitalist Transformation: Central Canada from the 1840's to the 1870's." Master's thesis, Carleton University, Ottawa.
1975 *The Emergence of the Canadian Working Class Movement 1845-1875.* Toronto: New Hogtown Press.
Laroque, Paul
1976 "Aperçu de la condition ouvrière à Québec (1896-1914)." *Labour/Le Travailleur 1.*
Laxer, Robert
1976 *Canada's Unions.* Toronto: James Lorimer & Co.
League for Social Reconstruction
1975 *Social Planning for Canada.* Toronto: University of Toronto Press (original 1935).
Levitt, Kari
1970 *Silent Surrender: The Multinational Corporation in Canada.* Toronto: Macmillan.
Lipton, Charles
1972 "Canadian Unionism." In *Capitalism and the National Question in Canada,* ed. Gary Teeple. Toronto: University of Toronto Press.
Lorimer, James
1975 "Big Business Probe of Big Business." *Globe and Mail,* 5 November.

Macdonald, R.D.S.
1980 "Fishermen's Income, Inputs and Outputs in the Fisheries Sector: The P.E.I. Case." *Canadian Issues 3:1 (Spring).*
Macpherson, C.B.
1953 *Democracy in Alberta: Social Credit and the Party System.* Toronto: University of Toronto Press.
1973 *Democratic Theory: Essays in Retrieval.* London: Clarendon Press.

1977   *The Life and Time of Liberal Democracy.* London: Oxford University Press.

1978   *Property: Mainstream and Critical Positions.* Toronto: University of Toronto Press.

Management Training Systems

1976   *Inco Consolidated Report, Ontario Division* (April).

Marfels, Christian

1977   *Concentration Levels and Trends in the Canadian Economy, 1965-1973.* Royal Commission on Corporate Concentration, Study no. 31. Ottawa.

Marx, Karl

1956   *Selected Writings in Sociology and Social Philosophy,* ed. T.B. Bottomore and M. Rebel. Harmondsworth: C.A. Watts and Co.

1963   *The Eighteenth Brumaire of Louis Bonaparte.* New York: International Publishers (original 1852).

1967   *Capital.* Vols. 1 and 3. New York: International Publishers (original 1867).

1967   *Capital.* Vol. 3. New York: International Publishers (original 1894).

1970   *The German Ideology.* New York: International Publishers (original 1845).

Marx, Karl, and Engels, Friedrich

1969   *Manifesto of the Communist Party.* Moscow: Progress Publishers (original 1848).

1970   *The German Ideology,* Part One, ed. C.J. Arthur. New York: International Publishers (original 1845).

Maslove, Allan M.

1972   *The Pattern of Taxation in Canada.* Economic Council of Canada. Ottawa: Information Canada.

McCallum, John

1980   *Unequal Beginnings: Agriculture and Economic Development in Quebec and Ontario until 1870.* Toronto: International Publishers.

Mealing, S.R.

1965   "The Concept of Social Class and the Interpretation of Canadian History." *Canadian Historical Review* 46 (September).

Moore, Barrington, Jr.

1966   *The Social Origins of Dictatorship and Democracy.* Boston: Beacon Press.

Moore, Bill

1978   "Staples and the Development of the Capitalist Mode of Production." Master's thesis, McMaster University, Hamilton.

Myers, Gustavus

1972   *A History of Canadian Wealth.* Toronto: James Lorimer & Co. (original 1914).

Naylor, R.T.
1972 "The Rise and Fall of the Third Commercial Empire of the St. Lawrence" and "Appendix: The Ideological Foundations of Social Democracy and Social Credit." In *Capitalism and the National Question in Canada*, ed. Gary Teeple. Toronto: University of Toronto Press.
Newman, Peter C.
1975 *The Canadian Establishment*. Toronto: McClelland & Stewart.
Niosi, Jorge
1979 "The New French-Canadian Bourgeoisie." *Studies in Political Economy* 1 (Spring).
Nock, David
1976 "The Intimate Connection: Links between the Political and Economic Systems in Canadian Federal Politics." Ph.D. thesis, University of Alberta, Edmonton.

Oliver, Michael, ed.
1961 *A Social Purpose for Canada*. Toronto: University of Toronto Press.
Olsen, Dennis
1977 "The State Elites." In *The Canadian State: Political Power and Political Economy*, ed. Leo Panitch. Toronto: University of Toronto Press.
1980 *The State Elite*. Toronto: McClelland & Stewart.
Ontario Department of Mines
1892 *Annual Report*. Reprinted in *Let Us Be Honest and Modest: Technology and Society in Canadian History*, eds. R. Sinclair, N.R. Ball and J.O. Petersen. Toronto: Oxford University Press, 1974.

Palmer, Bryan
1979 *A Culture in Conflict: Skilled Workers and Industrial Capitalism in Hamilton, Ontario, 1860-1914*. Montreal: McGill University Press.
Paltiel, K.Z.
1970 *Political Party Financing in Canada*. Toronto: McGraw-Hill.
1977 *Party, Candidate and Election Finance: A Background Report*. Royal Commission on Corporate Concentration, Study no. 32. Ottawa.
Panitch, Leo
1976 "Controls for Whom?" *This Magazine* 10 (February/March).
1977 "The Role and Nature of the Canadian State." In *The Canadian State: Political Power and Political Economy*, ed. Leo Panitch. Toronto: University of Toronto Press.
Parker, Ian
1977 "Harold Innis, Karl Marx and Canadian Political Economy." *Queen's Quarterly* 84:4 (Winter).

Parkin, Frank

1972   *Class Inequality and Political Order.* London: Paladine Press.

1974   "Strategies of Social Closure in Maintenance of Inequality." Presented at the Eighth World Congress of Sociology. Toronto (25 August).

Parsons, Talcott

1970   "Equality and Inequality in Modern Society or Social Stratification Revisited." In *Social Stratification,* ed. E.O. Laumann. New York: Bobbs-Merrill.

Pentland, H. Clare

1950   "The Role of Capital in Canadian Economic Development before 1875." *Canadian Journal of Economics and Political Science* 16:4 (November).

1953   "Further Observations on Canadian Development." *Canadian Journal of Economics and Political Science* 19:3 (August).

1959   "The Development of a Capitalistic Labour Market in Canada." *Canadian Journal of Economics and Political Science* 25:4 (November).

1960   "Labour and the Development of Industrial Capitalism in Canada." Ph.D. thesis, University of Toronto. Published as *Labour and Capital in Canada 1650-1860,* ed. Paul Phillips. Toronto: James Lorimer & Co., 1981.

1968   "A Study of the Changing Social, Economic and Political Background of the Canadian System of Industrial Relations." Draft Study prepared for the Task Force on Labour Relations. Ottawa.

1979   "The Western Canadian Labour Movement, 1897-1919." *Canadian Journal of Political and Social Theory* 3:2 (Spring-Summer).

Phillips, Paul

1977   "National Policy, Continental Economics and National Disintegration." In *Canada and the Burden of Unity,* ed. David Jay Bercuson. Toronto: Macmillan.

1979a "The National Policy Revisited." *Journal of Canadian Studies* 14:3 (Fall).

1979b "Clare Pentland and the Labour Process." *Canadian Journal of Political and Social Theory* 3:2 (Spring-Summer).

Porter, John

1955   "Elite Groups: A Scheme for the Study of Power in Canada." *Canadian Journal of Economics and Political Science* 21.

1956   "Concentration of Economic Power and the Economic Elite in Canada." *Canadian Journal of Economics and Political Science* 22.

1957   "The Economic Elite and the Social Structure in Canada." *Canadian Journal of Economics and Political Science* 23.

1961   "Freedom and Power in Canadian Democracy," In *A Social Purpose for Canada,* ed. Michael A. Oliver. Toronto: University of Toronto Press.

1965 *The Vertical Mosaic: An Analysis of Social Class and Power in Canada.* Toronto: University of Toronto Press.
1970 "Research Biography on a Macrosociological Study: The Vertical Mosaic." In *Macrosociology: Research and Theory*, eds. James S. Coleman, Amitai Etzioni and John Porter. Boston: Allyn and Bacon.
1978 "Comments by John Porter." *Alternate Routes* 2.
1979 *The Measure of Canadian Society.* Toronto: Gage Publishing.
Poulantzas, Nicos
1975 *Classes in Contemporary Capitalism.* London: New Left Books.
Power Corporation
1975 Submission of the Power Corporation of Canada, Ltd., to the Royal Commission on Corporate Concentration. Montreal (14 November).
Pratt, Larry
1976 *The Tar Sands: Syncrude and the Politics of Oil.* Edmonton: Hurtig.
1977 "The State and Province-Building: Alberta's Development Strategy." In *The Canadian State: Political Power and Political Economy*, ed. Leo Panitch. Toronto: University of Toronto Press.
Presthus, Robert
1973 *Elite Accommodation in Canadian Politics.* Toronto: Macmillan.
Pritchard, James
1972 "Commerce in New France." In *Canadian Business History, Selected Studies, 1497-1971*, ed. D.S. Macmillan. Toronto: McClelland & Stewart.

Regehr, T.D.
1977 "Western Canada and the Burden of National Transportation Policies." In *Canada and the Burden of Unity*, ed. David Jay Bercuson. Toronto: Macmillan.
Reynolds, Lloyd G.
1940 *The Control of Competition in Canada.* Cambridge, Mass.: Harvard University Press.
Richards, John, and Pratt, Larry
1979 *Prairie Capitalism: Power and Influence in the New West.* Toronto: McClelland & Stewart.
Roberts, Wayne
1976 *Honest Womanhood: Feminism, Femininity and Class Consciousness among Toronto Working Women, 1893 to 1914.* Toronto: New Hogtown Press.
Robin, Martin
1967- "The Working Class and the Transition to Capitalist Democracy in
68 Canada." *Dalhousie Review* 47.
Rotstein, Abraham
1977 "Innis: The Alchemy of Fur and Wheat." *Journal of Canadian Studies* 12:5 (Winter).

Royal Commission of the Relations of Labour and Capital 1889
1973 *Canada Investigates Industrialism,* ed. Greg Kealey. Toronto: University of Toronto Press.

Ryerson, Stanley
1960 *The Founding of Canada: Beginnings to 1815.* Toronto: Progress Books.
1962 "Conflicting Approaches in the Social Sciences." *Marxist Quarterly* 1 (Spring).
1968 *Unequal Union: Confederation and the Roots of Conflict in the Canadas, 1815-1873.* Toronto: Progress Books.
1975 Introduction to *A History of Canadian Wealth* by Gustavus Myers. Toronto: James Lorimer & Co.

Sacouman, R. James
1979 "The Differing Origins, Organisation and Impact of Maritime and Prairie Co-operative Movements to 1940" and "Underdevelopment and the Structural Origins of Antigonish Movement Cooperatives in Eastern Nova Scotia." In *Underdevelopment and Social Movements in Atlantic Canada,* eds. Robert J. Brym and R. James Sacouman. Toronto: New Hogtown Press.

Scheinberg, Stephen
1973 "Invitation to Empire: Tariffs and American Economic Expansion in Canada." *Business History Review* 47.

Schwindt, R.
1977 *The Existence and Exercise of Corporate Power: A Case Study.* Royal Commission on Corporate Concentration, Study no 15. Ottawa.

Scott, Bruce
1976 "A Place in the Sun: The Industrial Council at Massey-Harris, 1919-1920." *Labour/Le Travailleur* 1.

Scott, Stanley
1977 "A Profusion of Issues: Immigrant Labour, the World War, and the Cominco Strike of 1917." *Labour/Le Travailleur* 2.

Smart, John
1973 "Populism and Socialist Movements in Canadian History." In *(Canada) Ltd.,* ed. Robert Laxer. Toronto: McClelland & Stewart.

Smith, Adam
1869 *The Wealth of Nations.* London: McCulloch.

Statistics Canada
1970 *Incomes of Canadians.* Ottawa.
1971 *Canada's International Investment Position, 1926 to 1967.* Ottawa.
1977 *Perspective Canada II: A Compendium of Social Statistics.* Ottawa.
1978a 1971 *Census of Canada. Profile Studies: The Industrial Structure of Canada's Labour Force.* Cat. #99-715, vol. 5, pt 2 (Bulletin 5.2-4). Ottawa (February).

1978b *Canada's International Investment Position, 1974*. Ottawa.

Stelter, Gilbert A.
1974 "Community Development in Toronto's Commercial Empire: The Industrial Towns of the Nickel Belt." *Laurentian University Review* 6:3.

Stephenson, Marylee, ed.
1977 *Women in Canada*. Rev. ed. Toronto: General Publishing.

Stevenson, Garth
1977 "Federalism and the Political Economy of the Canadian State." In *The Canadian State: Political Economy and Political Power*, ed., Leo Panitch. Toronto: University of Toronto Press.

Tawney, R.H.
1978 "Property and Creative Work." In *Property: Mainstream and Critical Positions*, ed. C.B. Macpherson. Toronto: University of Toronto Press (original 1920).

Teeple, Gary
1972 "Land, Labour and Capital and Pre-Confederation Canada." In *Capitalism and the National Question in Canada*, ed. Gary Teeple. Toronto: University of Toronto Press.

Trebilcock, Michael J.
1975 "Winners and Losers in the Modern Regulatory State." University of Toronto, Faculty of Law.

Trofimenkoff, Susan Mann, and Prentice, Alison, eds.
1977 *The Neglected Majority: Essays in Canadian Women's History*. Toronto: McClelland & Stewart.

Trudeau, Pierre Elliott, ed.
1974 *The Asbestos Strike*. Toronto: James Lorimer & Co. (original *La Grève de l'amiante*, 1956).

Tulchinsky, G.
1972 "The Montreal Business Community, 1837-1853." In *Canadian Business History, Selected Studies, 1497-1971*, ed. D.S. Macmillan. Toronto: McClelland & Stewart.

Urquhart, M.C., and Buckley, K.A.H.
1965 *Historical Statistics of Canada*. Toronto: University of Toronto Press.

Veltmeyer, Henry
1979 "The Capitalist Underdevelopment of Atlantic Canada." In *Underdevelopment and Social Movements in Atlantic Canada*, eds. Robert J. Brym and R. James Sacouman. Toronto: New Hogtown Press.

Warwick, Donald P., and Craig, John G.
1975 "The Social Consequences of Corporate Concentration in Canada."
      A brief submitted to the Royal Commission on Corporate Concentra-
      tion. Toronto (16 December).
Watkins, Mel
1977 "Underdevelopment and Development." In *Déné Nation: The Colony
      Within*, ed. Mel Watkins. Toronto: University of Toronto Press.
Whitaker, Reginald
1976 Introduction to the Carleton Library Edition of *William Irvine, The
      Farmer in Politics*. Toronto: McClelland & Stewart.
Williams, Richard
1977 "Fish . . . or Cut Bait!" *This Magazine* 11:3 (May-June).
1979 "Inshore Fishermen, Unionization and the Struggle against Under-
      development Today." In *Underdevelopment and Social Movements
      in Atlantic Canada*, eds. Robert J. Brym and R. James Sacouman.
      Toronto: New Hogtown Press.
Wright, Eric Olin
1978 *Class, Crisis and the State*. London: New Left Books.

Zeitlin, Maurice
1974 "Corporate Ownership and Control: The Large Corporation and the
      Capitalist Class." *American Journal of Sociology* 79:5.